JOURNAL OF GRECO-ROMAN CHRISTIANITY AND JUDAISM 19

Journal of Greco-Roman Christianity and Judaism

Volume 19 (2023)

edited by

Stanley E. Porter,
Matthew Brook O'Donnell,
and Wendy J. Porter

PICKWICK *Publications* • Eugene, Oregon

JOURNAL OF GRECO-ROMAN CHRISTIANITY AND JUDAISM

Wipf & Stock
An Imprint of Wipf and Stock Publishers
199 W. 8th Ave., Suite 3
Eugene, OR 97401

www.wipfandstock.com

HARDCOVER ISBN: 979-8-3852-1913-1

Journal of Greco-Roman Christianity and Judaism

Volume 19   2023

CONTENTS

EDITORIAL STATEMENT

The *Journal of Greco-Roman Christianity and Judaism* (*JGRChJ*) has now completed volume 19 and continues to advance its study of the texts, languages and cultures of the Greco-Roman world of early Christianity and Judaism.

JGRChJ is pleased to publish only the highest quality articles that examine the ways in which the Greco-Roman world was the world of the New Testament and early Judaism. As the articles here indicate, the broad scope of this journal includes articles on many areas of relevance to the journal's aims and emphasizes a range of possible approaches and bodies of material. We encourage contributors to draw various areas of related knowledge together in their submissions.

For the online publication of the journal, see www.jgrchj.net (or www.mcmasterdivinity.ca for the link). The print form has the same pagination as the electronic form. The only changes are to correct mistakes and fix editorial inconsistencies.

JGRChJ is housed at McMaster Divinity College and is published under the ISSN 1467–1085 (e-ISSN 1467–1093). Manuscripts (electronic copy, preferably in Word, accompanied by a PDF) and editorial correspondence should be addressed to Stanley E. Porter, Senior Editor, at the address below. *JGRChJ* accepts books for possible review (no promises are made, as the number of books far outstrips possible reviewers). Those wishing to contribute book reviews should feel free to contact the Senior Editor. The reviews are posted exclusively online, but review articles of several volumes on the same topic may appear in the printed edition.

Those who wish to continue to receive *JGRChJ* as it appears in print may place a standing order with Wipf & Stock, by directly contacting them at Orders@wipfandstock.com. You may also contact them at this address:

Wipf and Stock Publishers
199 West 8th Avenue, Suite 3
Eugene, OR, USA 97401-2960
Tel: (541) 344-1528; Fax: (541) 344-1506

We encourage those interested in receiving the print copy of *JGRChJ* to establish their standing order as soon as possible.

We continue to invite as many contributors as possible to consider *JGRChJ* to be their primary outlet for substantial and expert work in the areas within the journal's purview.

Professor Dr Stanley E. Porter, Senior Editor
Dr Matthew B. O'Donnell and Dr Wendy J. Porter, Editors

Journal of Greco-Roman Christianity and Judaism
McMaster Divinity College, 1280 Main St. W.
Hamilton, ON, Canada L8S 4K1

princpl@mcmaster.ca
www.jgrchj.net

[*JGRChJ* 19 (2023) 9-39]

STEPHEN'S USE OF ΧΕΙΡΟΠΟΙΗΤΟΣ IN ACTS 7.48 AND ITS MEANING IN JEWISH AND GRECO-ROMAN LITERATURE

Tyler Hallstrom

Asbury Theological Seminary, Wilmore, KY

1. Introduction

Luke's interest in the temple has been regarded as 'sufficiently clear and widely acknowledged',[1] yet agreement on whether Luke maintains either a fundamentally positive or negative portrayal of this establishment in Luke–Acts remains elusive.[2] An adjoining complexity relates to discerning Stephen's own view of the temple through an analysis of his speech in Acts 7.1-51 and especially vv. 46-50 which contains his most poignant statements on the temple. Dennis D. Sylva notes that interpretations of these

---

1.   Peter Head, 'The Temple in Luke's Gospel', in T. Desmond Alexander and Simon Gathercole (eds.), *Heaven on Earth: The Temple in Biblical Theology* (Carlisle: Paternoster Press, 2004), pp. 101-19 (101). One finds in Luke–Acts, therefore, 39 uses of ἱερόν and 6 instances of ναός. On the use of οἶκος and τόπος for references to the temple, some of which are regarded as 'uncertain', see p. 108.

2.   For a survey of scholarship, see the overview in Francis D. Weinert's article, who nevertheless complains that while the temple in Luke–Acts 'is widely recognized by commentators as a prominent motif in Luke's work … few have pursued this topic with any rigor' ('Luke, the Temple and Jesus' Saying about Jerusalem's Abandoned House [Luke 13:34-35]', *CBQ* 44 [1982], pp. 68-76 [68]). Head, writing over 20 years after Weinert, also bemoans that 'there does not seem to be a really adequate treatment of the history of research in this area' ('Temple in Luke's Gospel', p. 104 n. 12). For a more recent, albeit brief, survey of scholarship on the topic, see Steve Smith, *The Fate of the Jerusalem Temple in Luke–Acts: An Intertextual Approach to Jesus' Laments over Jerusalem and Stephen's Speech* (LNTS, 553; London: Bloomsbury, 2017), pp. 6-8.

verses fall into three major categories: those who see them (1) as signifying a replacement of the temple; (2) as signifying a rejection and condemnation of the temple; or (3) as signifying an affirmation of God's transcendence of the temple.[3] The thesis that Stephen rejects the temple is taken up, for example, by Charles Talbert, who claims, 'Stephen's speech says that the very existence of the temple involves faithlessness to Moses and the pattern of worship he received from God.'[4] Similarly, Richard Pervo avers that Acts 7.48-50 indicates that Solomon's construction of the temple 'must be judged a mistake'.[5] Among the arguments advanced in support of this thesis is the claim that Stephen's use of χειροποίητος ('handmade') in 7.48, because of its use in the LXX to denote idols, indicates that the construction of the temple was itself an act of idolatry akin to the construction of the golden calf.[6] For

3.   Dennis D. Sylva, 'The Meaning and Function of Acts 7:46-50', *JBL* 106 (1987), pp. 261-75 (261); cf. p. 261 n. 4 for an extensive bibliography of advocates for each view.

4.   Charles H. Talbert, *Reading Acts: A Literary and Theological Commentary on the Acts of the Apostles* (RNTS; Macon, GA: Smyth & Helwys, rev. edn, 2005), p. 63. Concerning the relationship between Luke's view and Stephen's view on the temple, Talbert claims, 'Stephen's evaluation of the temple is different from that of the author of Luke–Acts,' where the former is negative and the latter positive (*Reading Acts*, p. 63). In contrast, Craig S. Keener (*Acts: An Exegetical Commentary* [4 vols.; Grand Rapids: Baker Academic, 2012–2015], II, p. 282) notes the challenge of recovering Stephen's view apart from Luke's: 'Those who think Stephen regarded the temple's construction as, indeed, wrong go beyond the evidence of the text; this cannot be Luke's view (cf. Luke 19.46; Acts 2.46), and we cannot certainly reconstruct Stephen's view apart from Luke's text.'

5.   Richard I. Pervo, *Acts: A Commentary* (Hermeneia; Minneapolis: Fortress Press, 2009), p. 191.

6.   Thus, Marcel Simon writes, 'χειροποίητο[ς] is the technical term, so to say, by which the Septuagint and the Greek-speaking Jews describe the idols. In Stephen's speech, the same kind of expression is used in relation to the worship of the golden calf ... This similitude of expression puts the making of the calf and the building of the Temple on the same level: they are both idolatrous actions' ('Saint Stephen and the Jerusalem Temple', *JEH* 5 [1951], pp. 127-42 [133]). Similarly, Pervo writes, 'by inference, innuendo, and insinuation, the temple of Solomon (and its successors) is drawn into the belly of the golden calf' (*Acts*, p. 189). Todd C. Penner (*In Praise of Christian Origins: Stephen and the Hellenists in Lukan Apologetic Historiography* [New York: T. & T. Clark, 2004], p. 317) also avers, 'The

others, however, the use of χειροποίητος denotes not the intrinsic status of the temple as an idol but only that Stephen finds his accusers to have adopted an idolatrous attitude toward the temple.[7] Although scholars argue their case by appealing in a general manner to the meaning and function of χειροποίητος in Hellenistic Judaism, there nevertheless exists a lacuna of detailed study on how this decisive term was employed throughout the LXX specifically and Jewish and Greco-Roman sources more broadly. In part, one may question whether any evidence may be found in the LXX use of χειροποίητος for viewing the handmade entity as something not intrinsically idolatrous in its creation but a legitimately constructed entity which was merely subsequently viewed with an idolatrous attitude.

The present article seeks to analyze more closely the instances of χειροποίητος in Greco-Roman and Jewish literature to enhance precision regarding how the term was employed, with a view toward assessing the claim that Stephen was criticizing an illegitimate attitude rather than an ille-

---

building of the temple is ... interpreted as an act of disobedience and, as a result, not surprisingly linked to idolatry as a "thing made by human hands".'

7.   'The use of "made with human hands" may suggest that the attitude of the people had become idolatrous' (I. Howard Marshall, 'Acts', in G.K. Beale and D.A. Carson [eds.], *Commentary on the New Testament Use of the Old Testament* [Grand Rapids: Baker Academic, 2007], p. 568). Here Marshall ('Acts', p. 568) seems to retreat from his position in his 1980 commentary, writing, 'the text seems to suggest not that Solomon was wrong to build the temple (contra Marshall 1980: 146; see Evans 1993b: 197), but that those people are wrong who think that God dwells there and is confined to this one place' (cf. Craig A. Evans, 'Prophecy and Polemic: Jews in Luke's Scriptural Apologetic', in Craig A. Evans and James A. Sanders [eds.], *Luke and Scripture: The Function of Sacred Tradition in Luke–Acts* [repr., Eugene, OR: Wipf & Stock, 2001], p. 198). Similarly, James D.G. Dunn (*Beginning from Jerusalem* [Christianity in the Making, 2; Grand Rapids: Eerdmans, 2009], p. 270) says that χειροποίητος 'is an astonishing term to find in a Jewish description of the Jerusalem Temple' since it 'was Hellenistic Judaism's dismissive description of "the idol".' However, Dunn posits that the point is not that the Temple was intrinsically idolatrous, but that 'the implied criticism is hard to avoid: the attitude of Stephen's accusers to the Temple was nothing short of idolatrous!' (cf. 'Yes, Stephen criticizes the temple, but not for what it is; rather, he is finding fault for how it is viewed' [Darrell L. Bock, *Acts* (BECNT; Grand Rapids: Baker Academic, 2007), p. 302]). See also to this effect David W. Pao, *Acts and the Isaianic New Exodus* (WUNT, 2/130; Tübingen: Mohr Siebeck, 2000), p. 207.

gitimate edifice. The study will proceed, first, by situating the use of χειροποίητος in 7.48 within the context of Stephen's overall speech in 7.2-53. Secondly, a brief examination of χειροποίητος in Greco-Roman texts will provide a broader foundation for assessing its usage than has traditionally been offered in scholarship and highlight the unique emphasis undertaken in its LXX usage. Thirdly, a close examination of χειροποίητος in Jewish literature—and particularly in the LXX—will seek to establish the manner in which the term was employed and how these usages compare with Acts 7.48. Finally, a limited survey of χειροποίητος in the New Testament and the cognate term ἀχειροποίητος will illuminate the way in which other New Testament authors might have employed the term and to what degree their usage comports with that found in the LXX.

2. *Χειροποίητος in its Acts 7 Context*

Attempts to analyze Stephen's speech in Acts 7.2-53 are problematized, *inter alia,* by the abundance of literature that attends to it,[8] with Heinz-Werner Neudorfer noting that contemporary study of the speech inevitably must address the three primary areas of inquiry which surround it, namely, its historical, literary and theological dimensions.[9] While a full analysis of Stephen's speech remains outside of the scope of the present study, it may nevertheless be briefly observed how χειροποίητος in 7.48 fits within the larger narrative.[10] Philip E. Satterthwaite has drawn attention to narrative

---

8.   E.g., I. Howard Marshall (*Acts: An Introduction and Commentary* [TNTC, 5; Downers Grove, IL: InterVarsity Press, 1980], p. 139 n. 8) notes that 'the literature is immense'. Smith (*Fate of the Jerusalem Temple*, p. 140) points to 'the vast scholarly literature on this speech' which 'contains substantial disagreement'. Likewise, Steve Walton writes that 'Stephen's speech ... has been a storm center in scholarship' ('A Tale of Two Perspectives', in T. Desmond Alexander and Simon Gathercole [eds.], *Heaven on Earth* [Carlisle: Paternoster Press, 2004], pp. 135-49 [135]).

9.   Heinz-Werner Neudorfer, 'The Speech of Stephen', in I. Howard Marshall and David Peterson (eds.), *Witness to the Gospel: The Theology of Acts* (Grand Rapids: Eerdmans, 1998), pp. 275-94 (276).

10.   As Chris Bruno, Jared Compton, and Kevin M. McFadden (*Biblical Theology according to the Apostles: How the Earliest Christians Told the Story of Israel* [NSBT, 52; Downers Grover, IL: IVP Academic, 2020], p. 55) write, 'While some

proportions in Acts and emphasizes that Luke dwells on an event when it plays a critical thematic and structural role in the overall strategy of the book.[11] Accordingly, the considerable length of this speech points to its important role as a turning-point in the narrative wherein the gospel is no longer preached only to Jews and only in Jerusalem.[12] This speech inaugurating the broadening of the gospel is, for Luke Timothy Johnson, the interpretive key to all of Luke–Acts.[13]

The raison d'être for this pivotal speech is as a response to the dual accusations in Acts 6.13, framed by the narrator as false charges, that Stephen spoke against the temple and against the law.[14] Jacques Dupont offers a widely accepted analysis of the rhetorical structure of the speech as dividing into the following: (1) *exordium* (7.2a); (2) *narratio* (7.2b-34); (3) transition/*propositio* (7.35); (4) *argumentatio* (7.36-50); and (5) *peroratio* (7.51-53).[15] It is in the final verses of Stephen's *argumentatio* that he claims, ἀλλ᾽ οὐχ ὁ ὕψιστος ἐν χειροποιήτοις κατοικεῖ ('yet, the Most High does not dwell in houses made by human hands'),[16] which has led to one of the most de-

may debate its historicity and background, few can dispute that Stephen's speech in Acts 7 and its aftermath play a crucial role in the unfolding narrative of Acts.'

11. Philip E. Satterthwaite, 'Acts against the Background of Classical Rhetoric', in Bruce W. Winter and Andrew D. Clarke (eds.), *The Book of Acts in its Ancient Literary Setting* (BAFCS, 1; Grand Rapids: Eerdmans, 1993), pp. 337-80 (351). As I. Howard Marshall (*Acts*, p. 139) writes, 'If length is anything to go by, Stephen's speech is one of the most important sections of Acts.'

12. Satterthwaite, 'Acts against the Background of Classical Rhetoric', p. 351.

13. Luke Timothy Johnson, *The Acts of the Apostles* (SP; Collegeville, MN: Liturgical Press, 1992), p. 119 (cf. pp. 12-13). See also Bruno *et al.* (*Biblical Theology according to the Apostles*, p. 55) who find that the speech 'serves as a narrative hinge'.

14. Those who speak these charges are identified as 'false witnesses' (μάρτυρας ψευδεῖς) (Acts 6.13).

15. Jacques Dupont, 'La structure oratoire du discours d'Étienne (Actes 7)', *Bib* 66 (1985), pp. 153-67. Cf. Ben Witherington III (*The Acts of the Apostles: A Socio-Rhetorical Commentary* [Grand Rapids: Eerdmans, 1998], p. 260), who calls this 'the most persuasive analysis of the crucial Stephen speech'. See also Keener, *Acts*, II, pp. 1332-33; Bock, *Acts*, p. 277.

16. All translations taken from the NRSV unless otherwise noted. Likewise, translations of the LXX are taken from NETS unless otherwise noted. The term

bated issues regarding Stephen's speech, namely, whether or not it is critical of the temple.[17]

For Richard N. Longenecker, 'Stephen reaches the climax of his anti-temple polemic by insisting that "the Most High does not live in houses made by men".'[18] Steve Smith agrees that 'for many scholars, the language in Acts 7.46-48 confirms Stephen's overall negative attitude to the Jerusalem temple.'[19] James D.G. Dunn sees 7.48 as the climax of the theme of apostasy, which was interwoven throughout the speech's mention of the idolatry of the golden calf (7.39-41), where the similar language of 'the works of their hands' appears,[20] to the idolatry of planetary powers (7.42-43) and to the present idolatry of the temple (7.48-50).[21] Dunn stresses that the outspoken attack on the temple in 7.48 'is the most astonishing feature of the speech' and finds χειροποίητος to be the 'key word' in the text.[22] Likewise, Sylva in arguing against the notion that Acts 7.46-50 criticizes the temple and in advocating for the idea that it asserts God's transcendence over the temple, finds the use of χειροποίητος in 7.48 to be one of the three main obstacles to the acceptance of his thesis since it was employed for

'houses' does not appear in the Greek but is supplied by most translations as the implied noun.

17. As Witherington writes, 'The suggestion that the speech is temple critical is largely based on an assumed contrast between things made with human hands and things made by God, and secondarily on a perceived contrast between the tent of witness and the temple as a "house" built by Solomon for God' (*Acts*, p. 262).

18. Richard N. Longenecker, 'Acts', in Tremper Longman III and David E. Garland (eds.), *Luke–Acts* (EBC, 10; Grand Rapids: Zondervan, rev. edn, 2017), pp. 663-1102 (826).

19. Smith, *Fate of the Jerusalem Temple*, p. 169.

20. ἐν τοῖς ἔργοις τῶν χειρῶν αὐτῶν (7.41). A full consideration of this phrase goes beyond the limitations of the present study, though it may be noted that many see 'works of their hands' in 7.41 as parallel to 'handmade' in 7:48. If this is the case, then the idolatry connection is heightened. On this construction, see Bock, *Acts*, p. 298; Hans Conzelmann, *Acts of the Apostles: A Commentary on the Acts of the Apostles* (trans. James Limburg, A. Thomas Kraabel, and Donald H. Juel; Hermeneia; Philadelphia: Fortress Press, 1987), pp. 54-55.

21. Dunn, *Beginning*, p. 293.

22. James D.G. Dunn, *Unity and Diversity in the New Testament: An Inquiry into the Character of Earliest Christianity* (London: SCM, 3rd edn, 2006), p. 292.

idols in the LXX.[23] Given the importance of the term χειροποίητος in the debate regarding the temple yet the paucity of studies on it in the relevant literature, the present study seeks to establish a clearer picture on how χειροποίητος was employed in Greco-Roman, Jewish and New Testament literature.

3. Χειροποίητος in its Greco-Roman Context

Although the septuagintal influence on Stephen's speech has been widely recognized,[24] the use of χειροποίητος in Greco-Roman literature must be given due attention, too, for two reasons. First, it provides a contrast to the distinctive septuagintal usage. Secondly, χειροποίητος is also employed throughout the New Testament in a way that departs from this usage, and one should therefore resist the baseline assumption that the septuagintal usage necessarily predetermines its meaning. In discussions of the meaning of χειροποίητος, scholars frequently trace a direct line from the LXX to the New Testament with little to no consideration of how the term was employed in other literature relevant to the time. G.K. Beale, for example, in assessing the term writes 'the word "handmade" (χειροποίητος, *cheiropoiētos*) always refers to idols in the Greek OT and is without exception a negative reference, with overtones of idolatry, in the NT.'[25] First, however, the use of 'always' is problematic insofar as its use in Isa. 16.12 refers instead to a pagan sanctuary, and thus more accurate is the use of 'almost always' by scholars.[26] Secondly, the framing of the evidences leaves the impression that the

---

23. Sylva, 'Meaning and Function of Acts 7.46-50', p. 268.

24. See, e.g., F.F. Bruce, *The Book of the Acts* (NICNT; Grand Rapids: Eerdmans, 1988), p. 134. Cf. 'Stephen's speech is based primarily on the LXX and it uses the Old Testament in different ways' (Gerhard A. Krodel, *Acts* [ACNT; Minneapolis: Augsburg, 1986], p. 139).

25. G.K. Beale, *Colossians and Philemon* (BECNT; Grand Rapids: Baker Academic, 2019), p. 186. Curiously, the *NIDNTTE* similarly writes that χειροποίητος 'always' refers to idols in the LXX, yet later its only other comment on χειροποίητος downplays the idolatry connection, writing that 'in the NT it never refers to idols (in Eph. 2.11 it is used of circumcision; elsewhere, of temples)' (Moisés Silva, 'Χείρ', *NIDNTTE*, IV, p. 663).

26. See, e.g., Otto Bauernfeind, 'Ἐπαναπαύω', *TDNT*, I, p. 351, where the Isa. 16.12 exception is noted. Similarly, David W. Pao (*Colossians and Philemon*

New Testament usage containing 'overtones of idolatry' is necessarily determined by the LXX usage and ignores the data from broader Greco-Roman or other Jewish literature.[27]

Concerning its Greco-Roman usage, it should be noted that χειροποίητος means merely 'made by hand, artificial', with no necessary connotations of idolatrous practice.[28] Plato applies the term to a trench reported to be an enormous depth, a report which Plato doubts and finds 'incredible ... considering that it was made by hand (ὡς χειροποίητον ἔργον)'.[29] Similarly, Herodotus details Lake Moeris and comments on the parts of the lake which were evidently altered 'by men's hands' (χειροποίητος),[30] while Appian describes two legions traversing a road 'which had been thrown up artificially' (τῆς ὁδοῦ, χειροποιήτου).[31] Likewise, Arrian in describing the conquests of Alexander the Great speaks of an enormous rock upon which certain cities sought shelter and which had 'only one way up, made by hand and rough' (ἀνάβασιν χειροποίητον μίαν χαλεπήν).[32] One finds Polybius noting that the land connecting Carthage and Libya contains hills difficult to traverse 'with several passes to the country artificially cut in them' (χειροποιήτους ἐχόντων διεκβολὰς ἐπὶ τὴν χώραν).[33] Alternatively, Polybius also reflects a non-liter-

[ZECNT; Grand Rapids: Zondervan, 2012], p. 165) writes that χειροποίητος 'in the LXX is almost always used in reference to the idols made by human hands'. Cf. Smith, *Fate of the Jerusalem Temple*, p. 173; Conzelmann, *Acts*, p. 56; Pervo, *Acts*, p. 434 n. 88.

27.   See also the same situation in G.K. Beale, *The Temple and the Church's Mission: A Biblical Theology of the Dwelling Place of God* (NSBT, 15; Downers Grove, IL: InterVarsity Press, 2004), pp. 222-28.

28.   LSJ, *s.v.* 'χειροποίητος'. Cf. 'by the hand of man, artificial' (MGS, *s.v.* 'χειροποίητος').

29.   Plato, *Critias* 118c (Bury, LCL).

30.   Herodotus, *Hist.* 2.149 (Gódley, LCL). 'That it has been dug out and made by men's hands the lake shows for itself' (ὅτι δὲ χειροποίητός ἐστὶ καὶ ὀρυκτή, αὐτὴ δηλοῖ). In *Hist.* 1.195, Herodotus uses the word in describing Babylonian clothing, where 'every man has a seal and a carven staff' (σφρηγῖδα δὲ ἕκαστος ἔχει καὶ σκῆπτρον χειροποίητον).

31.   Appian, *Bell. civ.* 3.66 (White, LCL). Later this road is referred to as 'the high road above mentioned' (ἐς τὴν χειροποίητον ὁδόν) (see 3.67).

32.   Arrian, *Anab.* 4.28.3 (Brunt, LCL).

33.   Polybius, *Hist.* 1.75.4 (Paton, LCL). Elsewhere, he speaks of a road 'of singular natural and artificial strength' (ὀχυρότητι δὲ φυσικῇ καὶ χειροποιήτῳ

al use when he describes the ruthlessness of Hermeias who was guilty of 'trumping up false charges' (τοῖς δὲ χειροποιήτους καὶ ψευδεῖς ἐπιφέρων αἰτίας) as a judge.[34]

Further, Dionysius of Halicarnassus speaks of Rome's fortification, wherein some sections of the wall were 'fortified by nature', yet draws attention to one section 'strengthened artificially' (χειροποιήτως ἐστὶν ὀχυρόν).[35] Thucydides records how the Peloponnesians attempted to burn a city rather than siege it, and speaks of a fire greater than any he had seen which was 'kindled ... by the hand of man' (γε ἐκεῖνον τὸν χρόνον χειροποίητον εἶδεν).[36] The word appears also in a first- or second-century travel letter (P.Lond. 854) to denote that travelers go by ship 'in order that they may visit works of art made by hands' (ἵνα τὰς χε[ι]ροπ[οι]ή[τους τέ]χνας ἱστορήσωσι) on the banks of the Nile.[37] In assessing the function of χειροποίητος in the New Testament, therefore, it should be borne in mind that the term was employed frequently in Greco-Roman literature without reference to idolatry or an intended negative association with the referred-to hand-made creation. The translation sometimes given as 'artificial', which may carry a negative connotation in modern English, relates more instead to the distinction made by the author between what is natural and what is non-natural.[38] Assessments of New Testament texts where χειροποίητος appears,

διαφέρει) (4.64.9 [Paton, LCL]). Similar uses may be found in *Hist.* 9.27.4 to describe the 'artificially rendered' steepness of a rock, and in 10.10.12 (Paton, LCL), an 'artificial communication' opened between a lagoon and neighboring sea. In 14.10.5, χειροποίητος is compared with φυσικός to describe the construction of Tunis: 'both nature and art have contributed to render it a very strong place' (διαφέρει δ' ὀχυρότητι καὶ φυσικῇ καὶ χειροποιήτῳ). This contrast is also seen in 6.42.2 where he notes that the Greeks 'think artificial defences are not equal in value to the fortifications which nature provides' (οὐχ ὁμοίας εἶναι τὰς χειροποιήτους ἀσφαλείας ταῖς ἐξ αὐτῆς τῆς φύσεως) (Paton, LCL).

34. Polybius, *Hist.* 5.41.3 (Paton, LCL).

35. Dionysius of Halicarnassus, *Ant. rom.* 9.68.3 (Cary, LCL). In 10.16.5, Dionysius uses the term for 'the roads that had been built to the summits' (τὰς χειροποιήτους ὁδούς) (Cary, LCL).

36. Thucydides, *Hist.* 2.77.4 (Smith, LCL).

37. MM, *s.v.* 'χειροποίητος', p. 687.

38. See, e.g., the definition of 'artificial' as 'of a thing: made or constructed by human skill, esp. in imitation of, or as a substitute for, something which is made or occurs naturally; man-made' (OED, *s.v.* 'artificial').

therefore, should include in their analysis not simply a citation that the LXX uses χειροποίητος in a particular way but also an acknowledgment of its Greco-Roman usage (and broader Jewish usage) as well as arguments for why the LXX sense should be seen as predominating in the text.

4. Χειροποίητος in its Jewish Context

Whereas the Greco-Roman literature employed χειροποίητος as a way of contrasting natural walls with non-natural walls or to describe works of art, the notion of idolatry looms large over its use in the LXX. In relation to its use in Stephen's speech, it is often posited that χειροποίητος draws from the LXX sense of idolatry, yet that χειροποίητος does not denote an intrinsically idolatrous creation but refers to an entity legitimately constructed that was only subsequently viewed with an idolatrous attitude. However, few studies have investigated closely the use of χειροποίητος in the LXX, and the question remains whether linguistic justification may be found in the LXX for the assertion that χειροποίητος denotes extrinsic, rather than intrinsic, idolatry.[39] Thus, the following analysis will examine the appearance of χειροποίητος in Jewish literature, particularly the Septuagint and the pseudepigrapha where the term appears (Lev. 26.1, 30; Isa. 2.18; 10.11; 16.12; 19.1; 21.9; 31.7; 46.6; Dan. 5.4, 23; 6.28; Jdt. 8.18; Wis. 14.8; *Sib. Or.* 3.606, 3.618; 14.16; *Sib. Or. Frag.* 3.29). Likewise, a brief examination of how the term appears in Philo and Josephus will be undertaken.

Leviticus 26.1, 30

In Lev. 26.1, the substantive use of χειροποίητος appears in the prohibition against idols which further develops Lev. 19.4 and corresponds to Exod. 20.4.[40] Here the creation of χειροποίητα ('hand-made things') translates the Hebrew אלילם which indicates 'pagan gods, always derogatory as nonenti-

39. For the sake of convenience, 'intrinsic' idolatry will refer to entities which were idolatrous ipso facto in their creation, and 'extrinsic' idolatry will refer to entities which were legitimate in their own right, such as presumably the temple, which later became an idol by the attitudes of others.

40. René Péter-Contesse and John Ellington, *A Handbook on Leviticus* (UBS Handbook Series; New York: United Bible Societies, 1992), p. 401.

ties, idols'[41] and 'is used with debilitating intention and with scornful un-
dertones in all OT passages where it occurs'.[42] The term thus 'resembles
אֱלֹהִים, gods, and is used to affirm the nonexistence of such entities, identifying them solely with the physical object'.[43] This physical object is therefore rendered in the LXX by the substantive χειροποίητα where Yahweh
commands the blanket prohibition, οὐ ποιήσετε ὑμῖν αὐτοῖς χειροποίητα
('you shall not make for yourselves hand-made things,' Lev. 26.1). Thus,
Jacob Milgrom notes that this command against אלילם/χειροποίητα prohibits
not only their worship but also their possession and even their manufacture.[44] Here, however, in contrast to Dan. 5.4 which follows, χειροποίητα
does not stand by itself as a summary of all idols but exists as one among
four terms which are used cumulatively to issue a comprehensive ban on
idolatry.[45]

Later in the chapter, in v. 30, the term appears again, yet instead of denoting idols and translating אלילם, it denotes an incense altar, translating
חמן.[46] Thus, Yahweh declares, 'I will destroy your high places and cut down
your incense altars (והכרתי את חמניכם; τὰ ξύλινα χειροποίητα ὑμῶν). I will
heap your carcasses on the carcasses of your idols. I will abhor you'
(26.30).[47] Here, three observations may be noted. First, it is unclear whether
the referent of τὰ ξύλινα χειροποίητα (which translates חמנים), a term typically given as 'incense-altar', may properly be defined itself as an idol,

41. HALOT, s.v. 'אֱלִיל'.

42. Horst Dietrich Preuss, 'אֱלִיל', *TDOT*, I, pp. 285-87.

43. Judith M. Hadley, 'אֱלִיל', *NIDOTTE*, I, p. 411. She adds, 'This is specifically said in Ps. 96.5 = 1 Chron. 16.26: the gods (אֱלֹהֵי) of the people are nothing
(אֱלִילִים).'

44. Jacob Milgrom, *Leviticus 23–27: A New Translation with Introduction and
Commentary* (AB, 3B; New Haven: Yale University Press, 2001), p. 2279.

45. John E. Hartley, *Leviticus* (WBC, 4; Dallas: Word, 1992), p. 450; Erhard
S. Gerstenberger, *Leviticus: A Commentary* (trans. Douglas W. Stott; OTL;
Louisville: Westminster John Knox, 1996), pp. 402-3.

46. HALOT, s.v. 'חמן'; 'sun-pillar, used in idolatrous worship' (BDB, p. 329);
'incense altar' (DCH, III, p. 256). For a detailed discussion, see Baruch A. Levine,
Leviticus: The Traditional Hebrew Text with the New JPS Translation (JPS Torah
Commentary; Philadelphia: Jewish Publication Society, 1989), p. 188.

47. NRSV translation of the HB. NETS translates the LXX as 'and I will strip
bare your steles and utterly destroy your wooden handcrafted objects'.

which would soften the claim that χειροποίητος always refers to idols in the LXX, even though the altar is undoubtedly used in idolatrous practices.[48] Secondly, the LXX, although translating חמנים as εἴδωλα ('idols') elsewhere, here 'renders the word vaguely'[49] as 'wooden object made with hands'.[50] Thirdly, throughout Lev. 26.30-31, one finds the notion of legitimate edifices which had subsequently resulted in illegitimate worship and thus were to be destroyed by Yahweh. For example, the 'high places' in 26.30 'were apparently once considered legitimate',[51] and Gordon Wenham adds that here 'they seem to be regarded as legitimate,' though used in illegitimate ways.[52] Milgrom disagrees that 26.30 has any legitimate sites in view, but sees them as legitimate in 26.31, writing that 'if Israel were obedient, God would indeed look with favor on his people's sacrifices at their "sanctuaries".'[53] Although the reference to τὰ ξύλινα χειροποίητα does not appear to

---

48. τὰ ξύλινα χειροποίητα here translates את־חמניכם and indicates 'incense altars', whereas an indication of idols appears in the LXX as τῶν εἰδώλων ὑμῶν and translates גלוליכם. On the latter terms, εἴδωλον is a standard designation of idol ('fabricated/imaged deity, idol', BDAG, p. 281), as well as גלולים ('idols', HALOT, *s.v.* 'גלולים'). The precise nature and function of the חמן, writes Milgrom, however, is ultimately 'shrouded in darkness'. See the survey of views in Milgrom, *Leviticus 23–27*, p. 2318. Cf. H.G.M. Williamson who writes that חמן is 'an uncertain word often thought to refer to an incense altar but perhaps now better identified as a shrine' (*A Critical and Exegetical Commentary on Isaiah 1–27* [3 vols.; ICC; New York: T. & T. Clark, 2006], II, p. 427). The view that חמן in Lev. 26.30 denotes an idol is, however, advocated by Rashi: 'This was some sort of idol that they would set up on the roofs' (Michael Carasik [ed.], *The Commentator's Bible: Leviticus* [Philadelphia: Jewish Publication Society, 2009], p. 227).

49. G.A. Cooke, *A Critical and Exegetical Commentary on the Book of Ezekiel* (ICC; Edinburgh: T. & T. Clark, 1936), p. 73. Cf. 'The Gk translates this term with τεμένη (official place) (Ezek. 6.4, 6); ξύλινα χειροποίητα (wooden object made with hands) (Lev. 26.30); εἴδωλα (idol) (Isa. 27.9; 2 Chron. 14.4); ὑψηλά (high place) (2 Chron. 34.4, 7); and βδελύγματα (abomination) (Isa. 17.8)' (Hans Wildberger, *Isaiah 13–27* [trans. Thomas H. Trapp; CC; Minneapolis: Augsburg Fortress, 1997], p. 176).

50. Wildberger, *Isaiah 13–27*, p. 176.

51. Péter-Contesse and Ellington, *Handbook on Leviticus*, p. 415.

52. Gordon J. Wenham, *The Book of Leviticus* (NICOT; Grand Rapids: Eerdmans, 1979), p. 332 n. 11. Cf. Hartley, *Leviticus*, p. 467.

53. Milgrom, *Leviticus 23–27*, p. 2327.

have in view sites that were ever legitimate, they nevertheless are included alongside sites which seem to have lost their legitimacy due to the behavior and practices of the worshippers.[54] As Hartley thus writes regarding the sanctuaries, 'the people have turned the sanctuaries where Yahweh was once worshiped in purity into places where they follow worship practices like those of their neighbors,'[55] a notion not too distant from the suggestion that the Jerusalem temple in New Testament times had begun to be used improperly.

Isaiah 2.18; 10.11; 16.12; 19.1; 21.9; 31.7; 46.6

H.G.M. Williamson notes that 'idolatry is a concern of the whole of the book of Isaiah in all its major divisions,'[56] and χειροποίητος appears among its various designations for idols.[57] The difficulty in assessing the significance of word choice in the LXX of Isaiah relates, in part, to what I.L. Seeligmann describes as 'the excessive inconsistencies shown everywhere in the translation of our text in the interpretation of Hebrew words'.[58] Thus, for example, אלילם is translated in 2.18 as τὰ χειροποίητα, but in 2.20, as τὰ βδελύγματα. Seeligmann concludes that 'the great majority of inconsisten-

54. However, Milgrom writes that *Sipra* Beḥuqotay 6.4 suggests these sites included legitimate worship, since it interprets חמניכם as 'magical practices in Israel' where Milgrom thus notes that 'the *Sipra* is forced to render it this way because what sort of punishment is it to destroy *idolatrous* objects? The assumption must therefore be that *legitimate* worship is destroyed' (Milgrom, *Leviticus 23–27*, p. 2318 [emphasis original]).

55. Hartley, *Leviticus*, p. 467.

56. Williamson, *Isaiah 1–27*, I, p. 43. Cf. 'Both sections condemn the worship of idols but in entirely different ways. The terminology is different, and the monotonous harping on the manufacture of idols in Second Isaiah by way of dismissing idolatry as stupid (40.19-20; 41.16-17; 44.9-20; 46.5-7) is absent from First Isaiah' (Joseph Blenkinsopp, *Isaiah 1–39: A New Translation with Introduction and Commentary* [AB, 19; New Haven: Yale University Press, 2000], p. 89).

57. For a non-exhaustive sampling, see, e.g., βδέλυγμα (2.8, 'abomination'), χειροποίητος (2.18, 'works of their hands'), γλυπτός (10.10, 'graven images'), εἴδωλον (10.11, 'idol'), δένδρα (17.8, 'trees'), translating אֲשֵׁירֶהֶם 'Asherah pole', θεοὺς αὐτῶν (19.3, 'their gods'), ἄγαλμα (21.9, 'statues/images') and εἰκόνα (40.19, 'image').

58. I.L. Seeligmann, *The Septuagint Version of Isaiah and Cognate Studies* (FAT; Tübingen: Mohr Siebeck, 2004), p. 181.

cies here discussed must be imputed to the translator's unconstrained and carefree working method, and to a conscious preference for the introduction of variations.'[59] Likewise, Seeligmann finds 'throughout his work, traces of his attempts to express some idea or other which was dear to his heart, without bothering overmuch about the Hebrew original'.[60] Assessments of the use of χειροποίητος in the LXX broadly and Isaiah particularly, which contains half of the septuagintal references, must therefore take into account the degree to which the use of χειροποίητος by the translator arose from an unconstrained method and a preference for introducing variations, rather than necessarily a view that χειροποίητος was the preferred term for referring to idols.[61]

Nevertheless, it remains the case that χειροποίητος was frequently used by the translator of Isaiah to denote idols. Thus, in 2.18, the substantive τὰ χειροποίητα stands for אלילם. A change, however, occurs from 'hiding' to 'passing away': 'The idols shall utterly pass away'[62] to 'They will hide all the works of their hands.'[63] Isaiah 10.11 similarly uses the substantive τοῖς χειροποιήτοις to translate the אליל of Samaria, and the word occurs alongside a series of terms for idols.[64] Curiously, however, while both the idols of Samaria and Jerusalem will be destroyed, only the former are described with τοῖς χειροποιήτοις αὐτῆς whereas Jerusalem's idols are designated instead with τοῖς εἰδώλοις αὐτῆς (10.11).[65] Again, in 19.3, the substantive τὰ χειροποίητα translates אלילם, but this time it is describing the idols of Egypt

---

59. Seeligmann, *Septuagint Version*, p. 182.

60. Seeligmann, *Septuagint Version*, p. 205.

61. On idolatry in Isaiah, T.J. Meadowcroft (*Aramaic Daniel and Greek Daniel: A Literary Comparison* [JSOTSup, 198; Sheffield: Sheffield Academic, 1995], p. 113 n. 61) draws attention to an idolatry polemic in Daniel and points out that Seeligmann 'notes a similar polemic against idol worship in LXX Isaiah', adding, 'the references in Isa. 1.29; 27.9; 37.19; 41.28 and 57.5 are all interpretations rather than literal translations of MT.'

62. והאלילים כליל יחלף (2.18).

63. καὶ τὰ χειροποίητα πάντα κατακρύψουσιν (2.18).

64. See, e.g., τὰ γλυπτά in 10.10 and τοῖς εἰδώλοις in 10.11.

65. In the Hebrew, Samaria's idols are אליל and Jerusalem's idols are עצבים. Williamson writes, however, that 'it is difficult to know whether the word was chosen here for any reason other than variety of terminology' (*Isaiah 1–27*, II, p. 520).

(i.e. 'the handiworks of Egypt'). As with 2.18 and 2.20 above, however, one finds the LXX translator showing variety in how אלילם is translated. Thus, the אלילם of Egypt are given in 19.1 as τὰ χειροποίητα Αἰγύπτου, but the reference to Egypt's אלילם is given in 19.3 as τοὺς θεοὺς αὐτῶν instead. In 21.9, the LXX differs from the MT slightly in regard to describing how Babylon's gods have fallen. Thus, where the MT reads 'and all the images of her gods' (וכל פסילי אלהיה), the LXX breaks the construct into two units: 'and all her images and the works of her hands' (καὶ πάντα τὰ ἀγάλματα αὐτῆς καὶ τὰ χειροποίητα αὐτῆς).[66]

An injunction for Israel to dispense with their idols occurs in 31.7 where, in contrast to previous texts, the focus on the illegitimacy of handmade idols is stressed both in the LXX and in the MT.[67] The emphasis is particularly heightened in the LXX since it contains both τὰ χειροποίητα as the translation of אלילם—which stresses the handmade nature of the objects—and the explanatory clause τὰ χειροποίητα αὐτῶν τὰ ἀργυρᾶ καὶ τὰ χρυσᾶ, ἃ ἐποίησαν αἱ χεῖρες αὐτῶν ('their handiworks of silver and gold, which their hands have made').[68] Here, the use of τὰ χειροποίητα by the translator of Isaiah closely matches the thematic emphasis of the MT; thus, 'as expressed elsewhere, it is stressed that the אלילים (idols) are made with human hands; how then can they possibly represent a real deity? ... The judgment could only be: they are, as a glossator added, חטא (for sin).'[69] In contrast to previ-

---

66. George Buchanan Gray (*A Critical and Exegetical Commentary on the Book of Isaiah, I–XXXIX* [ICC; Edinburgh: T. & T. Clark, 1912], p. 357) suggests that the doublet in the LXX text possibly represents 'an early text which read פסיליה (= פ', בבל, Jer. 51.47) or אלהיה, only'.

67. The LXX differs slightly from the MT here in that the MT repeats אלילם wherein אלילי כספו ואלילי זהבו ('their idols of silver and idols of gold') becomes τὰ χειροποίητα αὐτῶν τὰ ἀργυρᾶ καὶ τὰ χρυσᾶ ('their handiworks of silver and gold').

68. The third person possessive forms appear in both the MT and the LXX, although some translations, such as the NRSV, read 'your idols of silver and idols of gold', presumably to match the second person forms that appear in the second half of the verse (אשר עשו לכם ידיכם חטא, 31.7b).

69. Wildberger, *Isaiah 13–27*, p. 225. Cf. 'These idols, as works of people's own hands, will prove to be worthless and ineffective (cf. 17.7-8; 2.20; 27.9)' (S.H. Widyapranawa, *The Lord Is Savior: Faith in National Crisis—A Commentary on the Book of Isaiah 1–39* [ITC; Grand Rapids: Eerdmans, 1990], p. 195). The MT emphasizes the sinfulness of the hand-made creation: אשר עשו לכם ידיכם חטא ('which your hands have sinfully made for you'). The LXX, Ethiopian and Arabic

ous instances, in 46.6, it is אל ('god, deity') which stands behind the LXX translation of χειροποίητα.[70] Here, as well, the use of χειροποίητα is particularly suitable insofar as the text narrates (and mocks) the manufacturing of powerless gods.[71]

Special note may be made of Isa. 16.12 insofar as τὰ χειροποίητα does not stand for an idol—translating אלילם or אל—but means a 'sanctuary'[72] (translating מקדש), which is a point frequently missed in descriptions of the LXX use of χειροποίητος.[73] Here, one may note again Seeligmann's observation regarding the inconsistent method insofar as all other references to מקדש in LXX Isaiah are given as ἁγίασμα ('sanctuary', 8.14; 63.18) or τὸν τόπον τὸν ἅγιόν μου ('my holy place', 60.13).[74] The use of τὰ χειροποίητα thus likely refers to the various local sanctuaries in which Moabites might idolatrously pray.[75] As John Goldingay writes, 'Yahweh joins in the lamenting at devastation that is coming on Moab and at the futility of its laborious

versions omit the חטא, however, and Wildberger sees it as a gloss. For a discussion, see John D.W. Watts, *Isaiah 1–33* (WBC, 24; Nashville: Nelson, rev. edn, 2005), p. 478.

70. HALOT, *s.v.* 'אֵל'. Thus, the singular subject and object ויעשהו אל ('and he makes it into a god', RSV) is rendered in the LXX by the plural subjects and objects, ἐποίησαν χειροποίητα ('they made handiworks').

71. Walter Brueggemann, *Isaiah 40–66* (Westminster Bible Companion; Louisville: Westminster John Knox, 1998), p. 89. Cf. Graham S. Ogden and Jan Sterk, *A Handbook on Isaiah* (2 vols.; UBS Handbook Series; New York: United Bible Societies, 2011), II, p. 1284.

72. HALOT, *s.v.* 'מִקְדָּשׁ'.

73. See, e.g., Beal (*Colossians and Philemon*, p. 186), who says, 'The word "handmade" (χειροποίητος, *cheiropoiētos*) always refers to idols in the Greek OT.' Cf. Frank Thielman, *Ephesians* (BECNT; Grand Rapids: Baker Academic, 2010), p. 160; Douglas J. Moo, *The Letters to the Colossians and to Philemon* (PNTC; Grand Rapids: Eerdmans, 2008), p. 197 n. 46; Johnson, *Acts of the Apostles*, p. 133. Others have rightly noted that Isa. 16.12 denotes not an idol specifically, but a pagan sanctuary, such as Bauernfeind, ''Επαναπαύω', I, p. 436 n. 1. This distinction is also reflected correctly in Rudolf Pesch, *Das Markusevangelium* (2 vols.; HthKNT; Freiburg: Herder, 2001), II, p. 433; Keener, *Acts*, II, p. 1416 n. 1169.

74. BDAG, *s.v.* 'ἁγίασμα'.

75. Wildberger, *Isaiah 13–27*, p. 151. Cf. Blenkinsopp's comments on 1QIsaᵃ (*Isaiah 1–39*, p, 297).

efforts in praying at its own sanctuary.'[76] Bruce Chilton notes that the Aramaic Targum to Isaiah refuses to translate מקדש here as מקדשא, since it reserves the term to designate Yahweh's temple,[77] and this may also stand behind the LXX preference for τὰ χειροποίητα rather than ἁγίασμα in the present passage.

The importance of understanding LXX Isaiah's use of τὰ χειροποίητα for Stephen's speech is seen not only in the fact that the speech draws extensively from the LXX, but also in that Acts 7:48 is immediately followed by a quotation from Isa 66.1-2 in the LXX: 'Yet the Most High does not dwell in houses made with human hands; as the prophet says, "Will you build for me, says the Lord, or what is the place of my rest?"' As Joseph Fitzmyer writes, 'He cites Isaiah's words, which sought to make Israel aware that a human construction of stone and wood, no matter how beautiful, could not really contain God.'[78] For Conzelmann, this Isaiah quotation 'is a clear rejection of the Temple', and he avers that this quotation must be seen against the backdrop of the use of χειροποίητος in LXX Isa. 16.12 'as a designation for a temple'.[79] Against Conzelmann, however, it may be noted how the LXX and Targum of Isa. 16.12 seem to have intentionally chosen translations of מקדש which would ensure that the reader does not confuse the legitimate temple of Jerusalem with the illegitimate temples/sanctuaries of Moab. One may question, therefore, the degree to which the LXX use of χειροποίητος in Isa. 16.12—which is apparently chosen to protect the legitimacy of the Jerusalem temple—may therefore count as evidence against the legitimacy of the Jerusalem temple.

Overall, it may be noted that, regarding the use of χειροποίητος, it refers to idols themselves with no suggestion of a legitimate edifice only later viewed idolatrously, although an exception is Isa. 16.12 which refers instead to a sanctuary. Inconsistency, nevertheless, abounds in LXX Isaiah's word choice, and it remains a possibility that χειροποίητος was chosen merely for

---

76. John Goldingay, *The Theology of the Book of Isaiah* (Downers Grove, IL: IVP Academic, 2014), p. 44.

77. Bruce Chilton, *The Glory of Israel: The Theology and Provenience of the Isaiah Targum* (JSOTSup, 23; Sheffield: JSOT Press, 1983), p. 18.

78. Joseph A. Fitzmyer, *The Acts of the Apostles: A New Translation with Introduction and Commentary* (AB, 31; New Haven: Yale University Press, 1998), p. 384.

79. Conzelmann, *Acts*, p. 56.

word variation. Likewise, at times, one finds that χειροποίητος fits within the larger emphasis on the intrinsic inferiority of handmade entities, such as Isa. 31.7-8. Lastly, the substantive τὰ χειροποίητα mostly appears throughout LXX Isaiah with qualified terms which make the idolatry clear by the context;[80] however, the use of the substantive alone in Acts 7.48 might instead stress not that the Most High does not dwell in idolatrous houses, but that he does not ultimately dwell in any handmade entity, whether legitimately constructed or not.[81]

Daniel 5.4, 23; 6.28
In contrast to the substantive τὰ χειροποίητα seen earlier, in Dan. 5.4, it is used attributively to modify εἴδωλον; thus, during Baltasar's feast, they were praising τὰ εἴδωλα τὰ χειροποίητα αὐτῶν ('their handmade idols', 5.4). First, it may be noted that the LXX translation summarizes the Aramaic which lists in greater detail the material composition of the idols.[82] Secondly, following the use of τὰ χειροποίητα, the LXX also expands the MT to emphasize the transcendental nature of Yahweh in contrast to the idols, with the LXX adding καὶ τὸν θεὸν τοῦ αἰῶνος οὐκ εὐλόγησαν τὸν ἔχοντα τὴν ἐξουσίαν τοῦ

---

80. Thus, e.g., Σαμαρείᾳ καὶ τοῖς χειροποιήτοις αὐτῆς ('to Samaria and to the works of her hands', 10.11), τὰ χειροποίητα Αἰγύπτου ('the handiworks of Egypt', 19.1), etc.

81. Thus, ἀλλ᾽ οὐχ ὁ ὕψιστος ἐν χειροποιήτοις κατοικεῖ (7.48), that is, 'but the Most High does not dwell in hand-made things'. Though many translations, such as NASB, NRSV, ESV, NIV, add 'houses', the term as such does not appear in the Greek. Sylva's point is well worth noting: 'If Luke had written in Acts 7.48 that God (*ho theos*) does not dwell in the temple (*hieron* or *naos*), this would have been a biting criticism of the temple. However, Luke did not write this but rather he wrote that the Most High (*ho hypsistos*) does not dwell in what is made with hands (*cheiropoiētois*).' Thus, Luke's purpose in 7.46-50 is to convey 'the idea of God's transcendence (*ho hypsistos*) of earthly (*cheiropoiētois*) places of worship in general, and of the temple in particular' ('Meaning and Function of Acts 7:46-50', p. 267).

82. Thus, ‎ושבחו לאלהי דהבא וכספא נחשא פרזלא אעא ואבנא ('[they] praised the gold and silver and bronze and iron and wood and stone gods'). John A. Cook notes that describing the gods in terms of their material is 'a common strategy of anti-idolatry rhetoric' (*Aramaic Ezra and Daniel: A Handbook on the Aramaic Text*, [Baylor Handbook on the Hebrew Bible; Waco, TX: Baylor University Press, 2019], p. 79).

πνεύματος αὐτῶν ('and they did not bless the eternal God who had authority over their spirit'). Later, in 5.23 the same essential construction, πάντα τὰ εἴδωλα τὰ χειροποίητα τῶν ἀνθρώπων ('all the idols made by human hands') is found summarizing the Aramaic.[83] Similarly, there is a stress on the transcendence of God over these handmade idols, as well as the added comparison between the ineffectiveness of humankind's hands with God's hands: they praised the idols made by human hands but 'did not bless the living God. And your spirit is in his hand'.[84] For Meadowcroft, the use of τὰ χειροποίητα in the LXX represents a greater emphasis on the monotheistic nature of Yahweh.[85]

Finally, the construction appears again, in 6.28, in a clause only in the LXX and not in the MT. While the MT focuses positively on Yahweh's deliverance of Daniel, the LXX contains the additional statement of Darius stressing the inferiority of handmade idols to Yahweh: 'I, Darius, will do obeisance and be subject to him all my days, for the handmade idols are not able to save (τὰ γὰρ εἴδωλα τὰ χειροποίητα οὐ δύνανται σῶσαι) as God redeemed Daniel.' Meadowcroft refers to the 'problematic reference to "idols made with hands"' as evidencing the interests of the LXX translator since 'there does not seem to be any need to refer to idols as they have not been an issue in this story.'[86] Therefore, 'The translator betrays his continuing interest in the issue of idolatry with this insertion' as well as representing an 'explicit manifestation of the concern for cultic purity'.[87] The use of χειροποίητος in LXX Daniel is notable, therefore, for the manner in which it particularly reflects the interest of the translator as well as its difference in syntactical construction; it always appears here as modifying τὰ εἴδωλα whereas other uses largely appear substantively. Likewise, here it may be noted that it always refers to intrinsically idolatrous creations, rather than denoting a legitimate creation subsequently made idolatrous.

---

83. Thus, ולאלהי כספא ודהבא נחשא פרזלא אעא ואבנא ('the gold and silver and bronze and iron and wood and stone gods').

84. καὶ τῷ θεῷ τῷ ζῶντι οὐκ εὐλογήσατε, καὶ τὸ πνεῦμά σου ἐν τῇ χειρὶ αὐτοῦ (5.23).

85. Meadowcroft, *Aramaic Daniel and Greek Daniel*, p. 80.

86. Meadowcroft, *Aramaic Daniel and Greek Daniel*, p. 113.

87. Meadowcroft, *Aramaic Daniel and Greek Daniel*, p. 113.

Judith 8.18; Wisdom of Solomon 14.8; Sibylline Oracles 3.606, 3.618; 14.62; Sibylline Oracles Fragments 3.29

The term χειροποίητος may likewise be found in some pseudepigraphal texts with a similar function to the examples already surveyed. In Jdt. 8.18, χειροποίητος modifies θεός to denote idols and stresses that the current generations did not bow to idols as in the past. Thus, there is no tribe or family who προσκυνοῦσι θεοῖς χειροποιήτοις ('worships gods made with hands'). The particular construction, θεοῖς χειροποιήτοις, writes Lawrence Wills, 'was a relatively recent term in Israel's critique of idolatry', although it was comparable to other uses of χειροποίητος.[88] Notable is the use of χειροποίητος in Wis. 14.8. Here, the author is found praising a piece of wood, namely, the Ark of Noah which conceptually may be regarded as being made by hands and as 'blessed' and an object 'by which righteousness comes'.[89] Yet, while the raft (σχεδίας) guided by Yahweh's hand (χειρί) is blessed, this creation is strongly contrasted with τὸ χειροποίητον: 'But the idol made with hands is accursed, and so is the one who made it—he for having made it, and the perishable thing because it was named a god' (14.8). Here, then, is perhaps the clearest use where the substantive τὸ χειροποίητον—without any contextual modifiers such as τὰ χειροποίητα Αἰγύπτου in Isaiah or without grammatical modifiers such as τὰ εἴδωλα τὰ χειροποίητα in Daniel—refers specifically to an idol. This is particularly noteworthy insofar as the Ark could properly be described as τὸ χειροποίητον ('a handmade thing'), yet here the term by itself does not refer to a handmade thing in general, but that which is intrinsically idolatrous and, as 14.8 says, 'accursed'.

In the *Sibylline Oracles*, χειροποίητος appears in 3.606 substantively as χειροποίητα to denote idols and in a context which stresses the transcendence of Yahweh and the shame associated with worshipping these handmade creations.[90] This transcendence is again heightened in 3.618 where

88. Lawrence Wills, *Judith: A Commentary on the Book of Judith* (ed. Sidnie White Crawford; Hermeneia; Minneapolis: Fortress Press, 2019), p. 266.

89. εὐλόγηται γὰρ ξύλον, δι' οὗ γίνεται δικαιοσύνη ('For blessed is the wood by which righteousness comes'). Here the reference to ξύλον may indicate any piece of wood through which righteousness comes, but would nevertheless include at least the Ark.

90. 'They were not willing to piously honor the immortal begetter of all men, but honored idols made by hand [χειροποίητα], revering them, which mortals themselves will cast away, hiding them in clefts of rocks, through shame' (*Sib. Or.*

χειροποίητος appears attributively alongside ἔργα: 'They will bend a white knee on the fertile ground to God the great immortal king, but all handmade works [ἔργα δὲ χειροποίητα] will fall in a flame of fire.'[91] Notably, in 14.62, χειροποίητος does not technically denote idols as such, but is used, perhaps for the first time, specifically with reference to a temple. While the text has in view the melting down of the idolatrous statues (ἱδρύματα) of the temples, it is nevertheless the temple itself to which χειροποίητος applies: ναῶν ἱδρύματα χειροποιήτων ('the statues of temples made by hands').[92] In *Sib. Or. Frag.* 3.29, one finds the attributive ἀγάλματα χειροποίητα ('handmade images') in a list of objects adored by the 'mindless ones', alongside living creatures such as snakes, dogs and cats.[93]

Philo and Josephus

In both Philo and Josephus, χειροποίητος is utilized in similar ways already surveyed, yet also departing in significant ways. Like the usage found in Greco-Roman literature, the term appears in Philo in non-idolatrous contexts which relate both to physical and non-physical realities. For example, in *Vit. Mos.* 2.51 it refers to the 'foundation of a man-made city' (πόλεώς τε χειροποιήτου κτίσιν ἀρχήν) with no suggestion of its idolatrous nature.[94] Similarly, it is used for non-physical referents such as in *Somn.* 2.215 where it refers to 'trouble' caused by human agency[95] or in *Flacc.* 62 where it refers to 'a famine artificially created' (λιμῷ χειροποιήτῳ).[96] To be sure, Philo

---

3.604-607; translation from J.J. Collins, 'Sibylline Oracles [Second Century B.C.– Seventh Century A.D.]', in James H. Charlesworth [ed.], *The Old Testament Pseudepigrapha: Volume 1—Apocalyptic Literature and Testaments* [Garden City, NY: Doubleday, 1983], pp. 317-472 [375]).

91. Collins, 'Sibylline Oracles,' p. 375.

92. Collins, 'Sibylline Oracles,' p. 462. Note, e.g., that both ναῶν and χειροποιήτων are in the genitive yet ἱδρύματα in the accusative.

93. Collins, 'Sibylline Oracles,' p. 471.

94. Philo, *Vit. Mos.* 2.51 (Colson, LCL).

95. Thus, in listing various natural disasters, such as 'a blazing conflagration or a thunderbolt or family, or plague or earthquake', he adds 'any other trouble either of human or divine agency' (κακὰ χειροποίητα καὶ θεήλατα) (Philo, *Somn.* 2.125 [Colson and Whitaker, LCL]).

96. Philo, *Flacc.* 62 (Colson, LCL). The use of the term for 'famine artificially created' (λιμὸν ... χειροποίητον) also appears in Philo, *Spec.* 3.203 (Colson, LCL).

does employ χειροποίητος with reference to idols, as in *Vit. Mos.* 1.303 which depicts the massacring of those 'who had taken part in the rites of these idols made by men's hands' (τοῖς χειροποιήτοις).[97] However, what is notable is the fact that Philo uses χειροποίητος in *Op. Mund.* 142 to denote a construction of stone and wood, yet what is described is neither an idol nor an idolatrous temple, but a dwelling place that would have been suitable for Adam except that it merely had not yet been created.[98] So, too, does Philo in *Vit. Mos.* 2.88, when discussing the tabernacle and the temple, speak of 'a temple of man's making [ἱερὸν χειροποίητον], dedicated to the Father and Ruler of All' with no suggestion that it is an idol.[99] Significant here is that Philo was writing in a Jewish context, on the topic of the Old Testament, and was thoroughly acquainted with the LXX; indeed, Peder Borgen finds that 'Philo builds his exegesis on the Greek text of the LXX.'[100] However, he nevertheless employs χειροποίητος without the LXX connotations or denotations of idolatry.

Josephus likewise retains various uses of χειροποίητος unrelated to idolatry, such as its use to describe 'an artificial rounded hill' near Jerusalem.[101] He similarly speaks of immense walls 'reared by human hands' (χειροποίητα

---

97.   Philo, *Vit. Mos.* 1.303 (Colson, LCL).

98.   'If we call that original forefather of our race not only the first man but also the only citizen of the world we shall be speaking with perfect truth. For the world was his city and dwelling-place. No building made by hand had been wrought out of the material of stones and timbers' (Philo, *Op. Mund.* 142 [Colson, LCL]).

99.   Philo, *Vit. Mos.* 2.88 (Colson, LCL).

100.   Peder Borgen, 'Philo of Alexandria', *ABD*, V, pp. 333-42 (336). Cf. 'Scripture, in the form of the LXX, was a central source of authority for Philo and the window through which he could … reach his audience' (J. Andrew Overman and William Scott Green, 'Judaism', *ABD*, III, pp. 1037-54 [1050]).

101.   Josephus, *War* 1.419 (Thackeray, LCL). Literally, Josephus writes, τὸν δὲ μαστοειδῆ κολωνὸν ὄντα χειροποίητον, that is, a hand-made hill 'in the form of a breast', on which see translator's note in *War* 1.419 (Thackeray, LCL). Later Josephus will speak of the mound as being 'entirely artificial' (πᾶν χειροποίητον) in *War* 1.420 (Thackeray, LCL). The same expression appears in *Ant.* 15.324 where Josephus speaks of a hill 'raised to a (greater) height by the hand of man [χειροποίητον] and rounded off in the shape of a breast' (Marcus and Wikgren, LCL).

τείχη μέγιστα)[102] or the 'artificial defenses' of a city.[103] Josephus, in *Ant.* 4.55, also uses the term similarly to the earlier mentioned reference in Thucydides, *Hist.* 2.77.4 when he writes that the fire in Num. 16.35 was 'a fire, the like of which had never in the record of history been made by the hand of man' (χειροποίητον).[104] Notably, therefore, while Josephus does make reference to idols elsewhere,[105] there does not appear to be any use of χειροποίητος in his corpus to denote idols specifically or even idolatry more broadly. The repeated use of χειροποίητος by Josephus and Philo, who are rightly regarded as 'among the primary representatives of Hellenistic Judaism extant today',[106] without intending a derogatory sense of 'idol', therefore, problematizes broad generalizations such as Dunn's that the word 'was Hellenistic Judaism's dismissive description of "the idol"'.[107]

Observations on Jewish Usage
The focus of the present article has been to provide a more nuanced and thorough study of χειροποίητος in antiquity insofar as the term has rightly been recognized as a crucial interpretive key in Acts 7.48 and the debate about Stephen's view of the temple. Before surveying in a briefer fashion the instances where the term appears in the New Testament, the following observations may be made. First, the data are not as straightforward as has often been indicated and thus one finds in a standard dictionary like *NIDNTTE* the problematic claim that χειροποίητος in the LXX 'always' refers

---

102. Josephus, *War* 4.614 (Thackeray, LCL).

103. Josephus, *War* 7.176 (Thackeray, LCL). Later he will speak of Herod's tower which had been strongly 'intrenched against an enemy's attack, both by nature and the hand of man', here using the adverb χειροποιήτως (Josephus, *War* 7.294 [Thackeray, LCL]).

104. Josephus, *Ant.* 4.55 (Thackeray, LCL).

105. For example, when he discusses the construction of altars and the worship of idols in *Ant.* 9.243, he speaks of altars (βωμός) and idols (εἴδωλον). Likewise, in *Ant.* 18.344, he notes the custom of Mesopotamians carrying their idols (τὰ ἀφιδρύματα τῶν θεῶν).

106. Urban C. von Wahlde, *Gnosticism, Docetism, and the Judaisms of the First Century: The Search for the Wider Context of the Johannine Literature and Why It Matters* (LNTS, 517; London: Bloomsbury, 2015), p. 107.

107. Dunn, *Beginning*, p. 270.

to idols,[108] yet, in Isa. 16.12, the reference is to a sanctuary and, in Lev. 26.30, the reference is arguably to an incense-altar. Secondly, one finds in the LXX use of χειροποίητος, a degree of translational inconsistency insofar as it is sometimes used as a summary statement of a multiplicity of idols and, other times, as merely a singular idol within a list of other idols. The אלילם of Egypt can be given in Isa. 19.1 as τὰ χειροποίητα Αἰγύπτου, yet Egypt's same אלילם can then be given in Isa. 19.3 as τοὺς θεοὺς αὐτῶν instead. The use of χειροποίητος at various places may thus be due to an unconstrained translational method, a preference for introducing variations, along with the particular agendas of the LXX translators in their polemic against idol worship. Thirdly, grammatical constructions comparable to Acts 7.48 (viz., ἀλλ' οὐχ ὁ ὕψιστος ἐν χειροποιήτοις κατοικεῖ) are exceedingly rare. Nowhere does χειροποίητος appear near κατοικέω ('dwell') and it almost always appears as χειροποίητα rather than the dative χειροποιήτοις, and never in the prepositional phrase ἐν χειροποιήτοις.[109] Further, the use of χειροποίητος almost always has grammatical and contextual indicators that idolatry is in view, such as being used as an attributive adjective alongside εἴδωλα or as speaking of τὰ χειροποίητα Αἰγύπτο, that is, handmade objects *of Egypt*. The clearest example of a stand-alone reference to τὸ χειροποίητον without contextual modifiers is Wis. 14.8 where it does refer to an idol and is described as accursed.

Fifthly, it should be noted that very frequently χειροποίητος is utilized in contexts where what is being stressed is the transcendence of Yahweh over that which is handmade (e.g., Dan. 5.4 or *Sib. Or.* 3.606, 3.618). Sixthly, in at least one instance, Isa. 16.12, the translational choice of χειροποίητος in the LXX, like the use of במה instead of מקרשא in the Targum, appears chosen to protect the legitimacy of the Jerusalem temple. Thus, using Isa. 16.12 as evidence against the Jerusalem temple appears, at best, precarious. Seventhly, the use of χειροποίητος in Wis. 14.8 is a notable example of where χειροποίητος does not denote simply any 'handmade object', since it is used after a reference to Noah's ark yet stands in contrast to it, to denote an idol particularly. Eighthly, it is important to observe that in all of the instances where χειροποίητος denotes idolatry, it refers to intrinsic rather than extrinsic idolatry. That is, χειροποίητος denotes constructions which were

---

108. Silva, 'Χείρ', IV, p. 663.
109. See, however, Jdt 8.18 and Isa. 10.11.

idolatrous in their very construction; one does not find instances where χειροποίητος refers to a legitimately constructed object which only later was turned into an idol by the perception of those interacting with it. This does not, of course, prevent Acts 7.48 from being interpreted as meaning that the temple is legitimate but that the religious leaders had begun to treat the temple idolatrously, only that support for this type of use is difficult to find in the LXX use of the term. Lastly, it should not be ignored that while the references in the LXX and Pseudepigrapha do denote idolatry, there exists a widespread and established use of χειροποίητος in both the Greco-Roman literature and in Jewish writers such as Josephus and Philo where the term appears in entirely non-idolatrous contexts. Clearly, in *Op. Mund.* 142, Philo does not draw from the LXX use of χειροποίητος to suggest that Adam should have lived inside of an idol or idolatrous dwelling, but instead merely means a handmade house which is contrasted with the natural earth. Too often discussions of χειροποίητος draw a direct line from the LXX to the New Testament, yet these examples show how frequently the term was being used in both Greco-Roman and Jewish contexts without any reference to the concept of idolatry but merely to denote something 'handmade'.

5. Χειροποίητος in its New Testament Context

In interpreting the use of Acts 7.48, the LXX usage has for many been determinative, and not unreasonably so, yet it is nevertheless important to compare this usage to that found in the New Testament. For example, although the *NIDNTTE* claims that χειροποίητος is 'always' used with reference to idols in the LXX, it finds that 'in the NT it never refers to idols', which suggests a curious dissonance between the two corpuses.[110] Lohse finds that 'in the NT χειροποίητος in every passage in which it is used sets forth the antithesis of what is made with men's hands to the work of God' yet leaves unaddressed the question of how the LXX use of idolatry does or does not relate to the passages.[111] In the New Testament, χειροποίητος is used in six

---

110. Silva, 'Χείρ', IV, p. 663-64.

111. Eduard Lohse, 'χείρ, κτλ', *TDNT*, IX, pp. 435-36 (436). Bauernfeind, ''Επαναπαύω', I, p. 436. Similarly, W. Rebell in summarizing in the New Testament simply quotes Lohse at this point. Likewise, while Acts 7.48 is mentioned where it is concluded that it does not express 'any fundamental criticism of the temple' but

places: Mk 14.58; Acts 7.48, 17.24; Eph. 2.11; Heb. 9.11, 24. Likewise present is the use of the term ἀχειροποίητος ('not made by hand')[112] which is not found in the LXX but appears in Mk 14.58, Col. 2.11 and 2 Cor. 5.1. These examples, like those surveyed, help to illuminate the manner in which Stephen's contemporaries employed the term.

In Mk 14.58, both χειροποίητος and ἀχειροποίητος appear in the context of the 'false testimony' against Jesus who was claimed to have said: 'I will destroy this temple that is made with hands (τὸν ναὸν τοῦτον τὸν χειροποίητον), and in three days I will build another, not made with hands (ἄλλον ἀχειροποίητον οἰκοδομήσω).'[113] If this represents Jesus' words, then it is possible that Jesus, like Stephen, characterized the temple establishment as idolatrous.[114] Others, however, while noting the LXX context, do not go so far as to say that Jesus identifies the temple as idolatrous but acknowledge that he is nevertheless critical of it (i.e. χειροποίητος means 'merely a human construction' and ἀχειροποίητος indicates 'built by God himself').[115] Sylva has argued that Mk 14.58 represents a misunderstanding by the accusers of how the χειροποίητος terminology was used by Jesus, and that Luke attempts to correct this misunderstanding. Thus, he writes,

> According to Luke, the Christian message is not that Jesus will destroy the temple "made with hands" (*cheiropoiēton*, Mk 14.58), but rather that God transcends (*ho hypsistos*, Acts 7.48) anything made with human hands (*cheiropoiētois*, Acts 7.48); the Christian message is not that Jesus will build another temple 'not made with hands' (*acheiropoiēton*, Mk 14.58), but rather that God's hands made all things (*hē cheir mou epoiēsen tauta panta*, Acts 7.50). In such a way, Luke attempts to explain the false witness that Jesus would destroy

'pick[s] up the idea of the limitation of the temple's significance', no mention of the LXX, idols or idolatry is made in the entire entry (W. Rebell, 'Χειροποίητος', *EDNT*, III, p. 464).

112. BDAG, *s.v.* 'ἀχειροποίητος'.

113. Bruce opines that the fact that Jesus said this statement 'is not likely to have been false on this point' (*Book of the Acts*, p. 150).

114. Craig A. Evans, *Mark 8:27–16:20* (WBC 34B; Nashville: Nelson, 2001), p. 446.

115. Mark L. Strauss, *Mark* (ZECNT; Grand Rapids: Zondervan, 2014), p. 654. Cf. Pesch, *Das Markusevangelium*, II, p. 434.

the temple *cheiropoiēton* and build another *acheiropoiēton* as a misunderstanding of how these *cheiropoiēton* terms were used.[116]

It is possible, therefore, that Jesus' use of χειροποίητος and ἀχειροποίητος deals more properly with God's transcendence, a notion likewise embedded in the LXX usage of the terms.

After the use of χειροποίητος in Acts 7.48, it is found again in 17.24 in Paul's statement of God's transcendence during his speech at the Areopagus. Thus, he declares, 'the God who made the world and everything in it, he who is Lord of heaven and earth, does not live in shrines made by human hands' (οὐκ ἐν χειροποιήτοις ναοῖς κατοικεῖ). Here the language fits most closely with Acts 7.48, although ναός has been specified. While idolatry is no doubt in view throughout the entire pericope,[117] L. Scott Kellum has suggested that the use of χειροποίητος 'is not the inflammatory statement of 7.48', and here draws on simply its Greco-Roman usage of 'hand-made' which 'would not be offensive to a Gentile about a pagan shrine'.[118] Instead, the function of the description may be to stress more broadly God's transcendence, as C.J. Hemer writes: 'The nature of God is thus explained against the backdrop of the Athenians' own terminology, as Paul gently exposes the inconsistency between the transcendent reality to which their thinkers aspired and the man-made images of Athens.'[119]

In both Eph. 2.11 and Col. 2.11, Paul uses the language of χειροποίητος and ἀχειροποίητος as applied to circumcision. Paul speaks of Jews having merely 'a physical circumcision made in the flesh by human hands' (ἐν σαρκὶ χειροποιήτου; Eph. 2.11) and those in Christ being 'circumcised with a spiritual circumcision', as some translate it, or more literally, 'a circumci-

116. Sylva, 'Meaning and Function of Acts 7:46-50', pp. 270-71.

117. C.K. Barrett writes that the word 'cannot fail to recall its frequent use in OT denunciations of idolatry' (*A Critical and Exegetical Commentary on the Acts of the Apostles* [2 vols.; ICC; New York: T. & T. Clark, 2004], II, p. 840). See also Keldie Paroschi who notes 'the narrative framing of the speech [in Acts 17.22-31] around the issue of idolatry' ('On God's Side of History: Time and Apocalyptic History in Paul's Speech at the Areopagus', *AUSS* 59 [2022], p. 239 n. 65).

118. L. Scott Kellum, *Acts* (EGGNT; Nashville: B&H Academic, 2020), p. 204. Cf. Flavien Pardigon, *Paul against the Idols: A Contextual Reading of the Areopagus Speech* (Eugene, OR: Pickwick, 2019), p. 155 n. 70.

119. Colin J. Hemer, *The Book of Acts in the Setting of Hellenistic History* (ed. Conrad H. Gempf; Winona Lake, IN: Eisenbrauns, 1990), p. 423.

sion without hands' (περιτομῇ ἀχειροποιήτῳ; Col. 2.11). Here, Paul appears to be using the term in its more generic sense of 'handmade' rather than importing notions of idolatry, although he may nevertheless have intended to draw on general negative connotations of the term.[120] This, then, would represent important New Testament evidence for χειροποίητος departing from LXX usage. Alternatively, some have found the LXX use as determinative in the present passage, and thus Nijay K. Gupta writes that 'By using this term, then, in Col. 2.11, Paul is alluding to the over-reliance on physical circumcision as a kind of reverence for what is merely "handmade"—tantamount to idolatry.'[121] Notably, this view of the use of χειροποίητος is similar to the extrinsic view of idolatry concerning Acts 7.48. That is, if Paul employs χειροποίητος to mean not that circumcision at its inception was intrinsically idolatrous but that it has only become idolatrous because of subsequent attitudes toward the practice, then this would lend support to the view that Stephen does not mean that the temple at its inception was intrinsically idolatrous but only means that the temple became idolatrous because of subsequent attitudes toward the edifice.

In Heb. 9.11 and 9.24, χειροποίητος appears, yet the difficulty in taking the term as denoting an idol relates to the fact that it is applied to the tabernacle which God himself commanded. The author indicates that Christ has entered 'through the greater and perfect tent (not made with hands [οὐ χειροποιήτου], that is, not of this creation)' (9.11) and again that he 'did not enter a sanctuary made by human hands [χειροποίητα ... ἅγια], a mere copy of the true one, but he entered into heaven itself' (9.24). Again, in 8.2 the

---

120. A number of commentators thus note that the LXX employs the term to denote idols, but find that this sense is not carried over to Paul's usage here, such as Thielman, *Ephesians*, p. 160; Harold W. Hoehner, *Ephesians* (Grand Rapids: Baker Academic, 2002), p. 354; Clinton E. Arnold, *Ephesians* (ZECNT; Grand Rapids: Zondervan, 2010), p. 154; Andrew T. Lincoln, *Ephesians* (WBC, 42; Dallas: Word, 1990), p. 136.

121. Nijay K. Gupta, *Colossians* (SHBC; Macon, GA: Smyth & Helwys, 2013), p. 94. Cf. 'Here, in noting the circumcision that is "not performed by human hands", therefore, Paul is indirectly accusing those who emphasize physical circumcision of worshiping false gods' (Pao, *Colossians and Philemon*, 165). Beale also opines that the reference 'indicates that to continue to affirm circumcision as the true identity marker of God's new-covenant people is idolatrous' (*Colossians and Philemon*, p. 187).

author stresses that Christ is now a 'minister in the sanctuary and the true tent that the Lord, and not any mortal, has set up'. Yet the function of the text is not to stress that the handmade tabernacle was idolatrous, but that it was merely a copy and an imperfect representation of the heavenly tabernacle.[122] Indeed, the author is clear that Moses constructed the handmade Tabernacle according to God's command, indicating that Moses was told, 'See that you make everything according to the pattern that was shown you on the mountain' (8.5). Accordingly, Craig R. Koester, while acknowledging that the term χειροποίητος has a 'pejorative connotation and was used for idols', stresses that the author of Hebrews departs from such usage, writing, 'The author understood that the Tabernacle was made by hand, since Moses had "made" it at God's command (Heb. 8.5), although he did not consider the Tabernacle to be idolatrous.'[123] Both the tabernacle and the temple were handmade and temporary (cf. Mk 14.58; Acts 7.48) and stand 'in contrast to the heavenly tent that God set up (Heb. 8.2)', not because they were idolatrous but because they were merely copies.[124] Similarly, in 2 Cor. 5.1, the term ἀχειροποίητος is used to stress the earthly tent with the heavenly building 'not made with hands'. There appears little indication in the text that notions of idolatry are in view; rather, 'the description "not made with hands" (ἀχειροποίητος, *acheiropoiētos*) implies "not made by human effort or ability" and speaks of something that only God can do.'[125] Therefore, the application of the terms appears to have little relation to idolatry in the present

---

122. As William L. Lane stresses, 'the expression "true tabernacle" is used in contrast not to what is false but to what is symbolical and imperfect' (*Hebrews 1–8* [WBC, 47A; Dallas: Word, 1991], pp. 205-6).

123. Craig R. Koester, *Hebrews: A New Translation with Introduction and Commentary* (AB, 36; New Haven: Yale University Press, 1974), pp. 409-10. Cf. 'Χειροποιήτου, like χειροποίητα (v. 24), means "manufactured", not "fictitious" (as applied to idols or idol-temples by the LXX and Philo)' (James Moffatt, *A Critical and Exegetical Commentary on the Epistle to the Hebrews* [ICC; Edinburgh: T. & T. Clark, 1924], p. 120).

124. Koester, *Hebrews*, p. 410.

125. George H. Guthrie, *2 Corinthians* (BECNT; Grand Rapids: Baker Academic, 2015), p. 278. Victor Paul Furnish thus writes that the adjective merely 'describes what is "supernatural, immaterial, spiritual"' (*II Corinthians: Translated with Introduction, Notes, and Commentary* [AB, 32A; New Haven: Yale University Press, 1984], p. 266).

texts, and merely contrasts that which is handmade to that which is made by God. Concerning the New Testament usage, therefore, there exists an array of texts where the LXX usage of χειροποίητος with its relationship to idolatry does not appear to have a controlling force. Such uses provide a context for questioning the degree to which Acts 7.48 should, therefore, necessarily draw from the LXX sense of idolatry.

6. Conclusion

The present study has attempted to provide a more detailed account of the use of χειροποίητος in Greco-Roman and Jewish literature since a lacuna of such studies exists and the term occurs in a prominent place in Stephen's speech, as well as throughout the New Testament. Determination of how Stephen employs the term in Acts 7:48, as well as of his view of the temple more broadly, ultimately relies on a series of complex and interrelated interpretive questions that cannot be decided on word choice alone. Nevertheless, at least four conclusions from the data may be highlighted. First, while it is true that χειροποίητος was a term employed in describing idols, it is also true that in many of these instances this term appeared in conjunction with other terms which provided clear indications that the object was an idol; thus, the notion of idolatry was not necessarily derived from the internal semantics of χειροποίητος but came from the larger linguistic context. In the construction τὰ εἴδωλα τὰ χειροποίητα, for example, it is not that χειροποίητος stands alone substantively to denote an idol, but that τὰ εἴδωλα already indicates the idols and τὰ χειροποίητα stresses its handmade, material quality. Similarly, when χειροποίητος is employed in the LXX frequently the surrounding language makes clear that the focus is on transcendence. Secondly, a response to the charge that Stephen views the construction of the temple as idolatrous has been to claim that χειροποίητος denotes a legitimately constructed edifice merely subsequently viewed idolatrously. While possible, none of the instances of the term in the LXX are used in this way, although in the New Testament, Col. 2.11 may offer support.

Thirdly, though the LXX has undeniable significance on the language of the New Testament, the widespread and well-established usage of χειροποίητος in both Greco-Roman and Jewish literature as denoting 'handmade' with no connotations of idolatry should nevertheless not be ignored. It is significant that Philo can speak of the idea of Adam dwelling in a 'handmade' house of silver or gold without any indication that the concept of idolatry is anywhere in view. Likewise, several New Testament texts also appear to employ the term to indicate 'handmade' with no relation to idolatry. These factors should mitigate drawing too quickly a correlation between LXX usage and a particular text, since this correlation tends to ignore established usage in other Greco-Roman and Jewish literature. Lastly, Sylva has noted that an interpretive key to Acts 7.48 is recognizing that Stephen always refers to God with θεός in his speech, except for 7.48 where he changes to ὕψιστος 'the Most High'.[126] Rather than drawing from the conceptual pool of idolatry, Stephen may therefore employ χειροποίητος in the more general sense of handmade to stress Yahweh's transcendence over any handmade entity, whether legitimately constructed or not.[127]

126. Sylva, 'Meaning and Function of Acts 7:46-50', p. 267.

127. Accordingly, Sylva's observation has much to commend it when he writes, 'Luke's change in his manner of referring to God at this point (i.e. 7.48) in the Stephen episode is the result of his concern to convey in 7.46-50 the idea of God's transcendence (*ho hypsistos*) of earthly (*cheiropoiētois*) places of worship in general, and of the temple in particular' ('Meaning and Function of Acts 7:46-50', p. 267).

[*JGRChJ* 19 (2023) 40-72]

TRIAL BY ORDEAL: THE DEVELOPMENT OF
THE NERONIAN PERSECUTION

Daryn Graham

Independent Scholar, Sydney, NSW, Australia

Introduction

The 64 CE fire of Rome was a catalyst for change, and in relation to Christians living in the city, it was brutal. Along with Rome's rebuilding, persecution was enforced on a grand scale. Paul and Peter were killed, as were many other Christians who had done little to convict themselves in relation to the fire other than belong to the Christian faith. As this article demonstrates, these and other Christians were scapegoats for the fire that burned Rome in 64 CE. As punishment, many were killed, ultimately upon Nero's decision. This article also argues that members of other groups may have also been executed in the chaos and bloodlust of the persecution. Most were Christians, however. Ultimately, for falling out of imperial favour, many Christians found themselves victims of an emperor's cruelty. For this, the persecution may have extended beyond the confines of Rome although the main area of focus appears to have been Rome. Explored also is the argument that Paul was executed not immediately after his trial but during the persecution itself. Peter's execution and the possibility he held Roman citizenship are also discussed. Finally, the legacy of the remains of Paul and Peter is reflected upon. In this article, biblical and extra-biblical evidence is investigated through the lens of modern scholarship to offer a historical analysis of the topics outlined above, presented together as a whole in one article for the first time. It is affirmed that Nero was responsible for the persecution, that Christians were persecuted during it in solid numbers, that the confines of the persecution may not have been just the city of Rome and that Paul and Peter died as a result of it. It will also be affirmed that as Rome rebuilt, so did Christianity, with help from Christians further afield, including Antioch in Syria.

Blamed for the Fire

For the fire of 64 CE, Nero blamed a supposedly non-Roman religious group—the Christians—thereby seeking to galvanize support from patriotic religious Romans in his cause to eradicate the group from the city and to condemn it to persecution. As to who was responsible for suggesting to Nero to use these Christians as scapegoats, debate exists. As early as 1898, Philippe Fabia suggested that Poppaea Sabina, Nero's wife from 62–65 CE—whom Josephus described as a 'God-fearer' (θεοσεβής) at a time when Jews and Christians were at loggerheads in Rome over the trial of Paul in 63 CE—was the most likely candidate.[1] In 1959, Smallwood challenged this idea, pointing out that it was Poppaea who had Gessius Florus appointed procurator over Judea from 64–66 CE on account of her friendship with his wife—a procuratorship that would result in the outbreak of the First Jewish War (66–70 CE)— hardly the behaviour of a Jewish sympathizer.[2] Florus was an associate of G. Gessius Gallus, who was the Roman governor of Syria from 63 CE or 65 CE up to his death in 67 CE. While Florus was an antagonist towards the Jewish people at times, stirring Judean sentiment towards revolt against Rome, Gallus took an active role in the war that was to follow. At the outbreak of the war, Florus was replaced as procurator by Marcus Antonius Julianus over proceedings in Judea. These men worked with Florus in order to spark the outbreak and the First Jewish War in an administrative, orchestrated manner. Thus, it may be argued with some confidence that the appointment of Florus to the procuratorship of Judea was not the wisest move by Nero—and by implication, Poppaea—but was rather superficial, and not well thought through or considerably God-fearing in its extent.[3] In light of such a character profile

1.   Josephus, *Ant.* 20.195; Philippe Fabia, 'Le Règne et la Mort de Poppée', *Revue de Philologie, de Littérature, et d'Histoire Anciennes* 22 (1898), pp. 333-45 (336-37).

2.   E.M. Smallwood, 'The Alleged Jewish Tendencies of Poppaea Sabina', *JTS* 10 (1959), pp. 329-35.

3.   On Florus, see Josephus, *War* 2.14.5-9; 6.4.3; *Ant.* 20.11.1. On Gallus, see Josephus, *War* 2.14.3-4; 2.19.2, 9; *Ant.* 20.11.1; Tacitus, *Ann.* 5.10, 13; Suetonius,

of Poppaea, throughout the twentieth century most historians accepted that
she was most likely the one who in a fickle manner suggested to Nero to use
the Christians as scapegoats. However, it is often held that while Poppaea certainly encouraged Nero to officially blame the Christians, the idea may have
been first broached to her and to Nero by the praetorian prefect at the time of
the fire, Tigellinus.[4]

Poppaea is likely to have been born in Pompeii in Italy, given that her
father's family, known to history as the Ollii, derived from there as local
property owners.[5] In fact, the *gens Poppaea* owned at least five houses in
Pompeii, and Poppaea herself owned brick works property in nearby
Oplontis.[6] This renders Poppaea's family of affluent, but still fairly humble
origins compared to the wealth and prestige of Nero, whom she married—
leading to an influx of wealth and prestige into her own life in the city of
Rome, as she became empress over the Roman Empire. Her life was an example of impressive upward mobility through the ranks of Roman society.
The intelligence that inspired her to achieve this upward mobility marked her
as an influential character in the court of Nero. This influence over Nero had
been emerging strongly for many years leading up to the persecution of the
Christians in 64 CE. Thus, Tacitus states she became an intimate counsellor
of Nero from that time onwards.[7] However, the third-century CE Roman historian Cassius Dio also states that this influence extended to persuading Nero
to execute his own mother, and punishing his wife at the time.[8] Thus, while
her influence over others at the court of Nero included modelling lifestyle—
to the point of having fashionable beauty practices named after her—it also
extended over Nero to the point of killing. Poppaea died in 65 CE. She re-

Vesp. 4; E. Schürer, *History of the Jewish People in the Time of Jesus Christ* (New
York: Scribner, 1891), pp. 368-69.

4.   M. Cary and H.H. Scullard, *A History of Rome Down to the Reign of
Constantine* (New York: Bedford Books, 1983), p. 359; W.H.C. Frend, *The Rise of
Christianity* (Philadelphia: Fortress Press, 1984), p. 109; Michael J.G. Gray-Fow,
'Why the Christians? Nero and the Great Fire', *Latomus* 57 (1998), pp. 595-616.

5.   M. Della Corte, *Case ed abitante di Pompei* (Naples: Faustino Fiorentino,
3rd edn, 1965), p. 59.

6.   Miriam T. Griffin, *Nero: The End of a Dynasty* (New Haven: Yale University Press, 1984), p. 102.

7.   Tacitus, *Ann.* 15.61.

8.   Dio Cassius, *Hist. rom.* 61.12; 62.13.1, 4.

ceived a public funeral, and was embalmed and buried rather than cremated in the traditional Roman style; she was later deified by Nero.[9]

It is clear that Poppaea could not have foreseen the disaster that was Florus's governorship, having him appointed on the strength of her friendship with his wife alone, and although Poppaea did not embrace all Jewish traditions she most certainly admired and sympathized with Judaism. In 61 CE, she was instrumental in having Nero acquit the Jerusalem leaders in the 'Wall Case', which the Roman procurator Porcius Festus had brought against them for building a wall that screened-off the Temple from the Antonia.[10] Then, in 64 CE, at the request of a young Josephus, she persuaded Nero to pardon some Jewish priests sent to Rome a number of years earlier by the procurator Antonius Felix.[11] According to Pliny the Elder, Poppaea was obsessed with fashion, and in the words of Margaret H. Williams, who is to say this preoccupation of hers did not 'extend also into the sphere of religion'?[12] Indeed, given that Paul states in his letter to the Philippians that there were some of 'Caesar's household'—that is, occupiers and staff—that were new converts to the Christian faith, she may have heard of Christianity from them, and unhappy that this breakaway sect that undermined Jewish tradition had penetrated the palace, struck upon them as a group for Nero to blame after the fire.[13]

Precursors

Whatever Poppaea's role might have been, Nero took a leading role in his own decision making. He could see for himself Christianity's unpopularity in Rome, and knew full well the details with the aid of official records of how the tensions had reached flash point between Jews, Christians, and Romans during the principate of Claudius.[14] For, as the second-century CE Roman

9.   Juvenal, *Sat.* 1.155; Tacitus, *Ann.* 16.6; Dio Cassius, *Hist. rom.* 62.28.1-2; 63.26.3; Griffin, *Nero*, pp. 101, 103.

10.   Josephus, *Ant.* 20.182-196.

11.   Josephus, *Life* 13-16.

12.   Margaret H. Williams, 'θεοσεβὴς γὰρ ἦν—The Jewish Tendencies of Poppaea Sabina', *JTS* 39 (1988), pp. 97-111 (111).

13.   Phil. 4.22; Smallwood, 'Alleged Jewish Tendencies', p. 330.

14.   Daryn Graham, 'A World Aflame: Nero's Persecution of the Christians in AD 64', *Vox Reformata* 85 (2020), pp. 89-114 (94).

biographer Suetonius states, as a number of Jews repeatedly orchestrated disturbances 'at the instigation of Chrestus, he [Claudius] expelled them from Rome'.[15] Suetonius made this brief statement without any chronological markers, which makes it difficult to pinpoint the year this expulsion took place.[16] To complicate matters, Cassius Dio records another, separate event that took place under Claudius in 41 CE which has confused some scholars into thinking Dio and Suetonius described the same event.[17] These texts have also often been used to shed light on each other.[18] According to Dio, in the first year of Claudius's reign, the emperor wished to curb the Jewish presence in Rome, but could not expel the Jews from the city on account of their many numbers; he decided to ban their public meetings there instead. As Dio states,

τούς τε Ἰουδαίους πλεονάσαντας αὖθις, ὥστε χαλεπῶς ἂν ἄνευ ταραχῆς ὑπὸ τοῦ ὄχλου σφῶν τῆς πόλεως εἰρχθῆναι, οὐκ ἐξήλασε μέν, τῷ δὲ δὴ πατρίῳ βίῳ χρωμένους ἐκέλευσε μὴ συναθροίζεσθαι.

As for the Jews, who had again increased so greatly that by reason of their multitude it would have been hard without raising a tumult to bar them from the city [Rome], he [Claudius] did not drive them out, but ordered them, while continuing their traditional mode of life, not to hold meetings.[19]

The differences between this text and Suetonius's statement are evident. In Dio's passage, Claudius curbs his wish to expel the Jews while in Suetonius expulsion from Rome is carried out. This has prompted Slingerland to conclude that Dio and Suetonius describe different events—in 41 CE

15. Suetonius, *Claud.* 25.

16. Dixon Slingerland, 'Suetonius' "Claudius" 25.4 and the Account of Cassius Dio', *JQR* 79 (1989), pp. 305-22 (306).

17. A. Momigliano, *Claudius* (Greenwood, CT: Westport, 1981), p. 31; E.M. Smallwood, *The Jews under Roman Rule from Pompey to Diocletian* (Leiden: Brill, 1981), p. 215.

18. B. Baldwin, *Suetonius* (Amsterdam: M. Hakkert, 1983), p. 356; Slingerland, 'Suetonius' "Claudius" 25.4', p. 306.

19. Dio Cassius, *Hist. rom.* 60.6.6-7.

Claudius banned Jewish gatherings in Rome for concern of their growing presence there, while at a later date he carried out his expulsion.[20]

As to what that later date may be, two hypotheses exist. The first of these was proposed by Smallwood, who creatively argues that given Tacitus recorded a similar expulsion of Jews from Rome under Tiberius in 19 CE, it therefore makes sense that he also recorded the expulsion under Claudius. But, given our texts of Tacitus include only the years 46 CE to 54 CE of Claudius's principate, Tacitus must have placed it somewhere during the lost years of 41 CE to 46 CE of Claudius's reign.[21] Added to this, Smallwood argues that a comment by the first-century CE Jewish philosopher Philo provides credibility to this scenario. In his praise of Augustus, Philo—writing under the early reign of Claudius—states that Augustus 'neither ejected them [the Jews] from Rome...'.[22] Smallwood suggests that this shows the Jews were expelled by Claudius during the years covered by the lost sections of Tacitus's *Annals* in juxtaposition to Augustan policy.[23] However, as Slingerland points out, because we no longer possess these lost sections we cannot know this for certain. Furthermore, Philo might equally have been alluding to the expulsion under Augustus's immediate successor Tiberius, not Claudius.[24]

The second hypothesis relies on the testimony of the fifth-century CE historian Orosius, as he was preparing historical material for Augustine of Hippo for his mammoth *City of God*. According to Orosius, Josephus recorded that in the ninth year of the principate of Claudius, 'the Jews were expelled by Claudius from the city [Rome]'.[25] Although no such statement by Josephus exists in any of his extant works, Orosius's matter-of-fact language, and the verifiability of his claims at the time, make it likely that his attribution was

---

20. Slingerland, 'Suetonius' "Claudius" 25.4', p. 322; Dixon Slingerland, 'Suetonius Claudius 25.4, Acts 18, and Paulles Orosius' "Historium Adversus Paganos Libre VII"': Dating the Claudian Expulsion(s) of Roman Jews', *JQR* 83 (1992), pp. 127-44 (128, 144); Graham, 'A World Aflame', p. 96.

21. Smallwood, *Jews under Roman Rule*, pp. 212-13.

22. Philo, *Leg*, 23.243.

23. Smallwood, *Jews under Roman Rule*, pp. 213-14.

24. Slingerland, 'Suetonius', pp. 129-32.

25. Orosius, *Hist. adv. Pag.* 7.6.15.

legitimate.[26] In support of this hypothesis is the fact that Corinth was a Roman colony during those times, and thus was a likely destination for numbers of refugees expelled from Rome itself. Acts states that Aquila and Priscilla had been part of Claudius's expulsion, and had met Paul in Corinth during the proconsulship of Seneca's brother, Lucius Junius Gallio Annaeanus, over Achaea in 51–52 CE,

Μετὰ ταῦτα χωρισθεὶς ἐκ τῶν Ἀθηνῶν ἦλθεν εἰς Κόρινθον. καὶ εὑρών τινα Ἰουδαῖον ὀνόματι Ἀκύλαν Ποντικὸν τῷ γένει προσφάτως ἐληλυθότα ἀπὸ τῆς Ἰταλίας καὶ Πρίσκιλλαν γυναῖκα αὐτοῦ, διατεταχέναι Κλαύδιον χωρίζεσθαι πάντας τοὺς Ἰουδαίους ἀπὸ τῆς Ῥώμης

After this, Paul left Athens and went to Corinth. There he met a Jew named Aquila, a native of Pontus, who had recently come from Italy with his wife Priscilla, because Claudius had ordered all Jews to leave Rome.[27]

Because Acts actually states they came to Corinth from Italy, this may mean that they were part of the expulsion, which probably did take place in 49 CE, but sojourned throughout Italy for several years afterwards before leaving Italy for Corinth.[28]

As to whom 'Chrestus' might be, several theories exist. As pointed out by Koestermann and Benko, 'Chrestus' was a name that was very popular among slaves in Rome. Thus, these scholars argue, he must have been a historical person. But who that historical person might be, they argue, is unknowable.[29] Slingerland, however, through use of a different interpretation

---

26.   Peter Lampe, *From Paul to Valentinus: Christians at Rome in the First Two Centuries* (London: T. & T. Clark, 2003), pp. 11-16; Bernard Green, *Christianity in Ancient Rome: The First Three Centuries* (London: Bloomsbury, 2010), p. 25; Graham, 'A World Aflame', p. 97.

27.   Acts 18.1-2.

28.   Jerome Murphy-O'Connor, *St Paul's Corinth: Text and Archaeology* (Collegeville, MN: Liturgical Press, 2002), p. 159; Graham, 'A World Aflame', p. 97.

29.   E. Koestermann, 'Ein folgenschweres Irrtum des Tacitus (*Annals* 15.44.2f)', *Historia* 16 (1967), pp. 456-69; Stephen Benko, 'The Edict of Claudius of 49 CE and the Instigator Chrestus', *TZ* 25 (1969), pp. 406-18; Stephen Benko, *Rome and the Early Christians* (Bloomington: Indiana University Press, 1986), p. 18.

of Suetonius's language, argues this Chrestus may have been an adviser who influenced Claudius to expel the Jews.[30] However, a third more popular theory holds that Suetonius's 'Chrestus' was a garbled form of 'Christus'. As Tertullian of Carthage pointed out in the second century CE, 'Christus' was typically pronounced 'Chrestus' by Romans on account of their accent, which had flow-on effects in historical sources as Roman writers consistently recorded 'Christianos' as 'Chrestianos';[31] on this view the riots among Jews that caused Claudius's decree of expulsion had their origins in the preaching of the message of Jesus Christ by Christians also living there.[32] Most certainly, there are many accounts in Acts of Jewish Diaspora populations rioting at the introduction of the gospel by Paul to their parts of the world. Disturbances took place in Pisidian Antioch, Iconium, Lystra, Thessalonika, Beroea, and Corinth.[33]

This theory is, however, rejected by Green, who argues that since Dio states there were too many Jews to be expelled by Claudius in 41 CE, this must still have been the case in 49 CE.[34] Furthermore, since Acts names Christians Aquila and Priscilla, who were leaders of the Christian Church, as among those expelled, it must have been the Christians living in Rome who were expelled, not the Jews. Thus, whereas in Acts it is Paul and Barnabas who were expelled from the cities they preached among, in this case the entire Christian population of Rome was expelled.[35] Lampe agrees that Christians were expelled, but argues that since Aquila and Priscilla were key figures in the expulsion in Acts, Claudius's expulsion might have been confined to Christian leaders from Rome;[36] when Acts remarks that '*all* the Jews' were expelled from Rome (Acts 18.2), the word '*all*' ($\pi\tilde{\alpha}\varsigma$) can be seen as 'redactionally exaggerated': it was a preferred Lukan term, appearing 172 times in Acts, and 157 times in Luke.[37] However, Green's and Lampe's arguments

30.   Slingerland, 'Suetonius' "Claudius" 25.4', pp. 133-44.
31.   Tertullian, *Apol.* 1.3; *Nat.* 1.3; Tacitus, *Ann.* 15.44; Graham, 'A World Aflame', p. 99.
32.   Craig S. Keener, *The Historical Jesus of the Gospels* (Grand Rapids: Eerdmans, 2012), p. 66; Graham, 'A World Aflame', p. 99.
33.   See Acts 13.44–18.17.
34.   Green, *Christianity in Ancient Rome*, p. 26.
35.   See Rom. 16.3-5; 1 Cor. 16.19; Green, *Christianity in Ancient Rome*, p. 27.
36.   Lampe, *From Paul to Valentinus*, p. 14.
37.   Lampe, *From Paul to Valentinus*, p. 14.

are rejected by Slingerland, who points out that there is no evidence in Suetonius's statement that 'Jews' ought to be replaced with the word 'Christians'.[38] Thus, it may be argued that those expelled were most likely those who, as ringleaders of Jewish and Jewish-Christian circles, took part in the riots themselves, for there were many Jews in Rome who did not take part in the disturbances, and in any case were Roman citizens and who therefore could not be expelled from Rome lightly.[39]

The whole episode of 49 CE would leave a bitter taste not only between Jews and Christians living in Rome, but also Romans as well, and this spite would last up to 64 CE. Thus, in 61 CE, upon Paul's arrival in Rome, Acts states the local Jewish leaders there asked Paul with trepidation and curiosity, '... we would like to hear from you what you think, for regarding this sect we know that people everywhere speak against it'.[40] In these words we find evidence that disfavour by verbal condemnation was experienced by Christians in Rome as in other places throughout the empire by the time of the 64 CE persecution. No doubt, this disfavour, an aftertaste of events in 49 CE, independently inspired Nero to use the Christians in Rome as scapegoats for the Great Fire.[41] Whatever hand his wife Poppaea Sabina had in the affair, Nero was himself most certainly the leading and driving force in his choice of using Christians as scapegoats for the Great Fire. For good reason Tacitus states, 'Nero fabricated scapegoats.'[42]

The Persecution

As to what came next, Tacitus states,

> ergo abolendo rumori Nero subdidit reos et quaesitissimis poenis adfecit per flagitia invisos vulgus Christianos appellabat... sed per urbem etiam quo cuncta undique atrocia aut pudenda confluent celebranturque.

38. Slingerland, 'Suetonius', p. 143.
39. Lampe, *From Paul to Valentinus*, pp. 13-14; Graham, 'A World Aflame', p. 100.
40. Acts 28.22.
41. Graham, 'A World Aflame', p. 100.
42. Tacitus, *Ann.* 15.44; Graham, 'A World Aflame', p. 100.

Nero fabricated scapegoats—and punished with every refinement the notoriously depraved Christians (as they were popularly called) ... in Rome. All degraded and shameful practices collect and flourish in the capital.[43]

So reads our modern English translation of Tacitus. In fact, all modern versions of the Neronian narrative of Tacitus's *Annals* derive from a single manuscript from Monte Cassino, and some hypothesize that the section on Nero's persecution of the Christians has been inserted by a Christian copyist centuries ago.[44] Griffin has argued that on account of their protest against taking part in the state endorsed pagan religious ceremonies performed to appease the gods following the fire, the decision that Christians were guilty of the fire was fastened upon them by the Roman imperial court—at least, ostensibly and publicly for that reason.[45] According to our current version, Nero had self-acknowledged Christians arrested. Then, on their information given through interrogation—which meant torture—large numbers of others were arrested and condemned, as well. Tacitus does not state if these were more secretive Christians or if they were Christians at all; only that they were collectively despised as anti-social—a charge which could apply to Christians, but also to other groups as we shall see.[46]

According to Dando-Collins, clues to whom the original text of the *Annals* states were really arrested and condemned by Nero are found in the types of public executions meted out to them. According to Tacitus, those condemned were dressed in animals' skins and torn to pieces by dogs, while others were either crucified or impaled and set alight to serve as street lights at night. Nero hosted these spectacles in his own Gardens and in the Circus Flaminius.[47] Griffin argues that punishing these Christians with use as living torches fitted the crime of incendiarism—a charge with which Christians were charged *en bloc*.[48] Dando-Collins has also hypothesized that these types of punishments

---

43. Tacitus, *Ann.* 15.44.

44. Kelly Shannon, 'Memory, Religion and History in Nero's Great Fire: Tacitus, Annals 15.41-7', *ClQ* 62 (2012), pp. 749-65 (753, 758); Richard Carrier, 'The Prospect of a Christian Interpolation in Tacitus, Annals 15.44', *VC* 68 (2014), pp. 264-83 (264, 272, 281).

45. Griffin, *Nero*, pp. 132-33.

46. Tacitus, *Ann.* 15.44.

47. Tacitus, *Ann.* 15.44.

48. Griffin, *Nero*, p. 132.

would be more pertinent if they were meted out to Isis devotees, rather than Christians, and that a more accurate translation of the original text of the *Annals* should read, 'Nero fastened the guilt and inflicted the most exquisite tortures on a class hated for their abominations, followers of the cult of Isis, called Egyptians by the populace, which had taken root in Rome, where all things hideous and shameful find their centre and become popular.'[49] Dando-Collins points out that Isis devotees portrayed Egyptian gods and goddesses with animal characteristics, including Anubis, god of the dead, who had the head of a dog or jackal. Devotees of this sect also scorned touching dead animal products and wore only linen and papyrus clothing. Thus, Tacitus's statement that those arrested were dressed in wild animal skins and torn to pieces by dogs would have been of greater insult to an Isis devotee than any other religious group in Rome. Fire, also, played a key part in the religious observances of Isis devotees, and using it to kill those devotees that were condemned would have set a sobering example to other devotees of this sect in Rome and around the empire that Roman power was not to be trifled with. Given also that many of the arrested were crucified indicates that they were not Roman citizens, for crucifixion was banned for Roman citizens, which could imply that the majority of those arrested and condemned were 'Egyptians' as Dando-Collins argues.[50]

Dando-Collins thus casts doubt that Tacitus was referring to Christians when he states that 'large numbers of others were condemned'.[51] This line of argument is also endorsed by Shaw.[52] Jones, however, argues this line by pointing out that Paul's epistle to the Romans describes their faith as famous, apparently for their numbers as well as intensity of belief (Rom. 1.8)[53] Nonetheless, Dando-Collins draws attention to the many more devotees of Isis that resided in Rome. The cult of Isis had a long history of finding imperial disfavour in Rome. In 21 BC, Marcus Agrippa banned the cult in Rome,

49.   Stephen Dando-Collins, *The Great Fire of Rome: The Fall of the Emperor Nero and His City* (Cambridge: Da Capo Press, 2010), p. 13.

50.   Dando-Collins, *Great Fire of Rome*, pp. 13, 107-9.

51.   Tacitus, *Ann.* 15.44.

52.   Brent D. Shaw, 'The Myth of the Neronian Persecution', *JRS* 105 (2015), pp. 73-100 (96); Brent D. Shaw, 'Response to Christopher Jones: The Historicity of the Neronian Persecution', *NTS* 64 (2018), pp. 231-42.

53.   Christopher P. Jones, 'The Historicity of the Neronian Persecution: A Response to Brent Shaw', *NTS* 64 (2017), pp. 146-52.

and under Tiberius, Gaius, and Claudius, devotees of the cult were expelled from the capital. Finally, Dando-Collins puts forth, the term 'Christian' is a later name, and does not belong in the first century, and was not even used by the first-century Christians themselves.[54]

However, there are reasons to question Dando-Collins's eclectic argument. First, two first-century CE Christian biblical books, Acts and 1 Peter both use the term 'Christian' when describing Jesus' followers (Acts 11.26; 26.28; 1 Pet. 4.16). Intriguingly, this term has unique origins. According to Acts, Christians were first called by that term, by outsiders in the city of Antioch where many Christians lived, for following Jesus, whom they called Christ (Greek for 'Messiah') (Acts 11.26). This fact accounts for why the Christians of the Bible did not often call themselves Christians—it was a term used by others to refer to them. Most Christians described themselves with other labels, such as 'believers' (Acts 2.44), 'children of God' (Rom. 8.16), 'children of light' (Mt. 5.14; Lk. 11.35; 2 Cor. 6.14; Eph. 5.8-11; 1 Thess. 5.5) and members of 'The Way' (Acts 9.2, 23; 22.4; 24.14, 22), so used because Jesus taught that he is 'the way, the truth, and the life' (Jn 14.6) and as one converts one becomes one with the Spirit of Jesus (Eph. 1.22-23). Thus, when outsiders including Josephus, Tacitus, Suetonius, and Pliny the Younger labelled 'Christians' by that term, they confirmed the Acts account.[55]

Moreover, when we turn to other facts in the story, we find more complications with Dando-Collins's scenario. The 'large numbers' of 'others' (*multitudo ingens*) Tacitus states were arrested and condemned need not have implied numbers as large as one might initially imagine, for elsewhere in his *Histories* Tacitus uses similar language to describe just twenty executions (*immense strages*). However, in this case Tacitus was probably referring to more than those numbers, and only in regard to Christian ringleaders that were rounded up and executed, not simply their executed followers—who could have constituted a large number.[56] Hence, in his *Annals* Tacitus rhetorically evokes mental imagery of crowds of many victims being arrested and condemned, but in fact such a dramatization exaggerates the number of those

54. Dando-Collins, *The Great Fire of Rome*, pp. 8-13.
55. Josephus, *Ant.* 18.3; Pliny the Younger, *Ep.* 10.96; Tacitus, *Ann.* 15.44; Suetonius, *Nero* 16.
56. Tacitus, *Hist.* 1.47.2.

executed, as was his aim in his *Histories*.[57] As for the methods of rounding up, no extant ancient literature records it. However, Clement states that 'envy' (ἔριν) and 'strife' (ζῆλος) brought down Paul, and they may have done so in regard to other Christians, in Rome, at the time of the persecution (1 Clem. 5). This statement is of consequence, because Paul states in Philippians that he was opposed in Rome by Christian preachers who preached the gospel out of 'envy' (ἔριν) and 'rivalry' (θρόνον). Although Paul tried to reconcile with them, it may be argued they had something to do with those who informed on him as to his whereabouts, to Nero or to other Roman authorities, leading to his arrest, and eventual execution. Peter may have suffered the same fate. They were, after all, public figures in Rome, and as leaders of the Christian church there, they were technically speaking, ringleaders of Nero's propagated enemies. If so, these and others like them, including pagans and Jews in Rome, could very well have done likewise, and informed on Christians hiding throughout Rome, to Roman authorities (Phil. 1.15).

The number of those executed in this persecution need not have been only Christians. Christian numbers were still relatively small in Rome—compared to the rest of the population of Rome—however, the large numbers of 'others' also rounded up, according to Tacitus, were so precisely because they were 'detested' for their similar 'anti-social tendencies'. These 'others' might have included devotees of Isis, even many, which would mean that what we have here are Christians and Isis devotees being associated and linked together in blame and condemnation: first Christians, then Isis worshippers. Being dressed in animal skins may not have been meant as a religious insult, either, at least to the Christians among the condemned—these Christians may have been dressed in them simply in order to invite the dogs' appetites, by which they were executed. Crucifixion, as well, would have evoked the image of the death of Jesus by crucifixion in many onlookers' minds, adding to their torment. Finally, being lit up at night was a regular penalty for incendiarism, and might have been a method used by Nero to mock the Christian teaching that Christians were sons of light, not darkness (Mt. 5.14; Lk. 11.35; 2 Cor. 6.14; Eph. 5.8-11; 1 Thess. 5.5).[58] If this scenario is accurate—which endorses our current translation of Tacitus as correct and not doctored by a medieval Christian copyist—then these punishments would have added to the insult to both

57. Green, *Christianity in Ancient Rome*, p. 52.

58. B.H. Warmington, *Nero: Reality and Legend* (London: Chatto and Windus, 1969), p. 126.

Christians in Rome, and to the many 'others' that Tacitus states were executed throughout Rome, including perhaps a number of Isis devotees.[59]

Nero's persecution was not an empire-wide systematic proscription. Or,
so it seems. It appears to have been confined to the city of Rome, largely.
However, according to Bible commentators, there is some evidence of abuse
of Christians throughout the empire in 1 Peter. According to Thurston, Peter's
reference to the 'fiery ordeal coming upon you' in that letter, written to the
early Christians of Asia Minor, among others, must be a reflection of the same
punishments Nero inflicted upon the Christians of Rome coming upon the
Christians of Asia Minor too (1 Pet. 4.12).[60] Others see a causal link between
Peter's reference to the suffering 'for the name [of Christ]' and Pliny the
Younger's query to the emperor Trajan in 110 CE as to whether or not Christians in Bithynia be punished for the 'name itself' (1 Pet. 4.14).[61] Peter's
statement is to be 'prepared to give a defence', which has been argued by
Williams to imply that Peter was readying Christians in Asia Minor for formal
judicial interrogation before Roman magistrates (1 Pet. 3.15).[62] But others
view Peter's words, 'the same sufferings being experienced by your fellow
Christians throughout the world', to be proof that Nero's persecution was an
official empire-wide policy of persecution. In any event, although the bulk of
the persecution may have derived from, appeared in, and been elongated in
Rome, because Christians fell out of imperial favour there, the possibility that
violence against Christians besmirched the entire empire cannot be discarded
lightly (1 Pet. 5.9).[63]

Pliny's correspondences with Trajan reveal that there was no official
policy proscribing Christianity up to that time in 110 CE.[64] The 'fiery ordeal'
that Peter describes may have been a reference to the kind of punishments he
saw being inflicted on Christians in Rome, which he suspected were imma-
nent for the Christians in places like Asia Minor, at the time of writing (1 Pet.

---

59. The authenticity of this passage is endorsed by Warmington, *Nero*, p. 126;
Jürgen Malitz, *Nero* (Oxford: Oxford University Press, 2005), p. 69.

60. R.W. Thurston, 'Interpreting First Peter', *JETS* 17 (1974), pp. 171-82.

61. Pliny the Younger, *Ep.* 10.96; Martin Williams, *The Doctrine of Salvation
in the First Letter of Peter* (Cambridge: Cambridge University Press, 2011), p. 6.

62. Williams, *Doctrine of Salvation*, p. 6.

63. Williams, *Doctrine of Salvation*, p. 6.

64. Pliny the Younger, *Ep.* 10.96-97; Williams, *Doctrine of Salvation*, p. 6.

4.12).[65] Peter's reference to abuse 'for the name', and a need to give a 'defence', may be more likely closely linked to the verbal abuse that Christians suffered around the empire at the time that Peter, which Peter refers to throughout the letter, for there is no mention explicitly of physical attacks. But of course, verbal attacks can sometimes lead to physical violence.[66] As for Peter's comment that other Christians 'throughout the world' were undergoing the same sufferings as those in Asia Minor, this may denote that the same verbal abuses levelled at Christians around the empire were experienced by the Asian Christians, as well.[67] In short, Peter wrote his letter to encourage Christians in Asia to stand firm in the face of the attacks and to not escalate matters. They faced these attacks on account of their association with Christ, at the time, and the unpopularity from falling from imperial favour, during Nero's persecution, which is evidenced from his repeated references to verbal attacks against Christians throughout the letter (1 Pet. 2.11-12, 23; 3.9, 16; 4.3-4).[68]

Connecting Nero with the Fire and the Persecution

Pliny the Elder, Suetonius and Cassius Dio do not suggest that there were any Christians punished on the premise of proof for lighting, and spreading, the fire. Pliny refers briefly to the fire, but makes no mention of the Christians at all in his *Natural History*.[69] Suetonius describes the fire and Nero's actions against the Christians in separate chapters of his life of Nero.[70] Dio includes a detailed description of the fire but makes no mention of Christians in relation to it.[71] In more recent times, Shaw has argued that the persecution of the Christians under Nero did not happen in the way that Tacitus describes it, at all.[72] Wilken and Shaw both point out that under Nero, the term 'Christian',

---

65. Larry H. Helyer, *The Life and Witness of Peter* (Downers Grove, IL: InterVarsity Press, 2012), p. 163.

66. Williams, *Doctrine of Salvation*, p. 6.

67. Williams, *Doctrine of Salvation*, p. 6.

68. Williams, *Doctrine of Salvation*, pp. 7-8; Helyer, *Life and Witness of Peter*, p. 163.

69. Pliny the Elder, *Nat.* 7.1.5-6.

70. Suetonius, *Nero* 16, 38.

71. Cassius Dio, *Hist. rom.* 62.16-17.

72. Shaw, 'Myth of the Neronian Persecution'.

used by Tacitus, was not widely used by followers of Jesus to describe themselves at the time.[73] Of course, though early Christians in the first century CE
clearly used the term 'Christian' to describe themselves at times, Paul describes them in his letter to the Romans as simply 'brothers and sisters',
'saints', and those 'called to belong to Jesus Christ our Lord' (Rom. 1.6; 14-
15; Acts 11.26; 26.28; 1 Pet. 4.16). Still, Wilken has argued that Tacitus
somehow used a second-century CE term which he drew from Pliny the
Younger during the latter's tenure as governor of Bithynia in the 110s CE—
during which time Tacitus composed his *Annals*.[74]

However, these omissions in Pliny, Suetonius and Dio can be accounted
for. Pliny described the 64 CE fire as 'the Emperor Nero's conflagration', but
his linking Nero with the fire served to cast the new Flavian dynasty in a more
favourable light. In his early career, Pliny served as a fellow officer of Titus.
Later, he was a member of Vespasian's advisory council, and around 77 CE
dedicated his *Natural History* to Titus. It was in his and the Flavian dynasty's
interest, therefore, to cast Flavian rule against the alleged low codes of moral
behaviour of their predecessor, Nero.[75]

Suetonius, too, had reasons not to mention the Christians. It was also char-
acteristic of him to write value-laden biography, although he did clearly make
use of official records, and other valuable ancient literary sources.[76] Thus,
Suetonius focuses on Nero's morals and personality, or lack thereof as the
case may be, glossing over major items and including scandal and gossip to
'impose order on the facts'—to put it in Wallace-Hadrill's words—while
painting his literary portrait of Nero.[77] As far as Christianity was concerned,
Suetonius saw fit to gloss over its existence, for as a Roman, he held that
worship was a matter of ritual, not belief as espoused by early Christians.
Therefore, blaming Nero for the fire served Suetonius's purposes to erase
Christianity from history and enhance the dramatic defects of Nero's life, thus
keeping this emperor 'within the bounds of mortality' as Momigliano puts

73. Shaw, 'Myth of the Neronian Persecution', p. 89.

74. R. Wilken, *The Christians as the Romans Saw Them* (New Haven: Yale
University Press, 2003), pp. 48-49.

75. Pliny the Elder, *Nat.* 17.5; John F. Healy, *Pliny the Elder: Natural History.
A Selection* (London: Penguin, 1991), pp. ix-x, xiii.

76. Andrew Wallace-Hadrill, *Suetonius* (London: Bristol Classical Press,
1983), pp. 110, 141.

77. Wallace-Hadrill, *Suetonius*, pp. 13, 122-23, 202.

it.[78] Such drama was expected by Suetonius's equestrian readers, who found titillation and entertainment in the theatricality and melodrama of Nero's life. Suetonius delivered this to them in spades.[79]

Cassius Dio, like Suetonius, also seemingly abhorred Christianity. For Dio, innovations in religion like that of the Christians and the devotees of the cult of Isis were irrelevant to the traditional Roman social order.[80] For the period covered by this article in his *Roman History*, Dio does not refer to Christianity once. Perhaps his original references to Christianity were so hostile they were omitted by later Christian excerptors and epitomists of his work that have come down to us, or more likely, perhaps Dio felt Christianity deserved Roman persecution and thereby left out it of the pages of his traditional Roman history.[81]

Although Tacitus is our only main ancient historical source to draw a connection between the fire and the punishment of the Christians by Nero, he was not in fact the only ancient writer to do so. In fact, many early Christian writers also drew the same connection. The biblical source Hebrews mentions persecution under Nero as being 'full of suffering' (Heb. 10.32-33), and 1 Peter likens Rome at the time to Babylon (1 Pet. 5.13). Revelation—another first-century biblical source—also refers to 'the Beast' waging 'war against the saints' (Rev. 13.3-14), while the end of John's Gospel also alludes to the violent deaths that were to come to Jesus' disciples (Jn 21.18). More specifically, in addition to these biblical sources, *1 Clement*, written at the end of the first century or start of the second century in Rome itself, describes the persecution and execution of those Christians who lived under Nero, includ-

78.   A. Momigliano, *The Development of Greek Biography* (Cambridge, MA: Harvard University Press, 1971), p. 100. See also Wallace-Hadrill, *Suetonius*, pp. 190, 202; Tomas Hägg, *The Art of Biography in Antiquity* (Cambridge: Cambridge University Press, 2012), p. 271.

79.   Donald Mellor, *The Roman Historians* (London: Taylor and Francis, 1999), pp. 149, 152-54.

80.   Fergus Millar, *A Study of Cassius Dio* (Oxford: Clarendon Press, 1964), p. 108; Adam A. Kemezis, *Greek Narratives of the Roman Empire under the Severans: Cassius Dio, Philostratus and Herodian* (Cambridge: Cambridge University Press, 2014), p. 280.

81.   Millar, *Study of Cassius Dio*, p. 179.

ing Peter and Paul (1 Clem. 5).[82] Furthermore, the *Ascension of Isaiah*, a Syrian manuscript dated to 70–120 CE, also refers to Nero's persecution against 'the plant which the Twelve Apostles of the Beloved will have planted'.[83] Likely from Rome from around the same time, the *Shepherd of Hermas* makes clear reference to the 'crucifixions, and wild beasts for the sake of his [Jesus'] name'[84]—precisely the same punishments Tacitus states were used by Nero in the aftermath of the Great Fire—while the *Apocalypse of Peter*, a manuscript from Syria or Alexandria from 115–50 CE, talks about Nero as 'the son of the one who is in Hades' and as a persecutor of the Church.[85] Of course, this last source may base its claims upon a reading of Tacitus. However, the designation of Nero appears original. In fact, it may be argued that each built upon earlier written and oral historical traditions, with their own unique features, that may not be entirely unhistorical embellishments. Furthermore, although these early Christian references to the persecution under Nero are highly stylized and religious in tone, Lans and Bremmer conclude they clearly stem from a historical persecution of the Christians by Nero for their alleged incendiarism of the Great Fire, for 'it is highly unlikely that Nero made such an impact on the early Christian imagination if the link between him and the Christians was the result only of a later incidental association'.[86]

82. O. Zwierlein, *Petrus in Rom: Die literarischen Zeugnisse* (Berlin: de Gruyter, 2010), pp. 245-331; O. Zwierlein, *Petrus und Paulus in Jerusalem und Rom: Vom neuen Testament zu den apokryphen Apostelakten* (Berlin: de Gruyter, 2013), pp. 89-104, 276-79, 285-90.

83. *Mart. Ascen. Isa.* 4.1-4.

84. Herm. Vis. 1.1.1.

85. T. Nicklas, 'Jewish, Christian, Greek? The Apocalypse of Peter as a Witness of Early Second Century Christianity in Alexandria', in L. Arcari (ed.), *Beyond Conflicts: Cultural and Religious Cohabitations in Alexandria and Egypt between the 1st and 6th Century CE* (Tübingen: Mohr Siebeck, 2017), pp. 27-46; Jan N. Bremmer, 'The Apocalypse of Peter as the First Century Martyr Text: Its Date, Provenance and Relationship with 2 Peter', in J. Frey, M. den Dulk and J. van der Watt (eds.), *2 Peter and the Apocalypse of Peter: Towards a New Perspective* (Biblical Interpretation, 174; Leiden: Brill, 2019), pp. 75-98.

86. Birgit Van der Lans and J.N. Bremmer, 'Tacitus and the Persecution of the Christians: An Invention of Tradition?', *Eirene* 53 (2017), pp. 299-331 (316).

In addition to these sources, later during the mid-second century CE, Melito, Bishop of Sardis, stated that Nero made many false accusations against many Christians, and was persuaded to do this by many malicious slanderers, who might have been a group of mainstream Jews in Rome at the time.[87] Around the same time, Tertullian of Carthage also stated that Nero persecuted many Christians.[88] A century and a half later, Eusebius of Caesarea also recorded that Nero persecuted the Christians of Rome, after the Great Fire of 64 CE.[89] Lactantius also, around the same time, recorded that Nero persecuted the Christians.[90] The fourth-century CE Roman emperor, Julian the Apostate, did not leave behind any blame for the 64 CE fire on the Christians, in any of his extant writings, either.[91] Finally, in the fifth century CE, Orosius reported that Nero had been responsible for the fire, and complicit in its extent, and compliant to his own desires to persecute the Christians of Rome immediately after the Great Fire of 64 CE. These sources appear to build upon the claims made by earlier sources, with largely unique evidence not entirely made explicit by Tacitus and Clement. Thus, all of these sources appear not to be following each other blindly, but to be supporting each other through similar, though not entirely the same, historical claims. All of this evidence, compiled with the evidence in Tacitus, contextualizes it to such a degree as to conclusively show that Nero was responsible for the Great Fire of 64 CE, and the aftermath, including the persecution of the early Christians of Rome in that year, and for a duration afterwards.[92]

Paul and Peter

There is some interesting circumstantial evidence that suggests that Paul might have died sometime shortly afterwards following his first hearing—an

87. Eusebius, *Hist. eccl.* 4.13.18; 4.26.2-14.

88. Tertullian, *Apol.* 2.6; 5.3; *Scorp.* 15.3; *Nat.* 1.7.8.

89. Eusebius, *Hist. eccl.* 2.25.4; 3.1.2; 3.33.1-4.

90. Lactantius, *Mort.* 2.5-7; 12-15; Eusebius, *Hist. eccl.* 8.6; J. Rougé, 'L'incendie de Rome en 64 et l'incendie de Nicomédie en 303', in *Mélanges d'histoire ancienne: Offerts à William Seston* (Publication de la Sorbonne, 9; Paris: E. de Boccard, 1974), pp. 433-41; Shaw, 'Myth of the Neronian Persecution', p. 93.

91. Anthony A. Barrett, *Rome Is Burning: Nero and the Fire that Ended a Dynasty* (Princeton: Princeton University Press, 2020), p. 290 n. 100.

92. Orosius, *Hist. adv. Pag.* 7.7.

argument presented by McKechnie. For, between 62 CE and 65 CE, Poppaea Sabina, Nero's wife, had been a holder of Jewish beliefs and held clout among palace officials and to a degree over Nero himself. At her apparent request, Nero ruled in favour of Jewish Temple priests over others in every trial brought before him. Thus, McKechnie argues that Paul's trial was decided in this same way, and that Nero ruled in favour of Paul's accusers. This would apparently mean that Paul was beheaded shortly thereafter, a full year prior to the outbreak of the Neronian persecution.[93] In support of McKechnie's conclusion is the notion that there is certainly no direct ancient information, contemporaneous with Paul, about the outcome of his trial. Most certainly, as Haacker puts it, the trial's 'outcome is left open to the imagination (or the memory) of the readers'.[94] However, as Wilson points out, Acts was completed before Paul's trial began.[95] Furthermore, there is the early tradition that Paul was executed during the persecution of 64 CE—a tradition that draws upon many ancient sources, both written and oral, kept alive in the source material that is extant.[96]

In contravention to McKechnie's argument, according to the first-century CE Christian leader Clement of Rome, Paul was acquitted by Nero. He then adds that Paul then went ahead on a mission to Spain as he had hoped to do while penning his letter to the church in Rome (Rom. 15.24, 28; 1 Clem. 5).[97] Needless to say, Clement's proof about Rome is not conclusive, but rather informs us that by the time *1 Clement* was written, Clement and others believed he had travelled west to the Iberian peninsula deliberately on a mission to the 'limit of the west', as Clement reported.[98] These words may be based on nothing more than Paul's brief statement in Romans that he had wished to

93. Paul McKechnie, 'Judaean Embassies and Cases before Roman Emperors, AD 44–66', *JTS* 56 (2005), pp. 339-61.

94. Klaus Haacker, 'Paul's Life', in James D.G. Dunn (ed.), *The Cambridge Companion to St Paul* (Cambridge: Cambridge University Press, 2003), pp. 19-33 (31).

95. A.N. Wilson, *Paul: The Mind of the Apostle* (London: Sinclair-Stevenson, 1997), p. 248.

96. F.F. Bruce, *Paul: Apostle of the Free Spirit* (Exeter: Paternoster, 1977), p. 441.

97. Bruce, *Paul*, p. 447.

98. David L. Eastman, *Paul the Martyr: The Cult of the Apostle in the Latin West* (Atlanta: Society of Biblical Literature, 2011), pp. 18-19, 144-46.

travel to Spain to teach there (Rom. 15.24, 28).[99] Or, arguably, Clement was trying to give hope, and direction, to Christians fearful or suffering during, or after, Domitian's (reigned 81–96 CE) contemporaneous persecution against the Christians in Rome. This tradition continued well into the second and third centuries. In the *Acts of Peter*, a Gnostic historical work written around 180 CE, and the *Muratorian Fragment*, from a list of New Testament books drawn up in Rome in the late second century CE, most particularly in the Varcelli manuscript in Latin, Paul was acquitted. Then, he travelled to Spain from Italy, immediately following his acquittal by Nero's court.[100]

Although we do not possess a detailed account or explanation of the proceedings of Paul's trial in 63 CE, leading up to the persecution, specifically since public records of hearings were discontinued as a phenomenon in Rome around 50 CE, we do know details of how Nero conducted trials.[101] Acts does not record how Paul was tried, perhaps to leave out a parallel trial with Jesus Christ's own, and perhaps because Luke was not there to witness it and had no access to eye-witnesses, which he often relied upon when writing Acts (Lk. 1.2).[102] Still, Suetonius provides us with data on how Nero conducted his trials. Every trial lasted for one day, after which on the following day Nero would deliver his verdict and findings. Each trial Nero conducted opened with the prosecution team delivering evidence, arguments and findings. After their case was heard, the defence team would then present their own and any overriding evidence. Finally, Nero would write-up his deliberations before retiring and delivering his verdict and sentence the following day.[103] Accusers on the part of the plaintiff would accuse the defendant of breaking Roman law (*iniuria*).[104] Paul could have been accused by any number of these. However, if an accuser was found to have accused falsely (*calumnia*)

---

99. Bruce, *Paul*, p. 447.

100. Bruce, *Paul*, p. 449.

101. Bruce W. Winter, 'Acts and Food Shortages', in D.W.J. Gill and C. Gempf (eds.), *The Book of Acts in its First Century Setting: Volume 2. Graeco-Roman Setting* (Grand Rapids: Eerdmans, 1994), pp. 59-78.

102. J. Albert Harrill, *Paul the Apostle: His Life and Legacy in their Roman Context* (Cambridge: Cambridge University Press, 2012), p. 70.

103. Suetonius, *Nero* 15.

104. O.F. Robinson, *The Criminal Law of Ancient Rome* (Baltimore: Johns Hopkins University Press, 1995), p. 50.

before Nero, he was open to prosecution himself, and the punishment for this was death (Acts 24.1-2).[105]

As for the defendant, it was permissible for him or her to be present in the court, as a legal right. Defence could present witnesses, even if subpoenas were not enforced, and present documents, including official and unofficial government records, official complaints, official and unofficial letters, and any business memoranda;[106] the stakes were extremely high. Under Nero, the outcome could mean execution for either side. For instance, inciting public riots (*vis*), whether by Paul or the officials of states he travelled around, had the penalty of execution, and assembling a crowd or mob to do violence to an individual like Paul, or to the Roman state (*maiestas* and *perduellio*) by someone like Paul, also carried the death penalty.[107] In order to help him reach his verdict after each case was presented, Nero had the benefit of a panel of jurists, called a *consilium*—although their role was not to deliver the verdict, but to simply advise Nero as he formulated his if required (Acts 25.12).[108] The internal evidence in Acts and the New Testament does not repudiate the case that Paul was arguably tried before Nero in this traditionally Neronian manner (Acts 25.11; Eph. 6.19-20; Col. 4.3).[109]

As to who represented the apostle as his leading attorney, Mauck suggests it may have been Theophilus, to whom Luke's Gospel, and its sequel Acts, were addressed. Theophilus was a Roman official who sought from Luke his 'orderly account' to reach 'certainty' concerning Paul and his Christian faith.[110] Mauck detects that he held investigator (*cognitionibus*) powers and the skills of a rhetorician.[111] Mauck and Haacker argue that Luke composed his 'brief' to Theophilus on Paul's behest, and also to convert each reader and

---

105. Robinson, *Criminal Law*, pp. 5, 99, 102.

106. Winter, 'Acts and Food Shortages', p. 309; Robinson, *Criminal Law*, p. 5.

107. Robinson, *Criminal Law*, pp. 74-75, 78, 80; Irina Levinskaya, *The Book of Acts in its First Century Setting: Volume 5. Diaspora Setting* (Grand Rapids: Eerdmans, 1996), p. 6; John W. Mauck, *Paul on Trial: The Book of Acts as a Defense of Christianity* (Nashville: Nelson, 2001), pp. 12-13.

108. Robinson, *Criminal Law*, p. 10.

109. Mauck, *Paul on Trial*, pp. 14-17.

110. See the salutation 'Most Excellent' (Lk. 1.3; Acts 23.26). On Luke's purposes to write Theophilus defence material for Theophilus on behalf of Paul, see Lk. 1.1-4; Mauck, *Paul on Trial*, pp. ix, 21-23.

111. Mauck, *Paul on Trial*, pp. 26-28.

listener to faith in Christ, as his mentor Paul tried to do while providing a defence before Agrippa I (Acts 26.28).[112] This explains why Luke so heavily incorporated defence material against any potential charge that could have been brought against Paul.[113] Among those included are the discourses that proved Paul did not incite rebellion against the Jewish Temple or against Rome itself, nor that his Christ had any designs on strict temporal power, either. In all, some fifty-nine arguments laid bare by Luke refuting all incriminating evidence and charges have been detected in Luke's account of Paul's life in Acts by Mauck.[114]

We also have solid biblical evidence of the adventures of Paul after his trial, before the persecution. 1 Timothy and Titus appear both to have been written in Macedonia. In Paul's letter to Titus, Paul leaves Crete after a visit there and heads to Macedonia. In 1 Timothy, Paul asks Timothy to meet up with him later in Nicoplis in Epirus. Possibly both epistles were written at around the same time in Macedonia, after a visit to Crete and just before a visit to Epirus (1 Tim. 1.3; Tit. 1.5; 3.12). Then, in 2 Timothy, Paul mentions his visits to the city of Corinth and Troas by the Aegean, before a visit to Miletus, another island of the Aegean Sea (2 Tim. 4.13, 20). In 2 Timothy, Luke is with Paul (2 Tim. 4.11). From there, Paul next appears in Rome as a victim of Nero's persecution. If he did find his way to Rome from Asia or Miletus, it is possible he was arrested, as Peter warned against in 1 Peter, when he requested Christians to be prepared to give a formal defence before antagonists and authorities, at around that time. Or it may be argued Paul journeyed by ship and land to Rome itself. It was at that time the Christians there faced pressure of many types owing to the escalating persecution, and Paul, as a leader of the Roman church together with Peter, and writer of the letter to the Romans—a scriptural letter—may have believed he needed to be there. In Acts 14:19-21 Paul was nearly killed in Lystra, or rather just outside it after preaching there. Then he recovered and re-entered the city and kept preaching, and won large numbers there over a period of time. Later, throughout Syria and Cilicia, after finding hardships in some of those parts, he returned 'strengthening the churches' (Acts 15.41). Furthermore, after being re-

112. Mauck, *Paul on Trial*, p. ix; Haacker, 'Paul's Life', p. 31.
113. Mauck, *Paul on Trial*, pp. 5-8.
114. See the 'Chart of Fifty-Nine Arguments in Defense of Paul' in Mauck, *Paul on Trial*, pp. 34-40.

leased from prison in Philippi, he returned to the believers in the city and encouraged them before leaving (Acts 16.40).

Indeed, in Romans, Paul dictated to his secretary, Tertius, that he (Paul) had hoped for so long to travel to Rome and spend some time there before sailing or trekking overland to Spain to preach and evangelize. Perhaps, he had hoped this journey to Rome would be a short one before making his way to Spain. In any event, although Paul had some time to go to Spain between his acquittal and the persecution, Paul's Pastoral letters do not mention any fond memories of Spain, nor any plans to go there in the immediate future. This silence is possibly evidence that Paul did not go to Spain and that Clement contrived the story, or heard of it, and presented it to other Christians under Domitian, in the hope to give them direction in the face of Domitian's persecution and perhaps a hint as to where to go to flee and find safety (Rom. 15.23-24).

These Pastoral letters have been the subject of conjecture for many years. The earliest copy of any of these letters comes from Egypt and is housed in the John Rylands University Library. It contains on one side excerpts of Titus 1:11-15, while on the other is part of Tit. 2:3-8. It is the earliest we have and is dated to around 200 CE, or slightly earlier. However, Polycarp's *Letter to the Ephesians* also makes many mentions of these letters, called the 'Pastoral Letters' by convention. This epistle is usually dated to around 120 CE.[115] Tertullian of Carthage notably wrote that Marcion (c. 85–160 CE) knew of these letters, but purposefully rejected including them in his canon of scripture. His contemporary Tatian (c. 120–80 CE), however, accepted them as worthy literature, but only Paul's letter to Titus as canonical Scripture.[116] The 'Pastoral Letters' bear striking resemblances to other Christian and Jewish writings, such as the *Testaments of the Twelve Patriarchs* and the Gospels and Acts.[117] They also have some traits similar to *Didache* (c. 100), *Didescalia Apostolorum* (200s CE), *Apostolic Church Order* (c. 300 CE),

---

115. K. Berding, 'Polycarp of Smyrna's View of the Authorship of 1 and 2 Timothy', *VC* 53 (1999), pp. 349-60; Paul Hartog, *Polycarp and the New Testament* (Tübingen: Mohr Siebeck, 2001); Raymond F. Collins, *1 and 2 Timothy and Titus* (London: John Knox, 2002), pp. 1-2.

116. Tertullian, *Marc.* 5.21; Collins, *1 and 2 Timothy and Titus*, p. 2.

117. See the farewell discourses of Lk. 22.25-38; Jn 13–16, and Acts 20.18-35; Collins, *1 and 2 Timothy and Titus*, p. 6.

Apostolic Constitutions (fourth century CE), and *Testamentum Domini* (fifth century CE).[118]

Some believe it is impossible to date the 'Pastorals' precisely even if their language in Greek has much in common with first-century Hellenistic literature stylistically.[119] However, Witherington believes they can be dated, in their present form, to between 65 CE and 95 CE. He has noticed that of the three-hundred-and-six Greek words used in Greek literature and the 'Pastorals', 278 come from works dated to prior to 50 CE. Furthermore, he notices that if Marcion knew of the epistles by the early second century, when he drew up his canon of scripture, then he knew and read them for many years prior to drawing it up.[120]

The 'Pastoral Epistles' are relevant when these letters' dates of authorship by Paul are repeatedly, and consistently, determined to be after his acquittal.[121] Eusebius and a consensus of commentators and modern historians place them after Paul's acquittal and before his death, during the persecution of 64 CE.[122] Still, some consider these 'Pastoral Epistles' to have been compilations of Paul's teachings, by friends and disciples, presented in a pseudonymous manner, with Paul as the 'author'.[123] But, of course, it is to be expected that some teachings in the Pastorals may have been longstanding, but other messages, like that which states that Paul expected his life to soon be poured out like a libation, more recent in inspiration (2 Tim. 4.6).[124] It is true, of the 901 words contained in the Pastorals, only 306 of these appear in other biblical Pauline letters—and of these, 121 appear in the second-century

118. Collins, *1 and 2 Timothy and Titus*, p. 6.

119. Collins, *1 and 2 Timothy and Titus*, pp. 9, 13.

120. Ben Witherington III, *Letters and Homilies for Hellenized Christians: Volume II. A Socio-Rhetorical Commentary on 1–2 Peter* (Downers Grove, IL: IVP Academic, 2006), pp. 53, 61.

121. Bruce, *Paul*, p. 443.

122. Eusebius, *Hist. eccl.* 2.22.2-8; M. Dibelius and H. Conzelmann, *The Pastoral Epistles* (Philadelphia: Fortress Press, 1976), pp. 3, 15-20, 126-32, 152-62.

123. P.N. Harrison, *The Problem of the Pastoral Epistles* (Oxford: Oxford University Press, 1921), pp. 93-97, 115-20; P.N. Harrison, *Paulines and Pastorals* (London: Villiers Publications, 1964), pp. 106-12; Arland J. Hultgren, 'The Pastoral Epistles', in James D.G. Dunn (ed.), *The Cambridge Companion to St Paul* (Cambridge: Cambridge University Press, 2003), pp. 141-55 (144).

124. Bruce, *Paul*, p. 443.

CE Apostolic Fathers and Apologists.[125] Most likely, the style of the Pastorals stands in partial juxtaposition to those of other biblical Pauline letters because Paul and Luke worked on these letters together. After all, in 2 Tim. 4.11, only Luke was with Paul, during the time of that letter's dictation and taking-down.[126] Indeed, the three 'Pastoral Epistles' are, as Harding notes, 'sufficiently similar in style to commend the view that they were written by the same person'.[127] In other words, Paul was released, wrote the Pastorals or dictated them to Luke, and was then arrested a second time, and executed in 64 CE. Therefore, the possibility that these letters were written by Paul in around 63 CE, and later slightly edited by Luke, who survived Paul, or by later followers of his between 65 CE and 95 CE, resulting in their present form, is an interesting scenario that cannot be easily discounted.[128]

Bruce suggested that Paul was acquitted by Nero and then travelled to the eastern Mediterranean before heading for Spain in the Mediterranean Sea's west. After that, he was arrested a second time by Nero during his persecution and killed.[129] Later, Murphy O'Connor reversed this order and says that after leaving Rome, Paul took a mission to Spain and then returned to his more familiar East, before dying at the hands of Nero.[130] But it is interesting that, in juxtaposition, *1 Clement* gives no mention of Paul's eastern activities, and the 'Pastorals' give not even the slightest hint that Paul even arrived in Spain. If *1 Clement* is based upon Paul's brief comment that he wished to visit Rome on the way to Spain, a mission that the New Testament nowhere refers to as taking place, then this would make Clement's proof redundant. In other words, the 'Pastorals' are realistic and reliable accounts to Paul's activities after his trial and pardon by the emperor Nero. For good reason, Clement stated Paul was heroic—a sentiment used by Eusebius in his estimation of the

125. Hultgren, 'Pastoral Epistles', p. 142.

126. C.F.D. Moule, 'The Problem of the Pastoral Epistles: A Reappraisal', *BJRL* 47 (1964–65), pp. 430-52 (430-36); A. Strobel, 'Schreiben des Lukas? Zum sprachlichen Problem der Pastoralbriefe', *NTS* 15 (1968–69), pp. 191-210 (191-94).

127. Mark Harding, 'The Pastoral Epistles', in Mark Harding and Alanna Nobbs (eds.), *All Things to All Cultures: Paul among Jews, Greeks, and Romans* (Grand Rapids: Eerdmans, 2013), pp. 328-52 (335).

128. J.N.D. Kelly, *A Commentary on the Pastoral Epistles* (London: A. & C. Black, 1963), p. 9; Bruce, *Paul*, p. 444.

129. Bruce, *Paul*, pp. 441, 445-46, 448, 450.

130. Murphy-O'Connor, *St Paul's Corinth*, pp. 359-65.

apostle being victorious. Intriguingly, Revelation calls each martyr the recipient of a victor's crown—the crown of life. That is, eternally. No doubt he received that too, as a worthy apostle on earth throughout his life (Rev. 2.10; 3.11; 1 Clem. 5).[131]

The Fates of Paul and Peter in Rome

From the Aegean region, Paul next appears in Rome as a victim of Nero's persecution. According to Gaius, a Christian writing in the late second century CE, Paul was arrested by guards in Rome and beheaded upon Roman authorities' orders, during the 64 CE persecution, beside the Ostian Way.[132] This is confirmed by parallel tradition in the *Acts of Peter and Paul*, from future decades, that Paul was beheaded at Aquae Salviae (now Tre Fontane), near the third milestone, on the Ostian Way, outside Rome's ancient Julio-Claudian walls (*Acts Pet.* 80). By the late second century CE, a monument had been erected on the site of Paul's tomb, a mile closer to Rome's walls than the site of his execution.[133] According to the *Calendar of Philocalus* (354 CE) and the *Liber Pontificalis* (530 CE), the body of Paul had been interred inside a catacomb by the Appian Way by the year 258 CE.[134] In the late fourth century CE, Ambrose of Milan associated this road with Paul and Peter. Pope Damasus (366–83 CE) declared that the bodies of Paul and Peter had been interred in this same catacomb, in the part that extended under the Appian Basilica Apostolorum. Chadwick and Bruce also argue that this was temporarily so, due to the persecutions under the emperor Valerian (253–60 CE), especially in the year 258 CE.[135]

However, after the demise and death of Valerian, Paul's body was repeatedly moved back to his traditional tomb. Peter's was moved back to his on the Vatican Hill, also reputedly. Over Paul's original tomb, Constantine 'the Great' built a small basilica, around 324 CE. This was replaced in the late fourth century by a larger basilica. This structure remained in place until 16th

---

131. Eusebius, *Hist. eccl.* 2.25.
132. Eusebius, *Hist. eccl.* 2.25.7; 3.31.4.
133. Bruce, *Paul*, pp. 450-51.
134. H. Chadwick, 'St Peter and St Paul in Rome: The problem of the Memoria Apostolorum ad Catacumbas', *JTS* 8 (1957), pp. 31-52 (31-38).
135. Chadwick, 'St Peter and St Paul in Rome', p. 41 n. 2; Bruce, *Paul*, p. 451.

July 1823, when it sustained serious fire damage. It was rebuilt, and publicly reconsecrated, on 10th December 1854. It is now called 'The Basilica of St. Paul Outside the Walls'.[136]

As Potter has noted, Constantine 'the Great' often dedicated new churches throughout the city of Rome, at times converting old buildings that had public importance into new buildings for Christian worship. Thus, he built his basilica over the site of this earlier sacred site to Paul. The tradition surrounding this site was not his own invention, but rather built upon the existent tradition surrounding it. Thus, at once Constantine set in place his ambitions for Paul's reverence in this part of Rome, while setting it within his own ambitions to produce an 'architectural ode' that celebrated them as well.[137] For, as Drake has pointed out, as *pontifex maximus* Constantine was head of the Roman state religion. Therefore, under his reign, politics and religion were intertwined, as the emperor sought to encourage, through various means, correct belief (orthodoxy).[138] It was not to be the only church building built upon a sacred site to Christianity in the Roman world under Constantine. The 'Church of the Nativity in Bethlehem', the 'Church of the Ascension on the Mount of Olives', and the 'Church of the Holy Sepulchre', which were dedicated by the emperor's mother Helen and Bishop Macarius of Jerusalem, are three of the most notable church buildings built for Christian worship over older worship sites under Constantine 'the Great'. All of the buildings, including that which was built by Constantine 'the Great' over this sacred site to Paul, were built for various reasons, chief among them being the desire to honour the martyrs as a spur to fortitude under any future persecution that might eventuate throughout the Roman world.[139]

136. E. Kirschbaum, *The Tombs of St Peter and St Paul* (London: St. Martin's Press, 1959), pp. 165-72.

137. D. Potter, *Constantine: The Emperor* (Oxford: Oxford University Press, 2013), pp. 163-65.

138. H.A. Drake, 'The Impact of Constantine on Christianity', in N. Lenski (ed.), *The Cambridge Companion to the Age of Constantine* (Cambridge: Cambridge University Press, 2012), pp. 111-36 (114, 123).

139. J.W. Drijvers, *Helena Augusta: The Mother of Constantine the Great and the Legend of her Finding of the True Cross* (Leiden: Brill, 1992). See also G. Stemberger, *Jews and Christians in the Holy Land: Palestine in the Fourth Century* (Edinburgh: T. & T. Clark, 2000), p. 57; M. Edwards, 'The Beginnings of Christian-

Stephenson argues that other reasons on the part of Constantine to produce churches over sacred Christian sites, in Rome and elsewhere, included a desire to instill a 'coherent moral framework' with 'Christianity as a common faith'. This policy was set in place in order to appease God, while venerating houses of worship utilized by bishops and other clergy that were subordinate to Constantine, and his own religious powers as emperor and *pontifex maximus*.[140] As Drake points out, Constantine viewed bishops and clergy as fellow-players 'in the game of empire'.[141] With these newly dedicated places of Christian worship, together with bishops and clergy subordinate to him, Constantine set about putting into place the religious transformation of the Roman world. Toleration and freedom of worship for Christians throughout Rome and its empire were of paramount importance to him, raising the political and social status of Christians under his banner of imperial rule, and thereby consolidating power in his hands further.[142]

During excavations of 'The Basilica of St. Paul Outside the Walls', two slabs were found underneath the position of the high altar, bearing the words PAVLO and APOSTOLO MART (To Paul, Apostle and Martyr). Epigraphists have dated the lettering to the reign of Constantine. It is believed they once belonged to a memorial that was once situated somewhere in Constantine's basilica for Paul on this site. Of course, there may have been damage to Paul's bones if they had survived the centuries and still remained there by the nineteenth century. However, they may have been reinterred underneath the new high altar, upon the church's direction.[143] If so, they may still be there. In 2006 a stone sarcophagus was discovered, underneath the new high altar, into which Vatican archaeologists drilled. Inside, they found ancient purple linen, gold, blue textiles, red incense, protein, limestone, and fragments of bone. Pope Benedict XVI announced in 2009 that these once

ization', in N. Lenski (ed.), *The Cambridge Companion to the Age of Constantine* (Cambridge: Cambridge University Press, 2012), pp. 137-58 (144-45).

140. P. Stephenson, *Constantine: Roman Emperor, Christian Victor* (New York: Overlook Press, 2015), pp. 234, 256, 258.

141. H.A. Drake, *Constantine and the Bishops: The Politics of Intolerance* (Baltimore: Johns Hopkins University Press, 2000), p. 73.

142. T. Barnes, *Constantine and Eusebius* (Cambridge, MA: Harvard University Press, 1981), pp. 49-52, 56-57; T. Barnes, *Constantine: Dynasty, Religion and Power in the Later Roman Empire* (Oxford: Blackwell, 2014), pp. 84, 93.

143. Kirschbaum, *Tombs*, pp. 179-84; Bruce, *Paul*, p. 451.

belonged to someone who lived in the first or second centuries CE. Whilst it cannot be established that these belonged to Paul, it is possible that bone traces found inside this sarcophagus might have, once.[144]

Peter's death is just as interesting, if not more macabre. Crucifixion was a form of execution used by Nero for Christians during his persecution. Early tradition states that Peter was crucified upside-down. Tertullian mentions Peter being executed by crucifixion.[145] This is confirmed by Eusebius, who in the early fourth century CE recorded that Peter was crucified head-down upon request,[146] and Jerome confirms this also, writing around the same time, that he was executed by these means and buried somewhere in the Vatican hill.[147] Although it cannot be ruled out that Peter purchased Roman citizenship, allowing him to take a more central role within the church in Rome, crucifixion was not usually reserved for Roman citizens. But Helyer reflects that 'occasionally Roman soldiers did crucify people in various positions just to satisfy their sadistic impulses'. Thus, Helyer concludes, the idea that Peter was executed under Nero's persecution by crucifixion—which may have been extremely rare for Roman citizens to undergo, or perhaps Roman citizens by birth—is not implausible.[148]

Rome Rises from the Ashes

The damage done to Rome by Nero's persecution was immense, especially to Christians living there. Still, Christians rebuilt a new church there together with Christians from abroad, most notably from Syria.[149] After Peter's death,

144. Stephen Brown, 'Pope Says Bone Fragments Found in St Paul's Tomb' (June 28, 2009), see online: https://www.reuters.com/article/us-italy-saint-bone-idUSTRE55R22O20090628.

145. Tertullian, *Scorp.* 15.

146. Eusebius, *Hist. eccl.* 3.1.

147. Jerome, *Vir. ill.* 1.

148. Seneca the Younger, *Dial.* 6; Josephus, *War* 5.449-551; Y. Yadin, 'Pesher Nahum (4QpNahum) Reconsidered', *IEJ* 21 (1971), pp. 1-12; Helyer, *Life and Witness of Peter*, p. 197.

149. Juvenal, *Sat.* 3.62. On the rise of Christianity in Antioch generally, see Magnus Zetterholm, *The Formation of Christianity in Antioch: A Social-Scientific Approach to the Separation between Judaism and Christianity* (London: Routledge, 2003).

Linus presided over the running of the church in Rome, and after him, Anenclitus. After him, there ascended the brilliant Clement. He had known Paul, as had perhaps the previous leaders of Rome. He was a gifted rhetorician, a learned teacher of the Bible and literature, and a wise Christian. He too was a man who was all things to all people, like Paul. In *1 Clement*, he tells the story of the Phoenix: an Arabian bird that lives in Arabia, but flies west over the Red Sea to die and be reborn in Heliopolis ('City of the Sun' in Greek) in Egypt. Like a butterfly, the Phoenix re-emerges new, and as it grows bird-like it becomes a great Phoenix—a king of a bird that sings. According to Clement this bird is a symbol of the resurrection (1 Clem. 25). Very cross-like: life from death, and also very much like the church in Rome, which came back to life after the persecutions of Nero and Domitian, who died in 98 CE. Clement may have learned the story of the Phoenix from Paul. After all, Galatians states that Paul spent much time in Arabia after his conversion, and as someone who lived in Gentile Tarsus in Cilicia, and elsewhere throughout the Gentile world, Paul probably knew such myths. It could be argued that Paul had given instructions to Clement to spread the story of the Phoenix, to help the people have hope in the resurrection before, during and after times of persecution (Gal. 1.17).

By the end of the first century CE, Clement wrote to the churches of Corinth, not just as the church leader in Rome, but with authority as a universal teacher and pastor, giving advice to Christians living there. Although *1 Clement* displays signs of originative and emergent primacy of the Roman church over others,[150] the primacy of the church in Rome over all others of the Roman Empire in the late first century CE was not firmly established. Therefore, it cannot be confirmed, for that early stage.[151] However, *1 Clement* is a communal letter, written to the large Christian community of Corinth at that, which led the churches of all of Achaea. Therefore, the Roman church most certainly reserved the right to much honour over other Christian communities around the world.[152] *The Shepherd of Hermas*, also believed by modern historians to have been written in Rome in the late first century CE to

150. L.L. Welborn, 'Roman Political Ideology and the Authority of First Clement', in Mark Harding and Alanna Nobbs (eds.), *Into All the World: Emergent Christianity in its Jewish and Greco-Roman Context* (Grand Rapids: Eerdmans, 2017), pp. 372-92 (374).

151. Welborn, 'Roman Political Ideology', p. 373.

152. Welborn, 'Roman Political Ideology', p. 377.

early second century CE, likewise exhibits interests in the administration, running and conduct of Christian churches, throughout Rome and foreign places.[153] Thus, by the time these works were written, the church in Rome showed more than signs of surviving. It was also thriving, empowered among Christians, within the city of Rome and throughout the empire. This indicates the tenacity of its love for God, for themselves and for others—and for the message of Christ, intended for all the world. For this, one can give much credit to the likes of Paul and Peter. Their message of the gospel was based on God and the themes of Jesus Christ—the re-emergent life from apparent death into the kingdom of God, and the resurrection for us at the end of time, once again into the kingdom of God.[154]

Conclusion

This article has demonstrated that Christianity is like a phoenix rising from the ashes: it lives on despite Nero's persecution. It thrives, in part due to the likes of Paul and Peter who paid the ultimate price during Nero's persecution for their part in the promotion and development of Christianity in Rome and perhaps elsewhere. Their legacy continued even in Rome, as Rome rebuilt and rose from the ashes of the past, afresh and anew. No doubt, Christians were instrumental in the eventual rebuilding of Rome, following the fire of 64 CE, only to be persecuted in Nero's persecution. However, many Christians clearly survived in Rome despite the persecution and were in time joined by other Christians from around the empire, including Antioch, in support for their presence in Rome, if not their lives. The bodies of Paul and Peter were revered after their deaths, which is evident in a still-present Christian community, both during and after the persecution, and the reverence they were held in during their lives and times in the city of Rome itself. But, in the mayhem of Christianity's official disfavour in Nero's eyes, Roman society turned against the Church, and they died as a result. Still, their memory lived on, and

153. William L. Lane, 'Social Perspectives on Roman Christianity during the Formative Years from Nero to Nerva: Romans, Hebrews, 1 Clement', in Karl P. Donfried and Peter Richardson (eds.), *Judaism and Christianity in First-Century Rome* (Grand Rapids: Eerdmans, 1998), pp. 196-244 (236-37); Green, *Christianity in Ancient Rome*, pp. 52-56.

154. Green, *Christianity in Ancient Rome*, pp. 52-56.

many clamoured to rebuild the church of Rome, along with Rome itself, in the aftermath of the persecution, and indeed even the fire. That, in itself, is testament to the glowing examples of Paul and Peter to change people's lives for the better in Rome while still alive, and beyond. It is also testament to the lives of other Roman Christians, who followed their teachings and who followed Jesus Christ as Christians, but who lost their lives in the persecution. Their lives were also glowing examples of how the Christian faith changed the lives of many people for the better, who, while mortal, had hope beyond mortal death.

[*JGRChJ* 19 (2023) 73-93]

PAUL'S COLLECTION AND A SLAVE'S DILEMMA: GIVE TO THE POOR OR SAVE FOR FREEDOM?

Robin Thompson

Grand Canyon University, Phoenix, AZ

First Corinthians 16.1-2 reads, 'now concerning the collection for the saints, just as I directed the churches of Galatia, so you are to do also. On the first day of the week, each of you should set aside and save as he or she may prosper, so that when I come no collections need be made.'[1] This is the first time in the surviving correspondence to the Corinthian church that Paul mentions his collection. When this letter was read to the church, there would have been an economically-mixed group listening. Bruce Longenecker describes them as 'a community comprised of [*sic*] slaves, freedmen, artisans and families', which would have ranged from those with moderate surplus to those living below subsistence level.[2] In this church, we have textual evidence that some of the members were slaves: Paul directly addresses slaves in the church (1 Cor. 7.21-22), and he speaks of their baptism into the church (1 Cor. 12.13). While New Testament scholars often acknowledge the presence of slaves in the early church congregations, they seldom consider their life within those congregations. Therefore, in this article, I focus on the slaves who heard Paul's directive. In order to explore this topic, I discuss Paul's collection, present the reality of a slave's life in the first-century Mediterranean world, and then consider how a slave who was a Christ-follower might have responded to Paul's appeal. I propose that some slaves would have had the financial means to contribute to Paul's collection, but their contribution would have

---

1.   Translations are my own unless otherwise indicated.

2.   Bruce W. Longenecker, *Remember the Poor: Paul, Poverty, and the Greco-Roman World* (Grand Rapids: Eerdmans, 2010), p. 294.

come at the great cost of sacrificing money they were saving to purchase their freedom.

Paul's Collection

Paul specifically mentions his collection in three of his letters: 1 Cor. 16; 2 Cor. 8–9; and Rom. 15. Multiple churches were involved in the effort, including churches from Galatia (1 Cor. 16.1), Corinth/Achaia (1 Cor. 16.1-4; 2 Cor. 9.1-3; Rom. 15.25), and Macedonia (2 Cor. 8.1-4; Rom. 15.25). Richard Ascough comments, 'Paul's collection for the Jerusalem church was one of the major activities of his ministry during the 50s.'[3] According to Rom. 15.25-27, it is for the purpose of delivering this collection that Paul goes to Jerusalem before his planned trip to Rome and Spain. Most scholars associate this trip with the account in Acts where, upon his arrival in Jerusalem, Paul is soon arrested, ultimately appeals to Caesar, and is sent to Rome for trial (Acts 21–26). However, in Luke's account, there is only one obscure mention of the collection: 'After many years, I came bringing alms to my nation and to present offerings' (Acts 24.17).[4] This silence of Luke regarding the collection has led many scholars to speculate that it was not well-received by the church in Jerusalem.[5] While Paul does seem to indicate some anxiety about the how the Jerusalem church would respond (Rom. 15.30-31),[6] there is

---

3.   Richard S. Ascough, 'The Completion of a Religious Duty: The Background of 2 Cor 8.1-15', *NTS* 42 (1996), pp. 584-99 (586 n. 6). Longenecker attempts to pinpoint the beginning of these efforts to 53–54 CE (*Remember the Poor*, p. 344).

4.   Dieter Georgi, *Remembering the Poor: The History of Paul's Collection for Jerusalem* (Nashville: Abingdon, 1992), pp. 124-25; David G. Horrell, 'Paul's Collection: Resources for a Materialist Theology', *Epworth Review* 22 (1995), pp. 74-83 (75); S. McKnight, 'Collection for the Saints', in Gerald F. Hawthorne *et al.* (eds.), *Dictionary of Paul and his Letters* (Downers Grove, IL: InterVarsity Press, 1993), pp. 143-47 (144). Georgi notes, 'without the benefit of Paul's letters, modern historians would have no knowledge of Paul's collection' (*Remembering the Poor*, p. 69).

5.   Horrell, 'Paul's Collection', p. 75; A.J.M. Wedderburn, 'Paul's Collection: Chronology and History', *NTS* 48 (2002), pp. 95-110 (107).

6.   Horrell, 'Paul's Collection', p. 75; Keith F. Nickle, *The Collection: A Study in Paul's Strategy* (Studies in Biblical Theology, 48; repr., Eugene, OR: Wipf and Stock, 2009), pp. 14-15.

simply not enough evidence to know how the story of the collection actually ended.

Chronology and Terminology of the Collection
Some scholars point to Paul's statement in Gal. 2.10 to establish the begin-ning of the collection.[7] There, Paul comments that the leaders in Jerusalem ask that he and Barnabas 'remember the poor'. However, there is nothing in the context of this statement that serves to limit 'the poor' to those in Jerusalem. Longenecker observes that 'the earliest interpretations of Gal. 2.10 in the second through the mid-fourth centuries CE' did not understand 'the poor' in this manner.[8] Most scholars concur that, in Galatians, Paul is simply agreeing to continue the particularly Jewish practice of taking care of the poor in general;[9] there is consensus that Paul's statement in Galatians does not refer to his later collection.

The first time Paul specifically mentions the collection in his extant cor-respondence is in 1 Cor. 16.1-4. In vv. 1-2, he describes the work using the term λογεία, which 'is the general term for any kind of voluntary, or com-

7. In addition to Holl and Joubert mentioned previously, see also Abraham J. Malherbe, 'The Corinthian Contribution', *ResQ* 3 (1959), pp. 221-33 (222); Richard Last and Philip A. Harland, *Group Survival in the Ancient Mediterranean: Re-thinking Material Conditions in the Landscape of Jews and Christians* (London: Bloomsbury, 2020), p. 143.

8. Longenecker, *Remember the Poor*, p. 159.

9. Longenecker comments that taking care of the poor is 'one of Judaism's most socially distinctive features' (*Remember the Poor*, p. 203). David J. Downs ob-serves that 'for the most part, there was greater concern for the welfare of the poor among Jewish and Christian communities than one typically finds among pagan asso-ciations' (*The Offering of the Gentiles: Paul's Collection for Jerusalem in its Chronological, Cultural, and Cultic Contexts* [WUNT, 248; Tübingen: Mohr Siebeck, 2008], p. 110). While both Cicero and Seneca do acknowledge that money should be used to help those in need, 'the "needy" in question in both Cicero and Seneca's thought are respectable citizens, and not the most desperate members of their society' (see Anneliese Parkin, '"You Do Him No Service": An Exploration of Pagan Almsgiving', in Margaret Atkins and Robin Osborne [eds.], *Poverty in the Roman World* [Cambridge: Cambridge University Press, 2006], pp. 60-82 [62]). Philip A. Harland concludes that 'we do not know of any associations gathering funds for the poor' ('Associations and the Economics of Group Life: A Preliminary Case Study of Asia Minor and the Aegean Islands', *SEÅ* 80 [2015], pp. 1-37 [35]).

pulsory, monetary collection'.[10] Inscriptions and ostraca, however, indicate that this term was often used to describe collections taken up for religious purposes.[11] In v. 2, Paul goes on to say that 'on the first day of the week, each of you should set aside and save as he or she may prosper.' Paul does not ask for a specific donation, but that each person set aside funds according to their means. In v. 3, Paul refers to the collection as 'your gift'. The term used, χάρις, is one Paul uses repeatedly in reference to the work of the collection in his further correspondence, so we will discuss the significance of this term shortly.

The next time Paul discusses the collection is in the letter we call Second Corinthians, which is likely his fourth letter to the church in Corinth.[12] He allocates a considerable amount of time in this letter to the discussion of the collection—chs. 8–9. In these two chapters, Paul no longer refers to this work as a λογεία or collection, but instead uses several other terms: χάρις (8.6, 7, 19), διακονία (8.4; 9.1, 12, 13), εὐλογία (9.5), λειτουργία (9.12), and κοινωνία (9.13)—generous work, ministry, generous gift, service and sharing. James Harrison notes that these terms represent 'an impressive range of benefaction terminology and motifs'.[13] However, as Harrison notes, Paul is not simply urging the Corinthians to continue participating in the wider Greco-Roman system of reciprocity. We see this by his unusual focus on the concept of χάρις.[14] Julien Ogereau observes that 'no less than eight times is the term χάρις indeed employed to refer to either the collection per se, or to God's

10.   Julien M. Ogereau, 'The Jerusalem Collection as Κοινωνία: Paul's Global Politics of Socio-Economic Equality and Solidarity', *NTS* 58 (2012), pp. 360-78 (363); these two verses are the only time Paul uses this term to describe the collection.

11.   Adolf Deissmann, *Light from the Ancient East: The New Testament Illustrated by Recently Discovered Texts of the Graeco-Roman World* (trans. Lionel R.M. Strachan; repr., Grand Rapids: Baker, 4th edn, 1965), p. 105; Last and Harland, *Group Survival*, pp. 124-25.

12.   I hold the view that Second Corinthians was sent as one letter. But this view is not necessary to the following discussion.

13.   James R. Harrison, *Paul's Language of Grace in its Graeco-Roman Context* (WUNT, 172; Tübingen: Mohr Siebeck, 2003), p. 300.

14.   Harrison observes that 'while the range of circumlocutory terminology that Paul applied to the Jerusalem collection would not have occasioned surprise to readers of the honorific inscriptions, the profusion of χάρις as the leitmotiv of the collection certainly would' (*Paul's Language of Grace*, p. 343).

favour enabling [believers] to give' (2 Cor. 8.1, 4, 6, 7, 9, 19; 9.8, 14).[15] By shifting the focus away from the obligation inherent in the system of reciprocity, Paul provides an 'alternate vision of social relations by means of his theology of grace'.[16] John Barclay suggests that there are 'renegotiations of power and obligation that accompany the giving and receiving of gifts *in Christ*'.[17]

The final time Paul mentions the collection is at the end of his letter to the believers in Rome. Here he describes this work with the terms διαχονέω (15.25), κοινωνία (15.26), λειτουργέω (15.27) and καρπός (15.28). Only here, as the collection is being brought to completion, does Paul describe it as the fruit of his churches.[18]

Purpose of the Collection

Scholars have long debated why Paul initiated this collection and what the purpose of it was. It is beyond the scope of this article to engage the arguments, but the main suggestions are as follows: (1) financial relief for the

15. Ogereau, 'Jerusalem Collection', p. 364. Georgi comments that 'χάρις becomes the very *leitmotif* of chapter 8 and 9' (*Remembering the Poor*, p. 72).

16. Harrison, *Paul's Language of Grace*, p. 311 (see also 311 n. 86, 324)—contra Ascough, Peterman and Verbrugge who argue that Paul saw the collection as a religious obligation or duty (see Ascough, 'Completion', p. 599; Gerald W. Peterman, 'Romans 15:26—Make a Contribution or Establish Fellowship?', *NTS* 40 [1994], pp. 457-63 [460]; Verlyn D. Verbrugge, 'The Collection and Paul's Leadership of the Church in Corinth' [PhD diss., University of Notre Dame, 1988], pp. 234, 263).

17. John M.G. Barclay, *Paul and the Gift* (Grand Rapids: Eerdmans, 2015), p. 574 (emphasis original).

18. Grant R. Osborne explains that 'the offering is a *fruit* that the Jewish Christians will receive, possibly meaning that it is the "harvest" from the spiritual legacy that the Jewish people have given the Gentiles (Murray 1968; Moo 1996) or the visible demonstration of the *fruit* of Paul's mission (Morris 1988; Fitzmyer1993b; Cranfield 1979 takes both as possible' (*Romans* [The IVP New Testament Commentary Series; Downers Grove, IL: IVP Academic, 2004], p. 398 [emphasis original]). Robert Jewett, however, suggests that Paul is simply using the language of commerce, so that 'to seal the fruit of the Jerusalem offering is rather to guarantee its delivery against theft and embezzlement' (*Romans: A Commentary* [Hermeneia; Minneapolis: Fortress Press, 2007], p. 932).

poor believers in Jerusalem;[19] (2) a religious obligation placed upon Paul by
the Jewish leaders in Jerusalem (Gal. 2);[20] (3) a theological obligation of the
Gentile believers to the Jewish believers from whom they inherited their faith
(Rom. 15);[21] (4) an attempt to establish unity between the Gentile and Jewish
community of believers;[22] and (5) a symbol of the eschatological gathering
of the nations to Jerusalem.[23]

It is important to note that the conversation concerning the purpose of
Paul's collection continues because Paul himself never directly identifies the
purpose, other than to help alleviate the poverty of the Jerusalem believers (2
Cor. 8.4, 14; 9.12; Rom. 15.26). In his letter to the Roman churches, as the
collection nears completion, Paul does mention a type of material reciprocity
for spiritual blessings (Rom. 15.27). However, we have no knowledge of
what Paul communicated to his various churches—while the collection was
in process—as to a wider purpose for the collection. This lack of knowledge
concerning Paul's purpose is important to note: for when Paul asked his

19.   Downs, *Offering of the Gentiles*, p. 161; Horrell, 'Paul's Collection', p. 79;
Longenecker, *Remember the Poor*, p. 177; McKnight, 'Collection', p. 144; Justin J.
Meggitt, *Paul, Poverty and Survival* (SNTW; Edinburgh: T. & T. Clark, 1998), p.
159; Nickle, *Collection*, p. 142; Verbrugge, 'Collection', p. 233. Ogereau goes further, focusing on the term ἰσότης (2 Cor. 8.13, 14). He proposes that Paul is arguing
for 'a certain equality or fairness in the distribution of wealth within the early church'
('Jerusalem Collection', p. 364).

20.   Karl Holl, 'Der Kirchenbegriff des Paulus in seinem Verhältnis zu dem der
Urgemeinde', *Sitzungsbericht der Berliner Akademie* (1921), pp. 920-47; Stephan
Joubert, *Paul as Benefactor: Reciprocity, Strategy and Theological Reflection in
Paul's Collection* (WUNT, 124; Tübingen: Mohr Siebeck, 2000); contra Craig L.
Blomberg, *Christians in an Age of Wealth: A Biblical Theology of Stewardship*
(Grand Rapids: Zondervan, 2013), p. 116; Downs, *Offering of the Gentiles*, p. 72;
Georgi, *Remembering the Poor*, pp. 17-18; Wedderburn, 'Paul's Collection', pp. 96,
99.

21.   Ascough, 'Completion', p. 599; Nils Alstrup Dahl, *Studies in Paul: Theology for the Early Christian Mission* (Minneapolis: Augsburg Publishing House,
1977), pp. 22-39 (32); Peterman, 'Romans 15:26', p. 460; Verbrugge, 'Collection',
pp. 233, 263.

22.   Longenecker, *Remember the Poor*, pp. 177, 315 n. 38; Nickle, *Collection*,
p. 142; Peterman, 'Romans 15:26', p. 461; Verbrugge, 'Collection', p. 233; Last and
Harland, *Group Survival*, p. 143.

23.   Nickle, *Collection*, pp. 138-39.

churches to contribute financially to this project, the *rationale* for the project would have been a significant motivator (or demotivator) for the believers to give.

Motivation to Give to the Collection
Rather than an extended explanation of the purpose for the collection, what we have instead is a record of how Paul chose to ask and/or motivate his churches to give to it. In 1 Cor. 16.1-4, Paul simply directs the Corinthian church to gather the funds. The NET translation renders Paul's directive as a polite request: 'with regard to the collection for the saints, please follow the directions that I gave to the churches of Galatia.'[24] However, Paul chooses the verb διατάσσω to describe this directive, which carries the authoritative tone of command, and he uses imperatives in both verse one and two (ποιήσατε, τιθέτω).[25] Verlyn Verbrugge observes that Paul 'made no attempt to motivate them, nor did he cite any reasons why they should participate in this project. He felt his relationship with them was strong enough that he as their leader could take this authoritative approach with them.'[26] So while the collection in 1 Cor. 16 may have been presented as voluntary in regards to how each person prospered (and we will explore this in more detail to follow), the project as a whole was presented as something expected to be completed.

Paul's approach in Second Corinthians regarding the project is notably different from that taken in First Corinthians.[27] Scholars generally conclude

24. Here, the translators have rendered ποιήσατε as a 'request' type of imperative, adding 'please' for further politeness. The imperative initiates an event and is direct (2nd person), not indirect (3rd person). According to Joseph D. Fantin, the imperative in this context would not meet the 'qualifications' for a request imperative (*The Greek Imperative Mood in the New Testament: A Cognitive and Communicative Approach* [SBG, 12; New York: Peter Lang, 2010], pp. 263-70). Fantin explains that 'the imperative is strong-force unless there exists some feature to weaken the force' (p. 218); in the case of 1 Cor. 16.1, no such features are present.

25. See also Raymond F. Collins, *First Corinthians* (SP; Collegeville, MN: Liturgical, 1999), p. 677 n. 1.

26. Verbrugge, 'Collection', p. 79.

27. Malherbe notes that 'in 2 Corinthians Paul never uses the imperative in his discussion of the collection' ('Corinthian Contribution', p. 227). Verbrugge comments that 'Paul displays extreme hesitancy to tell the Corinthians to get on with the

that this letter was written only about a year after First Corinthians,[28] but since the Corinthians and Paul had been embroiled in difficult matters Paul addresses the church in Second Corinthians in a different manner than he did in First Corinthians.[29] In 2 Cor. 8, rather than with directives similar to those in 1 Cor. 16, Paul chooses to motivate the believers by way of example. He speaks first of the churches of Macedonia, who despite their deep poverty (βάθους πτωχεία) begged to participate (8.1-6); Paul identifies this work as the grace of God (8.1).[30] He then speaks of 'the grace of our Lord Jesus Christ' as the second and ultimate example (8.9). Paul reminds his listeners that though Jesus 'was rich, he become poor, so that you by his poverty might become rich'. As mentioned previously, in this chapter Paul repeatedly uses the term χάρις to describe the collection itself (8.6, 7, 19). And in ch. 9, he reminds the Corinthians that 'God is able to make all grace abound' to them, so that they 'may abound in every good work' (9.8).

However, in ch. 9, Paul also brings into play the Corinthians' honor. Paul has boasted to the Macedonians that 'Achaia has been prepared since last year,' and this has 'stirred up many of them' (9.2). In light of this, Paul urges the Corinthians to have the collection ready so that when he and the delegation from Macedonia arrive, the Corinthian believers will not be put to shame.[31]

project of the collection for Jerusalem ... It is hard to imagine a greater contrast to what he did in 1 Cor. 16.1-2' ('Collection', pp. 216-17).

28.   George H. Guthrie, *2 Corinthians* (BECNT; Grand Rapids: Baker Academic, 2015), p. 18; Colin G. Kruse, *2 Corinthians* (Nashville: B&H Academic, 2020), p. 34; Margaret E. Thrall, *A Critical and Exegetical Commentary on the Second Epistle of the Corinthians* (ICC; London: T. & T. Clark, 2004), p. 77.

29.   David E. Garland writes that 'the problems encountering Paul as he writes this letter are complex ... He must restore his relationship with the church so that he might continue to guide it in spiritual matters' (*2 Corinthians* [NAC, 29; Nashville: Broadman and Holman, 1999], p. 29). Linda L. Belleville observes that this letter 'comes at the tail end of a long and stressful exchange' (*2 Corinthians* [IVP New Testament Commentary; Downers Grove, IL: InterVarsity Press, 1996], p. 14).

30.   Guthrie notes that Paul offers 'the Macedonians as an example of how God has manifested his grace by doing a great work in, but also through, their churches' (*2 Corinthians*, p. 392).

31.   Hans Dieter Betz mentions that the names of those who did not follow through on public pledges 'used to be published in the Athenian Agora' (Betz, *2 Corinthians 8 and 9: A Commentary on Two Administrative Letters of the Apostle*

In summary, in this second correspondence, Paul states quite specifically that he does 'not say this as a command' (8.8), and he works carefully to inspire and motivate the Corinthians to give freely and generously.[32] He makes it clear that he desires that they offer what they give 'as a voluntary gift and not as an extortion' (NRSV), 'not reluctantly or under compulsion' (9.7). David Garland comments that 'Paul does not want the Corinthians to feel that this offering was somehow imposed upon them.'[33] Thus, his focus on χάρις is again significant. Nonetheless, Paul still communicates an expectation that the Corinthian church should participate.[34]

Slavery in the First-Century Mediterranean World

The Humanitarian View

Before we can consider how a slave who was a Christ-follower in the Corinthian church might have responded to Paul's appeal, it is necessary to briefly sketch the reality of a slave's life in the first-century Mediterranean world. There are some scholars today who argue for a humanitarian view of first-century slavery, especially in comparison to slavery in the American south. One New Testament scholar in a 2014 commentary on First Corinthians wrote,

> For the most part [slavery] provided generally well for up to one-third of the population in a city like Corinth or Rome. The household slave had considerable freedom and very often experienced mutual benefit along with the master. The owner received the benefit of the slave's services; and the slave had steady "employment," including having all his or her basic needs met—indeed, for many to be a slave was prefer-

Paul [Hermeneia; Philadelphia: Fortress Press, 1985], p. 96). While he is referring to something that took place centuries prior to the time of Paul, the honor/shame culture exemplified by this practice was pervasive throughout the centuries in the Mediterranean world.

32. Horrell, 'Paul's Collection', p. 77.
33. Garland, *2 Corinthians*, p. 404.
34. Blomberg, *Christians in an Age of Wealth*, p. 114.

able to being a freed person, whose securities were often tenuous at best.[35]

Another scholar working on the 2011 ESV translation team made this comment,

> For the average English reader, the word "slave" has irredeemably negative associations and connotations. In people's minds it's a permanent condition, whereas in the OT and certainly in the time of the NT it's temporary, it leads to a freedom. And it was often voluntary, at least in the first century ... It was often a situation that had status and carried considerable legal protections.[36]

This humanitarian view of first-century slavery was shared, for the most part, by classical scholars until the 1970s when a sea-change began to occur due to significant research in this area. The seminal works are by Keith Hopkins (1978), M.I. Finley (1980), Orlando Patterson (1982) and Keith Bradley (1984).[37] In 1984, Bradley wrote,

> The historiography of ancient slavery has been traditionally apologetic in one way or another and it is not until recent times that the realization has begun to set in among scholars that there is something distinctly unpalatable about slavery in antiquity. Indeed, in some quarters apologetic influences are still at work.[38]

As demonstrated above, these influences are unfortunately still at work in some New Testament circles even today. Thus, the need to consider here the life of a slave in the first century.

---

35.   Gordon D. Fee, *The First Epistle to the Corinthians* (NICNT; Grand Rapids: Eerdmans, rev. edn, 2014), p. 353.

36.   'ESV Bible Translators Debate the Word "slave" at Tyndale House, Cambridge', *YouTube*. https://www.youtube.com/watch?v=Mx06mtApu8k.

37.   Keith Hopkins, *Conquerors and Slaves* (Cambridge: Cambridge University Press, 1978); M.I. Finley, *Ancient Slavery and Modern Ideology* (New York: Viking, 1980); Orlando Patterson, *Slavery and Social Death: A Comparative Study* (Cambridge, MA: Harvard University Press, 1982); Keith R. Bradley, *Slaves and Masters in the Roman Empire: A Study in Social Control* (repr., New York: Oxford University Press, 1987).

38.   Bradley, *Slaves and Masters*, p. 19.

The Historical View

Entry into slavery was rarely voluntary. For much of Roman history, the two primary sources of slaves were conquered people and those born into slavery as children of slaves.[39] Babies could also be 'exposed' due to poverty or gender selection.[40] Some of these exposed infants were then taken by those who would raise them and sell them as slaves.[41] Walter Scheidel comments that 'this practice may conceivably have been the leading domestic source of freeborn slaves in the mature empire.'[42] Piracy, at times, was also a source of slaves.[43] If a family could not pay the ransom demanded for a kidnapped family member, the pirates then sold that person into slavery. Some have argued another source of slaves were people who sold themselves into slavery. This would have been the only voluntary method, and scholars debate just how often this actually occurred.[44] J.A. Harrill concludes his research into the question saying, 'there are, then, no grounds for seeing self-sale as a major source of slaves or as evidence for ancient slavery's relatively humane character.'[45]

In the later Roman Republic, slaves were not only used as manual laborers in the fields and mines, but they were also used for a variety of domestic chores to the point where a large number of domestic slaves was an indication

39. Keith R. Bradley, *Slavery and Society at Rome* (Cambridge: Cambridge University Press, 1994), pp. 32-33; Walter Scheidel, 'The Roman Slave Supply', in Keith R. Bradley and Paul Cartledge (eds.), *The Cambridge World History of Slavery* (4 vols.; New York: Cambridge University Press, 2011), I, pp. 287-310 (293-97); William L. Westermann, *The Slave Systems of Greek and Roman Antiquity* (Philadelphia: American Philosophical Society, 1955), p. 29.

40. For example, a husband tells his wife in a letter that 'if it is a boy, let it be; if it is a girl, cast it out' (P. Oxy. 744 [Hunt and Edgar, LCL]).

41. Bradley, *Slavery and Society at Rome,* p. 35; Westermann, *Slave Systems,* p. 30.

42. Scheidel, 'Roman Slave Supply', p. 298.

43. Bradley, *Slavery and Society at Rome*, p. 37; Scheidel, 'Roman Slave Supply', p. 297; Westermann, *Slave Systems*, p. 28.

44. Jennifer A. Glancy, *Slavery in Early Christianity* (Oxford: Oxford University Press, 2002), pp. 80-85; J. Albert Harrill, *The Manumission of Slaves in Early Christianity* (HUT, 32; Tübingen: Mohr Siebeck, 1995), pp. 30-31.

45. Harrill, *Manumission in Early Christianity*, p. 31. Contra Morris Silver, 'Contractual Slavery in the Roman Economy', *Ancient History Bulletin* 25 (2011), pp. 73-132.

of luxury and wealth.[46] Domestic slaves were the Rolexes and luxury cars of that period, what we know as 'conspicuous consumption'.[47] This increased demand for and use of slaves created a slave population in 'proportions never before known in antiquity, and never to be reached again'.[48] Scheidel estimates that there were 'between 1 and 1.5 million slaves in Italy at the peak of this labour regime, equivalent to some 15-25 per cent of the total population'.[49] He goes on to estimate 'between 5 and 8 million slaves in the Roman empire' as a whole.[50]

Slaves were bought and sold as property. There was no regard for children or family affiliation at the auction block. Keith Bradley presents records of slave sales from Egypt from the first century BCE to the fourth century CE. Only a few records show that young children were sold with their mother. Females were sold individually as young as four and male children as young as two.[51] As evidence that they were being sold as bodies, slaves were inspected with no regard to their personhood. Seneca comments, 'when you buy a horse, you order its blanket to be removed; you pull off the garments from slaves that are advertised for sale, so that no bodily flaws may escape your notice.'[52] For a female slave the humiliation was greater. Publius Vinicus described one female slave as 'she stood naked on the shore to meet the buyer's sneers; every part of her body was inspected—and handled'.[53]

---

46.   Westermann, *Slave Systems*, p. 100.

47.   Matthew J. Perry comments, 'Owners frequently used [male slaves] for "female" duties as a display of status. The underlying message of such staffing decisions was that owners were wealthy enough to use more expensive commodities (male slaves) than the work required' (*Gender, Manumission, and the Roman Freedwoman* [New York: Cambridge University Press, 2014], p. 185 n. 3). Hopkins notes that 'senators and knights maintained elaborate households staffed with hundreds of slaves, including cooks, scribes, librarians, doctors, name-callers, at once a mark of their culture, and of an extravagance which enhanced their status' (*Conquerors and Slaves*, p. 49).

48.   Westermann, *Slave Systems*, p. 63.

49.   Scheidel, 'Roman Slave Supply', p. 289.

50.   Scheidel, 'Roman Slave Supply', p. 293.

51.   Bradley, *Slaves and Masters*, pp. 53-57.

52.   Seneca the Younger, *Ep.* 80.9 (Gummere, LCL).

53.   Seneca the Elder, *Controv.* 1.2.3 (cited in Glancy, *Slavery in Early Christianity*, p. 86).

Once they were sold or were born as a slave into a household, they had no 'independent social existence: they were the absolute property of their masters with no legal rights.'[54] It is difficult to comprehend the trauma of their situation, they were 'deprived of a past and a future, unable to claim natal family or legitimate offspring'.[55] Even if a slave owner allowed a slave to 'marry' and have children, he could split up the family at any point. And while slave owners may not have done this very often, the fact that these 'forcible separations ... were possible and that from time to time they did take place was enough to strike terror in the hearts of all slaves and to transform significantly the way they behaved and conceived of themselves.'[56]

Slaves could be physically punished, sometimes brutally, without recourse. Ammianus Marcellinus reported that some slave owners 'are so strict in punishing offences, that if a slave is slow in bringing the hot water, they condemn him to suffer three hundred lashes'.[57] Sometimes a slave suffered from no action of his own. Plutarch records the story of a teacher who 'wanted to teach his students to be more frugal with their lunches, so he had a slave beaten during the afternoon lecture as a way to reinforce his message about the necessity of self-control'.[58] While these may be extreme examples, flogging was nonetheless a common experience for slaves. Slaves could also be branded, tattooed, and shackled.[59] If all this were not enough, 'enslaved girls, women, boys and young men were frequently sexual targets for their masters.'[60] Moses Finley comments that this sexual exploitation was 'treated as

---

54.   Clarice J. Martin, 'The Eyes Have It: Slaves in the Communities of Christ-Believers', in Richard A. Horsley (ed.), *A People's History of Christianity: Christian Origins* (7 vols.; Minneapolis: Fortress Press, 2005), I, pp. 221-39 (228).

55.   Carolyn Osiek, 'Family Matters', in Richard A. Horsley (ed.), *A People's History of Christianity: Christian Origins* (Minneapolis: Fortress Press, 2005), I, pp. 201-220 (209).

56.   Patterson, *Slavery and Social Death*, p. 6.

57.   Ammianus Marcellinus, *Rerum Gestarum* 28.4.16 (Rolfe).

58.   Martin, 'The Eyes Have It', p. 235, referring to Plutarch, *Mor.* 70e.

59.   Richard A. Horsley, 'The Slave Systems of Classical Antiquity and their Reluctant Recognition by Modern Scholars', in Allen Dwight Callahan *et al.* (eds.), *Slavery in Text and Interpretation* (Semia, 83/84; Atlanta: Society of Biblical Literature, 1998), pp. 19-66 (43).

60.   Glancy, *Slavery in Early Christianity*, p. 51.

a commonplace in Graeco-Roman literature from Homer on; only modern writers have managed largely to ignore it.'[61]

But the most significant difference between slave and free was that a slave lacked personhood.[62] While they lived in an honor/shame society, slaves could neither acquire honor, nor suffer shame. In addition, the absolute power an owner had to beat, sell or even kill his or her slave led to the dehumanization of the slave; Bradley comments that slavery 'was viewed in many ways as a state of living death'.[63]

Peculium and Manumission

At this point, it is important to comment on two areas of first-century slavery that often cause the modern reader to assume ancient slavery was more humanitarian than subsequent forms of slavery: peculium and manumission.

Roman slaves were given a *peculium*, a fund which legally belonged to the owner but was 'spoken of as, *de facto*, the property of the slave'.[64] A slaves could increase his or her *peculium* in a variety of ways, such as selling part of a food allowance (Seneca the Younger, *Ep.* 80.4), selling left-over food from the owner's table (Apuleius, *Metam.* 10.13-14) or receiving profits or earnings from business done for the owner (Dig. 2.13.4.3). The *peculium* could include non-monetary items such as farms, houses, slaves, and cattle (Dig. 15.1.57; 33.8.6), and thus could be quite valuable in some cases.[65] While there may have been some slaves who had such financial resources, these resources were never truly their own—they legally belonged to the owner, and both slave and owner were always aware of this reality.

Manumission takes place when a slave is set free by his or her owner. Both the Greeks and Romans regularly set slaves free. But there are two common misconceptions regarding this practice: (1) that most slaves were eventually freed; and (2) that slaves were set free at no cost to themselves. Only those slaves in close proximity to their masters could hope to achieve manumission.

---

61.   Finley, *Ancient Slavery and Modern Ideology*, pp. 163-64.

62.   Keith R. Bradley states it this way: 'the contrast between free and slave was thus a contrast between person and non-person' ('The Regular, Daily Traffic in Slaves: Roman History and Contemporary History', *CJ* 87 [1991], pp. 125-38 [137]).

63.   Bradley, *Slavery and Society at Rome*, p. 25.

64.   W.W. Buckland, *The Roman Law of Slavery: The Condition of the Slave in Private Law from Augustus to Justinian* (repr., New York: AMS, 1969), p. 187.

65.   Buckland, *Roman Law of Slavery*, p. 187.

Scholars have noted that manumission among rural slaves, who had far less interaction with their owners, probably rarely occurred.[66] The slaves who acquired manumission were a decided minority of slaves; as Hopkins concludes, 'most Roman slaves were freed only by death'.[67] Freedom was rarely given at no cost to the slave—it usually came at a price.[68] Under Greek manumission, the average release price would buy enough wheat to feed a poor family for three years.[69] Under Roman manumission, one of the lowest release prices found in sources was equal to a Roman soldier's earnings for over three years.[70] To save up such a large amount would likely have taken a slave years of service to their master. While some see manumission as evidence that first-century slavery was more humanitarian, the reality is that manumission served rather to perpetuate the institution of slavery: the owners used the slaves' desire for freedom to incentivize them to work hard and to be faithful.[71]

66. Henrik Mouritsen, *The Freedman in the Roman World* (Cambridge: Cambridge University Press, 2011), p. 204; Susan Treggiari, *Roman Freedmen during the Late Republic* (Oxford: Clarendon Press, 1969), pp. 106-7.

67. Hopkins, *Conquerors and Slaves*, p. 118.

68. Hopkins, *Conquerors and Slaves*, pp. 118, 131; Rachel Zelnick-Abramovitz, *Not Wholly Free: The Concept of Manumission and the Status of Manumitted Slaves in the Ancient Greek World* (Leiden: Brill, 2005), p. 208 n. 32 (she notes that 'most scholars believe that [payment of money for release] was the rule').

69. Hopkins, *Conquerors and Slaves*, p. 146.

70. The release price that Hermeros says he paid (Petron, *Sat.* 57) was comparable to what a Roman soldier earned in one year; Richard Duncan-Jones, *The Economy of the Roman Empire: Quantitative Studies* (Cambridge: Cambridge University Press, 2nd edn, 1982), p. 12; Bradley, *Slaves and Masters*, p. 107.

71. Hopkins explains, 'it was sensible for masters to opt for the carrot rather than or in addition to the stick. The prospect of buying freedom encouraged a slave to show both initiative and parsimony ... If the slave died before achieving liberty, the master pocketed his savings ... If the slave later bought full freedom, the master had recapitalized the slave's value and with the purchase money he could buy a younger slave to replace him' (*Conquerors and Slaves*, p. 147).

Paul's Collection and a Slave's Dilemma

Now that we have explored what the New Testament teaches about Paul's collection and what history reveals about slavery in the first century, we can turn our attention to the question of how a slave who was a Christ-follower in Corinth might have responded to Paul's appeal. While we cannot defini- tively answer this question, it is important to consider how these texts might have been understood by this particular group of people who were part of the Corinthian church.

We must begin by first acknowledging that there were undoubtedly slaves in the Christian assembly in Corinth and exploring briefly what their experi- ence within that assembly might have been.[72] Paul indicates their presence in the Corinthian community in 1 Cor. 7.21-22 and 12.13. While being a mem- ber of the Christian community provided spiritual equality among members (1 Cor. 12.13), we do not have much evidence of how that spiritual reality impacted a slave's social reality. Wayne Meeks comments that 'in any house- hold of any size there was an informal pecking order that was taken seriously, and the threshold between slave and free remained fundamental in a percep- tion of one's place in society.'[73] It is possible that being a part of the church provided these slaves a sense of honor and human dignity that they lacked outside of the church. However, Barclay notes that 'it is hard to imagine any slaves being given leadership roles, given their inability to predict their atten- dance from one meeting to the next and the difficulty of admonishing (1 Thess. 5.12) their social superiors.'[74] And given the sexual availability of slaves, Jennifer Glancy challenges the idea that all slaves would have been allowed 'full involvement in the Christian body'.[75] Thus, slaves were a part

72.   Dale B. Martin comments that 'though no one any longer accepts the older notion that Christianity was a "slave religion" or a movement comprising a huge number of slaves, it is universally recognized among scholars that Christian groups included slaves and freedpersons' ('Slave Families and Slaves in Families', in David L. Balch and Carolyn Osiek [eds.], *Early Christian Families in Context: An Interdis- ciplinary Dialogue* [Grand Rapids: Eerdmans, 2003], pp. 207-30 [207]).

73.   Wayne A. Meeks, *The First Urban Christians: The Social World of the Apostle Paul* (New Haven: Yale University Press, 2nd edn, 2003), p. 21.

74.   J.M.G. Barclay, 'Paul, Philemon and the Dilemma of Christian Slave- Ownership', *NTS* 37 (1991), pp. 161-86 (179).

75.   Jennifer A. Glancy, 'Body Work: Slavery and the Pauline Churches', in Pargas Damian Alan and Roşu Felicia (eds.), *Critical Readings on Global Slavery*

of the Corinthian assembly, but they may have had a liminal existence in that body of believers. Nonetheless, slaves would have been present when the letter we call First Corinthians was read to the church.

The way Paul introduces his discussion of the collection in First Corinthians indicates that the church in Corinth is already aware of the project, 'now concerning the collection for the saints ...' (16.1). In this letter then, Paul is simply instructing them *how* to gather the funds—he does not address *why* they should (16.2): 'on the first day of the week, each of you should set aside and save as he or she may prosper, so that when I come no collections need be made.'[76] Those who gathered to hear this letter read to the church would have heard Paul addressing each one of them without distinction: 'each of you (ἕκαστος ὑμῶν)'. Garland comments that Paul 'fully expects every member to take part in the project'.[77] This would include men and women, free people, freedpersons, and slaves, wealthy and poor.[78] Many of these people would have had limited resources. Since Paul is directing them to set aside something each week, this may indicate that 'the majority were not well off and had to set aside small sums carefully'.[79]

(Leiden: Brill, 2018), pp. 427-76 (475-76). See also Jennifer A. Glancy, 'Obstacles to Slaves' Participation in the Corinthian Church', *JBL* 117 (1998), pp. 481-501.

76. Some Greco-Roman associations required fees and fines that included non-monetary resources (i.e. bread, food, wine) (Harland, 'Associations', pp. 13-15). However, it is apparent that Paul is referring to a monetary collection since it is something that can be set aside and saved until he arrives.

77. David E. Garland, *1 Corinthians* (BECNT; Grand Rapids: Baker Academic, 2003), p. 754. Meggitt comments that 'it was not intended to be the work of a few wealthy members or congregations' (*Paul, Poverty and Survival*, p. 159).

78. Garland expects these slaves to participate in the collection: 'if free artisans, small traders, and slaves also give, then the gift will represent the entire body, not just a few wealthy donors' (*1 Corinthians*, p. 754). See also Pheme Perkins, *First Corinthians* (Paideia; Grand Rapids: Baker Academic, 2012), p. 676.

79. Craig L. Blomberg, *Neither Poverty Nor Riches: A Biblical Theology of Material Possessions* (NSBT; Grand Rapids: Eerdmans, 1999), p. 189. See also Collins, *First Corinthians*, p. 409. Longenecker comments that 'this advice makes the most sense if it is directed to those of ES5 [stable near subsistence level], and possibly ES6 [at subsistence level]. Those among ES7 [below subsistence level] would have had nothing to put aside, while those in ES4 [moderate surplus] would probably have had resources that are out of alignment with the kind of advice Paul offers' (*Remember the Poor*, pp. 253-54).

The opportunity for those with limited resources to participate in a project would not have been unique in the first century. Greco-Roman associations also had collections that allowed those in such circumstances to participate. While wealthy benefactors were usually an important source of funds,[80] there were collections that were set up specifically so that those with little surplus could contribute. Some collections 'set a minimum and a maximum contribution' while others 'had contributors all give the same—usually quite small—amounts'.[81] This latter method of collecting funds suggests that 'the act of giving, rather than the amount given, was what mattered.'[82] There were other collections that called on both citizens and non-citizens alike to contribute, thus allowing everyone to 'contribute to a common project and thus to "perform" their membership in the polis'.[83] These collections provide evidence that those outside the elite—those with limited resources—could and did contribute to collections for projects they found worthy of their participation. So, like these collections by Greco-Roman associations, Paul provided for all—regardless of means—to participate.

After directing the Corinthian believers to set aside funds each week, Paul states that each one should 'save as he or she may prosper (εὐοδῶται)'. This Greek term in the middle/passive can mean to have a good journey, have success, prosper.[84] The NRSV rendering of the term in this context as 'whatever extra you earn', perhaps captures the idea best. By using this phrase, Paul is not asking them to give in a sacrificial manner, to give beyond their means or to leave their own needs unmet.[85] Rather, when God prospers these Corinthian believers, Paul is encouraging them to set some of the surplus aside for this collection.[86] This implies then that some members at times would have nothing to set aside; in fact, they may never have anything to set

80. Harland, 'Associations', p. 6.
81. John S. Kloppenborg, 'Fiscal Aspects of Paul's Collection for Jerusalem', *EC* 8 (2017), pp. 153-98 (184) (attested by inscriptions of the third to first BCE centuries at Athens).
82. Kloppenborg, 'Fiscal Aspects', p. 185 (attested by inscriptions of the third to second BCE centuries on the Island of Kos).
83. Kloppenborg, 'Fiscal Aspects', p. 187.
84. BrillDAG, *s.v.* εὐοδόω; LSJ, *s.v.* εὐοδόω; BDAG, *s.v.* εὐοδόω;.
85. Garland, *1 Corinthians*, p. 754.
86. It is worth noting that this giving is likely above and beyond whatever funds each believer in Corinth gave to the local assembly.

aside as they regularly lived at or below subsistence level.[87] So then, we must come back around to the command that 'each of you should set aside and save' is qualified by the next clause, 'as he or she may prosper'. Not everyone listening to this letter would have the means to follow Paul's directive.

Someone might raise the question as to whether a slave would have the means to follow Paul's directive. As discussed earlier, slaves could have a *peculium*. Hopkins notes that 'many [privileged slaves] worked in positions in which they were able to make a profit for themselves.'[88] Thus, some slaves could prosper financially. This, of course, benefitted the master, for the slave was incentivized to work in a such a way that a profit was realized. However, it is important to realize that most of these slaves would have had a very specific purpose for this surplus: to purchase their freedom.

Someone might argue that such slaves were in a good situation and would not necessarily want freedom. What would these slaves gain by purchasing their freedom? Manumission provided release from being owned by another person, freedom from sexual exploitation and bodily punishment, the opportunity to establish and maintain a family that could not be forcibly separated or individually exploited, the ability to own property and benefit from it personally, and sometimes Roman citizenship. But even more significantly, freedom provided the return of human dignity.[89] There is much evidence that slaves longed and worked and sacrificed to achieve freedom.

In all likelihood, if they were able, slaves in the Corinthian assembly were longing and saving for their manumission. In fact, they may have found some hope when they heard Paul earlier in his letter encourage them to become free if they could (1 Cor. 7.21). So, when they were encouraged by Paul to set aside something when they prospered, how might they have responded? Did they take some of their freedom money and set it aside to give away?

About a year goes by and Paul sends another letter, and he addresses the topic of the collection again. This time he has much more to say about it. Many scholars conclude that the Corinthian church has been resistant or reluctant to participate in the collection, and Paul is writing to encourage them

---

87. Longenecker comments that 'if the destitute were excluded from contributing by default, it was not to their shame or detriment' (*Remember the Poor*, p. 285).

88. Hopkins, *Conquerors and Slaves*, p. 126.

89. For support of these arguments, especially the final one, see Robin G. Thompson, *Paul's Declaration of Freedom from a Freed Slave's Perspective* (BibInt, 210; Leiden: Brill, 2023), pp 45-47, 76-78.

and ensure that their promised gifts are ready when he arrives.[90] When listening to this letter, the slaves hear of the example of the Macedonians: how God's grace has enabled them to give out of their deep poverty—even beyond their ability (8.1-3). They then hear of Christ's example of becoming poor for their sake (8.9). However, Paul does qualify these statements by telling them their gift is 'acceptable according to what one has, not according to what one does not have' (8.12). He goes on to say that the Corinthians' 'abundance will meet [the saints'] need, so that one day their abundance may also meet [the Corinthians'] need, and thus there may be equality' (8.14 NET).

Some slaves listening to this letter would have little to no resources to give to anyone else. But being Christ-followers, would they nonetheless long to have the grace of God work in them and enable them to participate in the collection, just as their brothers and sisters in Macedonia? Perhaps they—like the Macedonians who gave out of their 'deep poverty'—would desire to give because they knew first-hand the hardship of privation.[91] Other slaves listening to this letter would have surplus in their *peculia*. This surplus would likely have been set aside to pay for their freedom. How would they hear that their surplus is to meet the needs of the saints in Jerusalem so that later those saints could meet their needs? Would those needs include help on the path to freedom?[92]

While we cannot definitely answer these questions, it is important that we consider their full implications. We should not be quick to offer easy—and perhaps comfortable—answers to these questions. We should not dismiss out-of-hand that the slaves in the community of the Corinthian church could

90.   For example, Belleville, *2 Corinthians*, pp. 208-9; Garland, *2 Corinthians*, p. 371; Horrell, 'Paul's Collection', pp. 74-75; Craig S. Keener, *1-2 Corinthians* (New Cambridge Bible Commentary; Cambridge: Cambridge University Press, 2005), p. 204; Jan Lambrecht, *Second Corinthians* (SP; Collegeville, MN: Liturgical, 1999), p. 102.

91.   As Parkin suggests, 'Those for whom the spectre of destitution held the most power were perhaps the most generous' ('You Do Him No Service', p. 72).

92.   There is evidence that both Christian and Jewish assemblies paid for the manumission of slaves, but the extant sources are later than the first century. See J.A. Harrill, 'Ignatius, Ad Polycarp. 4.3 and the Corporate Manumission of Christian Slaves', *JECS* 1 (1993), pp. 107-42; Last and Harland, *Group Survival*, pp. 176-77, 183.

have contributed to Paul's collection. And we must reflect on the deep sacrifice they would have made if they did so.

However, we cannot stop there in our consideration of these slaves who were members of the Corinthian assembly. We must also consider the other Christ-followers in the community—those who were freeborn or freedpersons. As they were setting aside funds from their surplus to meet the needs of unknown fellow believers in a faraway land, did they stop to consider the needs of the slaves among them? Did they see how desperately these slaves worked to save for their freedom, or was this so common they could easily look past the desperation? Was the surplus of these freeborn and freedpersons due, at least in part, to the exploitation of these very slaves? Was it easier to give this excess to a stranger far away who needed food than to sacrifice their lifestyle in some manner and give a slave (or help a slave buy) their freedom?

In conclusion, I suggest we not leave our questions for the Corinthian community in the first century; perhaps we ought to ask ourselves similar questions. What is the source of *our* surplus? Do we know if people are exploited so that we might maintain our current lifestyle? Is it easier for us to send money to organizations who serve the poor, the hurting, the displaced around the globe, than to change the way we live in order to truly help those who are exploited in our own midst? What does it say about us today, who give to those we do not know while we look past the needs of those we do?

[*JGRChJ* 19 (2023) 94-103]

A RESPONSE TO DAVID ALLEN'S
'A MODEL RECONSTRUCTION OF WHAT JOSEPHUS WOULD HAVE REALISTICALLY WRITTEN ABOUT JESUS'

Christopher M. Hansen

Independent Scholar, Grand Blanc, MI

In a recent article attempting a formidable reconstruction of a negative *Testimonium Flavianum* (*TF*), David Allen reconstructs part of his passages on the basis of Tacitus, *Ann.* 15.44. The authenticity of the *TF* has been long contested, though most scholars seem to agree that it was authentic in some capacity; various theories have been proposed.[1] A growing minority, however, has recently been contending that it was entirely inauthentic and that

---

1.   Fernando Bermejo-Rubio, 'Was the Hypothetical "Vorlage" of the "Testimonium Flavianum" a "Neutral" Text? Challenging the Common Wisdom on "Antiquitates Judaicae" 18.63-64', *JSJ* 45 (2014), pp. 326-65; John P. Meier, *A Marginal Jew: The Roots of the Problem and the Person* (New York: Doubleday, 1991), pp. 61-69; Paul Garnet, 'If the *Testimonium Flavianum* Contains Alterations, Who Originated Them?', in Elizabeth A. Livingstone (ed.), *Studia Patristica. Vol. XIX: Papers Presented to the Tenth International Conference on Patristic Studies held in Oxford 1987* (Leuven: Peeters, 1989), pp. 57-61. On the basis of Ulrich Victor, 'Das Testimonium Flavianum: Ein authentischer Text des Josephus', *NovT* 52 (2010), pp. 72-82, Zinner proposes that the entire *TF* is authentic (see Samuel Zinner, *The Infancy Gospels of James and Thomas and the Canonical Gospels in Conversation with Josephus* [Journal of Higher Criticism Supplement Series; Salem, NC: Journal of Higher Criticism, 2020], pp. 200-208). See also Alice Whealey, 'Josephus, Eusebius of Caesarea, and the Testimonium Flavianum', in Christoph Böttrich, Jenz Herzer and Torsten Reiprich (eds.), *Josephus und das Neue Testament* (Tübingen: Mohr Siebeck, 2007), pp. 73-116, who proposes that the vast majority of the *TF* is authentic.

none of it was original.[2] Allen's proposals are rather interesting for complicating the picture of the *TF*'s development and potentially finding pre-Eusebian layers present; however, I think that there are some weaknesses which can be noted, particularly in the passages where Allen utilizes Tacitus, and which ultimately render the reconstruction unconvincing upon closer scrutiny.

In this response, I wish to specifically argue against Allen's usage of Tacitus and contend that we cannot reconstruct those specific passages from Josephus on the basis of Tacitus's work. I argue there are a number of reasons for this: (1) that Tacitus's familiarity with Josephus is extremely questionable, given how his work fails to align with Josephus's own on numerous points; and (2) that the similarities between *Ann.* 15.44 and the *TF* either cannot be distinguished from Christian creedal statements, or are the result of Allen using Tacitus as a source for his reconstruction. This also calls into question other parts of the reconstruction as well, including what justifications Allen has for utilizing specific sources. As a result, while the reconstruction is rather attractive, it is unconvincing to me.

Allen's Reconstruction of Josephus

Allen's total reconstruction of the *TF* reads,

> And there was about this time a certain man, a sophist and agitator, if one may call him a man, for he was a deceiver and an imposter. A teacher of men who worship him with pleasure. [He claimed the Temple would be destroyed and that not one stone would be left standing on another and that it would be restored in three days.] And he led many of the Judeans, along with many of the Galilean (element) in a tumult. He was believed to be a King [for he opposed paying the tax to Caesar]. And many souls were roused, thinking that thereby the

2. Ken Olson, 'Eusebius and the "Testimonium Flavianum"', *CBQ* 61 (1999), pp. 305-22. Olson (p. 306) cites Tessa Rajak, *Josephus, the Historian and His Society* (Philadelphia: Fortress Press, 1984), pp. 67, 131 n. 13; J. Neville Birdsall, 'The Continuing Enigma of Josephus Testimony about Jesus', *BJRL* 67 (1985), pp. 609-22; Per Bilde, *Flavius Josephus between Jerusalem and Rome: His Life, his Works, and their Importance* (Sheffield: JSOT Press, 1988), pp. 222-23. See also Joshua Efron, *Studies on the Hasmonean Period* (Leiden: Brill, 1987), p. 333.

tribe of Judaeans could free themselves from the Romans. And, on the accusation of the first men among us, Pilate had condemned him to a cross. *Many of his followers, the Galileans and Judaeans, were slain and thus repressed for the moment. The movement again broke out with great abundance, when it was believed he appeared to them living again.* Those that followed him at first did not cease [worshipping] only him, who is their leader in sedition. And this tribe has until now not disappeared.[3]

The sections in brackets were Allen's own creations, which he posited were likely there as otherwise the reconstruction would be 'vacuous', as he states.[4] In what follows, I wish to complicate these readings and give reason as to why we should probably not accept them as going back to a pre-Eusebian *TF*. Additionally, I will raise some concerns with Allen's usage of the pre-Eusebian sources in general.

Source and Reconstruction Issues

Searching for outside attestation to the *TF* in wider Greco-Roman literature and thus the possibility to use it to reconstruct a pre-Eusebian variant of the passage is a notable endeavor, and a direct challenge to the recent inter-polation theories of Olson and others. However, there seems to be some rather questionable reasoning in place here, particularly where Tacitus's knowledge of the *TF* is concerned, and there are some distinct reasons for thinking that the texts are independent of each other.

First, outside of the *TF*, which is found in Josephus (*Ant.* 18.63-64) (which lies in contention at present), the only evidence which Allen is able to demonstrate which may point to Tacitus's knowledge of Josephus's writings is his description of the fall of Jerusalem and the fulfillment of the prophecy of Vespasian from *War* 6.312-13 (cf. Tacitus, *Hist.* 5.13).[5] The comparison,

---

3.   David Allen, 'A Model Reconstruction of What Josephus Would Have Realistically Written about Jesus', *JGRChJ* 18 (2022), pp. 113-43 (128-42) (emphasis mine). I have italicized some sections/one section that concern/s me in this current response, as they rely principally on the works of Tacitus for reconstruction (Allen, 'Model Reconstruction', pp. 139-40).

4.   Allen, 'Model Reconstruction', p. 132.

5.   Allen, 'Model Reconstruction', p. 139.

however, on closer inspection showcases a number of divergences.[6] For instance, Josephus claims that one million people were slain in the siege of Jerusalem. Meanwhile, Tacitus claims that it was 600,000 instead. Josephus never mentions this number anywhere. The sayings which the voices utter are different in Josephus's and Tacitus's works. In *War* (6.299-300) the voices of the multitude declare 'Let us remove hence.' Meanwhile, Tacitus's account indicates instead that the voices declare that the gods themselves are abandoning Jerusalem to its fate (*et audita maior humana vox excedere deos*), which is not in accordance with Josephus's text. Meanwhile, there are also other noted differences (was it Varus or Gratus who killed Simon of Perea? [see Tacitus, *Hist.* 5.9; cf. Josephus, *War* 2.57-59]). It is my view that Tacitus likely had no knowledge of Josephus, but instead the rather surface similarities are simply due to these being stories that fluctuated and circulated within the courts of Rome, accounting also for the even more variant version of events recorded in Suetonius, *Vesp.* 4-5. There seems to have been little consistency, and further as Olson has again pointed out, Josephus was not positively viewed by his Roman contemporaries, further decreasing chances of them reading his work at all.[7]

As I noted in my response to Mason, as well, it should be asked why this even matters? If Tacitus did rely on *War* this does not speak to whether or not he had access to the *Antiquities*. As I state,

> As we know from Tacitus's own reception history, it was not hard for an author with multiple titles to have only one which gets cited or acknowledged (as is the case with Tacitus's *Histories* while the *Annals* are virtually unknown until Sulpicius). Thus, demonstrating that Tacitus's *Histories* may have relied on Josephus's *Jewish War* [sic] has little bearing on whether Tacitus's *Annals* used Josephus's *Antiquities*.[8]

---

6. These are discussed in depth in Christopher M. Hansen, 'The Problem of Annals 15.44: On the Plinian Origin of Tacitus's Information on Christians', *JECH* 13 (2023), pp 62-80 (4-6).

7. This is again indebted to Olson, who pointed to Suetonius, *Vesp.* 5.6. One can add to this as well Dio Cassius, *Hist. rom.* 66.1 which has Josephus captured and then laughing at Vespasian saying that he would soon be freed. Josephus seems to have become a character for negative caricature, rather than a source of information.

8. Hansen, 'Problem of Annals 15.44', p. 5.

Given this, Allen would need to demonstrate clear reliance of Tacitus upon the *Antiquities* outside of the *TF* (as this is under question). This also leads us to a few issues specifically regarding the reconstruction as well, however.

Notably, Tacitus's version of events and Josephus, *Ant.* 18.63-64, especially on Allen's reading, are highly divergent to the degree that it is hard to see how Tacitus was reliant upon the version of the *TF* that Allen describes. For instance, while the neutral *TF* previously posited by Stephen Carlson and others was already problematic and showed numerous variances,[9] Allen's reconstruction only exacerbates the issue: Tacitus, as an example, never mentions any Γαλιλαῖος people at all. In fact, to the contrary, he mentions Judeans and Romans, instead. This was already a problem for Carlson and others who had to bridge the difference between the Ἰουδαίους and Ἑλληνικοῦ neutral reconstructions, and somehow map this onto Tacitus's *Iudaeam* on the one hand and Rome on the other (Rome being the *urbem* where horrible and pernicious superstitions always broke out). While identifying Ἑλληνικοῦ with Romans may be more understandable to an extent, the shift from Galileans to Romans is completely inexplicable in my view. How one could derive this from Tacitus's text is strange.

There are also details present in Tacitus's text which do not appear to have arisen from Josephus's either. For instance, Pilate is referred to as *procurator* in Tacitus's text,[10] but not in Allen's reconstruction of the *TF*, and Tacitus lacks any mention of the so-called 'first men' (πρώτων ἀνδρῶν); instead the blame is entirely on the procurator for these events. Since 'procurator' is likely an anachronistic title for Pilate,[11] it is apparent that this must have derived

9.   Hansen, 'Problem of Annals 15.44', pp. 5-6.

10.   Anthony A. Barrett (*Rome Is Burning: Nero and the Fire that Ended a Dynasty* [Princeton: Princeton University Press, 2020], pp. 170-74) posits that the reference to Pilate may be an interpolation. But there is no reason for thinking this (see Willem J.C. Blom, 'Why the Testimonium Taciteum Is Authentic: A Response to Carrier', *VC* 73 [2019], pp. 564-81 and Margaret H. Williams, *Early Classical Authors on Jesus* [London: T. & T. Clark, 2022], pp. 67-70).

11.   Fernando Bermejo-Rubio (*La invención de Jesús de Nazaret: Historia, ficción, historiografía* [Madrid: Siglo XXI de España Editores, 2021], p. 57) notes that the title of prefect was changed to procurator during the reign of Claudius. A curious—though unconvincing—argument that there was never any such change in titles and that they were used interchangeably or dually has been offered in Richard

from somewhere.[12] The Latin traditions titled Pilate as the procurator and Tacitus was of course very close with Pliny the Younger, including the fact that they exchanged work with each other and Tacitus would solicit Pliny for information.[13] Thus, it appears that this information would have been derived from Pliny's interrogations of Latin Christians in the early second century CE under Trajan. Allen himself admits that Tacitus likely used Pliny as a source, so why he needs recourse to the *TF* is strange, other than that he requires Tacitus for his reconstruction.[14] Notably, Tacitus's statement (as Olson has pointed out) looks almost identical to standard Christian creeds of the time:

> Our teacher of these things is Jesus Christ, who also was born for this purpose, and was crucified under Pontius Pilate, procurator of Judæa, in the times of Tiberius Cæsar; and that we reasonably worship Him, having learned that He is the Son of the true God Himself, and holding Him in the second place, and the prophetic Spirit in the third, we will prove.[15]

Tacitus also mentions that Jesus was known as *Christus* (i.e. the messiah), but this information appears nowhere in Allen's reconstruction, who instead refers to Jesus as a 'king' (βασιλεύς). As a result, we have to ask where does this come from? Again, the evidence best points to Pliny and his Latin Christian sources from Bithynia-Pontus. Why the *TF* is necessary at all for

Carrier, *Hitler Homer Bible Christ* (Richmond, VA: Philosophy Press, 2014), pp. 131-40.

12.   It is true that Josephus does refer to Pilate as 'procurator' elsewhere (see Paul R. Eddy and Gregory A. Boyd, *The Jesus Legend: A Case for the Historical Reliability of the Synoptic Jesus Tradition* [Grand Rapids: Baker Academic, 2007], p. 182). But because Allen has not established that Tacitus was reliant on *Antiquities* and there are the numerous divergences and because the only portion that Allen proposes of *Antiquities* that Tacitus used was the *TF* (where the title is not mentioned), there seems no reason to posit this as Tacitus's source of information. As such, we should look elsewhere.

13.   Anthony A. Barrett, Elaine Fantham, and John. C. Yardley, *The Emperor Nero: A Guide to the Ancient Sources* (Princeton: Princeton University Press, 2016), p. 165.

14.   Allen, 'Model Reconstruction', p. 139.

15.   Justin Martyr, *1 Apol.* 13 (William Edgar and K. Scott Oliphint [eds.], *Christian Apologetics: Past and Present, A Primary Source Reader* [2 vols.; Wheaton: Crossway, 2009], I, p. 48).

Tacitus's information, when he had Pliny at his disposal (and who was a known collaborator on Tacitus's projects), is unexplored by Allen. Given the differences between *Ann.* 15.44 and Allen's *TF*, and also between *Hist.* 5 and *War* 2-6, there seems to be little basis for positing any relationship. It is curious also that there are parts of Tacitus's testimony that Allen does not include, such as the reference to Christians as *odio humani generis* or having a 'hatred of the human race'.[16] No doubt, if Josephus was a polemicist against this 'tribe', he could have said such things.

Allen may ask about the similarities between Tacitus and Josephus, but these are inconsequential in no small part because the similarities are either (a) too close to Christian creedal statements to be of much use (i.e. we cannot distinguish between Tacitus using a creedal statement or Josephus), or (b) derived from Allen's reconstruction utilizing Tacitus. For instance, that both texts mention that movement was 'repressed' is only because Allen used Tacitus's text, thus, the similarity is of no utility as this would be entirely based on circular reasoning.

Given that Allen admits that Tacitus used other sources, which account for the discrepancies between Tacitus and Josephus, the question becomes why we need to posit he knew Josephus at all, except that Allen requires this for his reconstruction. If Tacitus used other sources and showcases numerous discrepancies with Josephus, what justification is there for thinking he knew Josephus at all? The far more parsimonious answer and the one best befitting the evidence at hand would simply be that Tacitus only used his Greco-Roman sources, and probably had no knowledge of Josephus's work. It seems that Allen's proposal is based entirely on the fact that Tacitus provides convenient statements that build up his idea of the *TF*, but I have argued that there is little to no evidentiary basis for this. Excising the questionable passages based on Josephus still leaves Allen's reconstruction as partially coherent, as seen here:

> And there was about this time a certain man, a sophist and agitator, if one may call him a man, for he was a deceiver and an imposter. A teacher of men who worship him with pleasure. [He claimed the Temple would be destroyed and that not one stone would be left

---

16.   This specific polemic is particularly Tacitean, comparable to *Hist.* 5.5 where he describes Jews similarly as having this loathing for non-Jews (*adversus omnis alios hostile odium*).

standing on another and that it would be restored in three days.] And he led many of the Judeans, along with many of the Galilean (element) in a tumult. He was believed to be a King [for he opposed paying the tax to Caesar]. And many souls were roused, thinking that thereby the tribe of Judaeans could free themselves from the Romans. And, on the accusation of the first men among us, Pilate had condemned him to a cross. Those that followed him at first did not cease [worshipping] only Him, who is their leader in sedition. And this tribe has until now not disappeared.[17]

However, this greatly reduces the seditiousness of Jesus and also then raises some questions about what happens with the crowds he roused in a tumult as well. If only he were punished, what happened to the rest of his followers, who were riotous? The narrative seems incomplete as a result of this.

Additionally, it does call the veracity of other parts of this reconstruction into question. Allen's reconstruction, though attractive, is based in no small part on largely reading around various texts of figures like Celsus and Tacitus and then picking fragments from among them that would contextually fit the passage as Allen envisages it, but the basis for doing so seems limited. For instance, Allen notes how Origen claims that Jews did not connect the deaths of John and Jesus together, and it is apparent that *Antiquities* 18 does not either; therefore, it is likely that Origen may have relied upon Josephus. As Allen notes, 'In *Antiquities* it does not connect the Baptist movement with the Jesus movement.'[18] This reasoning is unconvincing on a number of points. First, it is an argument from silence, wherein Allen is asserting reliance on the basis of an absence of information on Josephus. Neglecting the debate on whether or not the Baptist passage is authentic, which has come to the fore in recent years (and recently argued to be an interpolation by Origen himself),[19] this argument is based entirely on a lack of information. Should we also conclude that Origen had access to oral history and traditions eventually to be passed down in the Babylonian Talmud, because they also do not make such

17. Allen, 'Model Reconstruction', pp. 128-42.
18. Allen, 'Model Reconstruction', p. 120.
19. Clare K. Rothschild, 'Echoes of a Whisper: The Uncertain Authenticity of Josephus' Witness to John the Baptist', in David Hellhom (ed.), *Ablution, Initiation, and Baptism: Late Antiquity, Early Judaism, and Early Christianity* (3 vols.; Berlin: de Gruyter, 2011), I, pp. 255-90; Rivka Nir, 'Josephus' Account of John the Baptist: A Christian Interpolation?' *JSHJ* 10 (2012), pp. 32-62.

a connection between John and Jesus? I think not. Allen argues that *Cels*. 1.47 'contradicts the *TF* statement "he was the Christ," showing that that statement was not in the earlier version of the *TF*'.[20] This is, of course, a faulty argument for it would be easily surmised by any Christian that a Jewish author like Josephus would not consider Jesus the Messiah. This statement does not require that he had seen anything like a *TF*, and it would make just as much sense in the context of his combatting Celsus, as Celsus uses a Jewish source of his own. As such, here, Origen would want to note that Josephus has no bias in favor of Christianity, because that increases the reputability of the supposed statements which Origen attributes to him. It is also questionable how in Allen's reconstruction Origen, on the basis of Josephus's unnamed seditious actor, would have known this was about Jesus to begin with, as noted above. This is perhaps the most challenging for Allen's reconstruction, however, as his position that Jesus does not appear to have been named in the *TF* at all originally calls into question how he can clearly identify this unnamed seditious actor in the *TF* with Jesus as found elsewhere, and then utilize these texts to further justify his reconstruction. For instance, he does so with his utilization of 1 Thess. 2.14-16 and Jn 11.47-50, where he presumes that his unnamed seditious actor is Jesus and therefore justifies his reconstruction utilizing those passages on this basis. In fact, there seems to be little reason, in my view, to think that this *TF* that Allen has constructed necessarily discusses the historical Jesus. How later scribes came to believe it was Jesus in this passage appears to be a mystery, since there is no clear indication that Tacitus or others would have thought this, given they clearly gathered Jesus' title of *Christus* and such from other sources (as this title is not used in Allen's reconstruction). As Allen notes, Jesus not being named would be typical of others like 'The Egyptian' and 'The Samaritan', but if this is the case how we can distinguish that this figure is Jesus and not just another rabble rouser who was executed like the others is left an open question. Furthermore, how apologists like Eusebius and commentators like Tacitus made this identification is also unanswered, which again calls into question the reconstruction and also Allen's own ability to identify this figure with Jesus (which in turn calls into question the sources Allen uses to justify his reconstruction). In short, the methodology behind this reconstruction seems doubtful.

20.   Allen, 'Model Reconstruction', p. 120.

Conclusions

It appears that Allen's proposal, though attractive for its possibilities, is belabored with a number of methodological issues that prevent me from finding the reconstruction convincing. In the case of Tacitus, there does not appear to be any convincing reason for thinking that he relied upon any version of the *TF* or even any of Josephus's writings. The best which Allen and others have put forth is that Tacitus may have utilized Josephus's *War*, however, that Tacitus may have read *War* does not mean that he therefore had read *Antiquities*, as we know that it was quite plausible for an author of multiple works to only have one which was regularly read (as was the case with Tacitus, in fact). The supposed similarities between Tacitus and Josephus, in this case, are merely a result of the fact that Allen uses Tacitus as his source for reconstruction, thus, the similarity factor between *Ant.* 18.63-64 and *Ann.* 15.44 is inconsequential.

These problems also belie Allen's usage of other sources. A major issue for Allen's reconstruction is that he posits that Jesus was not originally named, which calls into question how any of the sources which supposedly used Josephus knew that this seditious actor (who looks virtually nothing like the Jesus of the Gospels) was Jesus in the first place. Most certainly, scribes like Tacitus could not have derived the terminology of *Chrestianos* and *Christus* from this version of the *TF*, as it is nowhere mentioned. The arguments for Origen utilizing the *TF* are likewise faulty and seem to posit little creative ingenuity on the part of the ancient apologist, such as the idea that his simple mention of Josephus not believing Jesus was the Messiah somehow indicates that Origen had read the *TF*. As noted above, if Origen had read Allen's *TF*, then there is no reason to think he would even conclude this figure was Jesus to begin with. Instead, it is easily explicable by the fact that Origen was simply stating an easily intuited fact about a Jewish author.

As such, these problems with his sources prevent me from thinking that Allen's reconstruction suffices, and further undermines the concept that there was a pre-Eusebian variant in circulation. In my opinion, a wholesale interpolation (as suggested by Olson and others) on the part of Eusebius appears more likely.

[*JGRChJ* 19 (2023) 104-27]

NO LONGER A PEOPLE-PLEASER:
NARRATIO AND DEFENSIVE REFUTATION IN GALATIANS 1.10–2.21

Kennedy K. Ekeocha

West Africa Theological Seminary, Lagos, Nigeria

Introduction

Ever since the landmark work of Hans Dieter Betz on Galatians,[1] there has been renewed interest in the rhetorical analysis of Paul's letters. Galatians represents perhaps the 'most obviously rhetorical of all of Paul's letters',[2] evincing his acquaintance with Greco-Roman rhetoric. Yet there is no consensus on the rhetorical genre of the letter.[3] Additionally, the place of 1.10 and, by extension, the nature and function of the *narratio* in chs. 1–2 continue to be disputed.[4]

---

1. Hans D. Betz, *A Commentary on Paul's Letter to the Churches in Galatia* (Philadelphia: Fortress Press, 1979).

2. Ben Witherington III, *New Testament Rhetoric: An Introductory Guide to the Art of Persuasion in and of the New Testament* (Eugene, OR: Cascade, 2009), p. 124.

3. It has been taken as forensic or apologetic rhetoric (Betz, *Commentary*), deliberative rhetoric (George A. Kennedy, *New Testament Interpretation through Rhetorical Criticism* [Chapel Hill: University of North Carolina Press, 1984]), a combination of both forensic and deliberative rhetoric (Richard Longenecker, *Galatians* [WBC, 41; Dallas: Word Books, 1990]) or epideictic rhetoric (James D. Hester, 'The Rhetorical Structure of Galatians 1.11–2.14', *JBL* 103 [1984], pp. 223-33).

4. In place of *narratio*, I will use the terms 'narration' (*diegesis*) and 'narrative' (*diegema*). This is purely stylistic. The latter two terms are often used interchangeably, although 'narrative' deals with one event while a 'narration' deals with many events pulled together (see George A. Kennedy [trans. and notes],

This study partially follows the analytical method outlined by George A. Kennedy,[5] while considering discussions on narratives in ancient rhetorical theory. It is argued in this article that, rather than limiting the *narratio* to 1.13–2.14, as many interpreters do, we should consider the entire section of 1.10–2.21 to constitute a coherent rhetorical unit that functions to demonstrate Paul's self-understanding. The unit portrays Paul as one who now only seeks to please God rather than people, and it represents his self-defensive refutation of a false narrative by which the Galatians are being persuaded against the true gospel. In other words, the *narratio* is an expansion and explication of 1.10 upon which the section depends for meaning.

Various Rhetorical Analyses of Galatians 1–2

Galatians 1.10, its relationship to the *narratio*, and how the latter functions are crucial for determining the rhetorical burden of the letter. Scholars have neither adequately appreciated this nor given it due consideration.

First, for many interpreters, Gal. 1.10 is only loosely appended to the preceding material with little or no rhetorical significance for what follows. According to Longenecker, most recent translators and commentators treat this verse as an emotional outburst that is to be related in some manner to the curses of vv. 8-9; it is to be set off as a separate paragraph or regarded as parenthetical within the paragraph.[6] Betz takes it as a mere literary transition between the *exordium* and the *narratio* (1.12–2.14) although he embeds it within the *exordium*.[7] This way of delineating the section is closely followed by many, as the following outlines show:

Progymnasmata: Greek Textbooks of Prose Composition and Rhetoric [Atlanta: Society of Biblical Literature, 2003]).

5.   Kennedy articulates a five-step procedure for analyzing New Testament letters rhetorically: (1) determine the rhetorical unit; (2) determine the rhetorical situation of the unit; (3) determine the species of rhetoric (forensic, deliberative or epideictic); (4) proceed to consider the arrangement of material in the text; and (5) evaluate or review the success of the rhetorical unit in meeting its rhetorical exigence and what its implication may be for the speaker or audience (*New Testament Interpretation*, p. 38).

6.   See UBSGNT, RSV, NEB and NIV (Longenecker, *Galatians*, p. 18).

7.   Betz, *Commentary*, p. 16.

Betz	Hester	Kennedy[8]	Witherington	Longenecker
Epistolary Prescript 1.1-5		Salutation 1.1-5	Epistolary Prescript 1.1-5	Salutation 1.1-5
Exordium 1.6-11	*Exordium* 1.6-10	Proem 1.6-10	*Exordium* 1.6-10	*Exordium* 1.6-10
Narratio 1.12–2.14	*Stasis* 1.11-12	Proof 1.11–5.1	*Narratio* 1.11–2.14	*Narratio* 1.11–2.14
	Transitio 1.13-14	[1st Heading 1.11-12]		
	Narratio 1.15–2.10	[Narrative 1.13–2.14]		
	Digressio 2.11-14			
Propositio 2.15-21		[*Epicheireme* 2.15-21]	*Propositio* 2.15-21	*Propositio* 2.15-21
		[2nd Heading 3.1]		

In his 1984 article, James Hester challenged Betz's separation of 1.11 from 1.12. He argued that the presence of γάρ in vv. 11 and 12 serves to unite the two verses which, as he claimed, represent the stasis of the *narratio*.[9] Yet Hester assigned 1.10 to the *exordium*, separating it from v. 11, and failed to see how the γάρ of v. 11 could equally unite it to v. 10. Hester's case at this point is, therefore, as flawed as the one he rejects. It is even more flawed because he separates vv. 13-14 and vv. 11-12 from the *narratio* which he only limits to 1.15–2.10. Hester's insistence on this structural move is based on the assumption that the only general guidelines laid down for *narratio* are that it be lucid, credible and brief.[10] It is unclear how 1.10 will impinge on lucidity and credibility if it were taken as part of the *narratio*. Hester's

8.   Culled from Kennedy, *New Testament Interpretation*, pp. 147-51.
9.   Hester, 'Rhetorical Structure', pp. 225-27.
10.   Hester, 'Rhetorical Structure', p. 228.

assumption, however, is not accurate. Credibility was certainly required, but ancient rhetors advised sacrificing brevity, for example, in difficult cases.[11] As will be explained shortly, lucidity and brevity were not qualities on which ancient rhetoricians agreed.

Further, Hester's labeling of 2.11-14 as *digressio* lacks merit.[12] Nothing in these verses interrupts the structure or linear progression of the narration. Nor do these verses conform to Quintilian's definition of digression (*parekbasis*).[13] In fairness, Hester later adopted a different view on 2.11-14, calling it a *chreia* instead, saying, 'I now believe that 2.11-14 is not a digression but a chreia, slightly expanded by Paul, and 2.15-21 the elaboration of the chreia.'[14] Still, 1.10 remains irrelevant to the *chreia*.

Kennedy simply describes 1.10 as 'a written aside which contributes to his [Paul's] ethos by its candor'.[15] Kennedy locates it in the *exordium* as do Ben Witherington and Richard Longenecker. Apart from the observation made by Robert G. Hall that 'most ancient rhetoricians would probably prefer to call the first heading (Gal. 1.10–2.21) a narration',[16] the strict exclusion of 1.10 from the *narratio* has not been seriously challenged. Hall agrees with Hester that 1.11-12 is the thesis of the *narratio* but suggests that v. 10 be included. In Hall's words, 'Paul wants to show that his gospel did not come from human beings but from God (Gal. 1.11-12) and that he does not seek human approval but divine (Gal. 1.10). Both these theses develop Paul's ethos, the overriding purpose of the narration in Galatians.'[17] This recognition is important, and yet it has been ignored by interpreters of the letter. Even so, Hall does not proceed to demonstrate it. By switching the order of 1.10-12, giving priority to vv. 11-12 ('concern for the gospel's divine origin') over against v. 10

11. See Kennedy, *Progymnasmata*, p. 29.

12. Hester, 'Rhetorical Structure', pp. 230-33.

13. This is *egressus* in Latin (see Quintilian, *Inst.* 4.2.13-15). For further critique of Hester, see Robert G. Hall, 'The Rhetorical Outline for Galatians: A Reconsideration', *JBL* 2 (1987), pp. 277-87.

14. Hester, 'Placing the Blame: The Presence of Epideictic in Galatians 1 and 2', in D.F. Watson (ed.), *Persuasive Artistry: Studies in New Testament Rhetoric in Honor of George A. Kennedy* (JSNTSup, 50; Sheffield: JSOT Press, 1991), pp. 281-307 (282).

15. Kennedy, *New Testament Interpretation,* p. 148.

16. Hall, 'Rhetorical Outline', p. 286.

17. Hall, 'Rhetorical Outline', p. 285.

('concern for Paul not being a human approval seeker'), he misses the crux of Paul's rhetorical burden. Apart from Hall's attempt, the wisdom of including v. 10 in the *narratio*, as constituting the thesis or, at least, as part of it, has won only a few advocates.

The second issue concerns the nature and function of the narration in Gal. 1–2 as a whole. Interpreters tend to follow two general paths.[18] First, a large majority of scholars argue that Paul is on the defensive. However, there is no consensus on what he is defensive about. The narration is taken to be (a) Paul's defence of his apostolic authority,[19] (b) Paul's defence against several other accusations or charges,[20] or (c) Paul's defence of his gospel.[21] Secondly, other scholars argue that the narration functions not as a defence but as Paul's presentation of himself as a paradigm in light of 4.12 where he appeals to the Galatians to imitate him.[22]

Each of these interpretations has merit, but they are also fraught with problems. For example, in the first category, the view that Paul is defending himself against charges is problematic because it usually depends on the mirror reading of several passages. According to George Lyons, 'The designation "mirror reading" arises from the presumption that what Paul

18.   For a discussion of the views, see Debbie Hunn, 'Pleasing God or Pleasing People? Defending the Gospel in Galatians 1–2', *Bib* 91 (2010), pp. 24-49; Justin K. Hardin, 'Galatians 1–2 without a Mirror: Reflections on Paul's Conflict with the Agitators', *TynBul* 65 (2014), pp. 275-303.

19.   J.B. Lightfoot, *St. Paul's Epistles to the Galatians: A Revised Text with Introduction, Notes, and Dissertations* (repr., Peabody, MA: Hendrickson, 1995), pp. 23, 71. See also F.F. Bruce, *Galatians* (Grand Rapids: Eerdmans, 1982), pp. 24-27; J.D.G. Dunn, *The Epistle to the Galatians* (Peabody, MA: Hendrickson, 1993), p. 67; and Longenecker, *Galatians*, p. 24. Galatians 1.1 is usually taken as an indicator of this view.

20.   Interpreters in (a) are most likely to be found here also.

21.   D.J. Verseput, 'Paul's Gentile Mission and the Jewish Christian Community: A Study of the Narrative in Galatians 1 and 2', *NTS* 39 (1993), pp. 36-58; J.S. Vos, 'Paul's Argumentation in Galatians 1–2', *HTR* 87 (1994), pp. 1-16. Vos describes the narration as 'apologetic in the sense of defending the truth of the gospel but not apologetic in the sense of taking a defensive position' (p. 15).

22.   Proponents of the paradigm view include George Lyons, *Pauline Autobiography: Toward a New Understanding* (SBLDS, 73; Atlanta: Scholars Press, 1985), pp. 96-105; Beverly R. Gaventa, 'Galatians 1 and 2: Autobiography as Paradigm', *NovT* 28 (1986), pp. 309-26.

denies, his opponents have asserted and/or that what he asserts, they have denied.'[23] Mirror reading as a hermeneutical approach has been under attack since the 1980s.[24] Debbie Hunn contends that one problem with mirror reading is that a given response may be provoked by more than one cause. For example, 1.10 may be Paul's response to a charge that he pleases people, not God, or it may be a veiled charge that his opponents are themselves people-pleasers.[25] Similarly, the view that Paul is defending the gospel, as argued by J.S. Vos, is problematic because it bases Paul's genuineness and that of the gospel on the content and tone of 1.6-9.[26] But these verses in themselves do not demonstrate that the gospel is genuine,[27] and, as will become clear shortly, the narration that follows is primarily concerned with Paul's ethos and, only secondarily, with the gospel.

The absence of any motif of *imitatio Pauli* within the narration itself detracts significantly from the claim that Paul is presenting himself as a paradigm for imitation as argued by Lyons and Beverly Gaventa. As Vos notes, Gal. 4.12 is in a different context and only a few elements in 1.13–2.14 have paradigmatic force.[28] Vos further adds that a great deal of Gal. 1.13–2.14, including details of Paul's journeys and his relation to the pillar apostles, would be irrelevant to the purpose of presenting himself as a paradigm.[29] Justin K. Hardin judges that 4.12 is too far removed from the narration to be an interpretative lens and concludes that the view that the narration is providing an example for the Galatians to emulate is un-successful.[30]

Considering these difficulties, Hunn and Hardin both start from the presupposition that mirror reading, as an interpretative method, cannot be trusted

---

23. Lyons, *Pauline Autobiography*, pp. 80-81.

24. See John M.G. Barclay, 'Mirror-Reading a Polemical Letter: Galatians as a Test Case', *JSNT* 31 (1987), pp. 73-93; Hunn, 'Pleasing God or Pleasing People?'; Hardin, 'Galatians 1–2'; Nijay K. Gupta, 'Mirror-Reading Moral Issues in Paul's Letters', *JSNT* 34 (2012), pp. 361-81.

25. Hunn, 'Pleasing God or Pleasing People?', p. 27.

26. See Vos, 'Paul's Argumentation', pp. 9-10.

27. For a critique of Verseput and Vos, see Hardin, 'Galatians 1–2', pp. 293-95.

28. Vos, 'Paul's Argumentation', p. 15.

29. Vos, 'Paul's Argumentation', p. 15.

30. Hardin, 'Galatians 1–2', pp. 292-93.

and therefore should be abandoned, although Hunn believes that a total jet-tisoning of the approach is unlikely to happen.[31]

Hunn's 2010 article is based on the understanding that Gal. 1.10 and 1.11-12 are inextricably connected. She notes that, while exegetes generally understand that Paul argues for the divine origin of his gospel on the basis that he sought to please God and not humans, they have not recognized the critical role of v. 10 in 1.10–2.21.[32] In other words, Hunn belongs to the category of interpreters who take the narration as defensive. She argues that the narration functions as proof of the divine origin of Paul's gospel, which is substantiated by the fact that Paul, after his conversion, only sought to please God rather than humans.[33] Hunn construes 1.10 as consisting of two mutually exclusive categories—pleasing people, on the one hand, and pleasing God, on the other. Thus, to make clear that his gospel is divine (vv. 11-12), Paul demonstrates that he seeks to please God (1.10) rather than people (1.10, 13-14). The demonstration begins at 1.15-17 and continues until 1.24.[34]

As Hunn argues, 'verses 13-24 … establish v. 10 [i.e.] that Paul no longer seeks to please people but God, and v. 10 gives the grounds for vv. 11-12 that his gospel is from God.'[35] But Paul must not only show that his gospel is divine, he must also show that he defended it when it was threatened, hence his reminiscence of the incidents in ch. 2.[36]

The important contribution of Hunn's work lies in the recognition that, rather than being a mere addendum to a rebuke, 1.10 serves as a foundational component in support of Paul's message.[37] However, Hunn's argument exhibits two important shortcomings. First, as Hardin rightly points out, the claim that 1.10 is a proof for 1.11-12 gets the logic backward.[38] Indeed, Hunn must have read the text in the reverse order to arrive at the logic she perceives. Read linearly, vv. 11-12 and what follows serve to substantiate the point made in v. 10, not the other way round. Secondly, like Hester's claim that 1.11-12

31. Hunn, 'Pleasing God or Pleasing People?', p. 29.
32. Hunn, 'Pleasing God or Pleasing People?', p. 34.
33. Hunn, 'Pleasing God or Pleasing People?', p. 34.
34. Hunn, 'Pleasing God or Pleasing People?', p. 37.
35. Hunn, 'Pleasing God or Pleasing People?', p. 38.
36. Hunn, 'Pleasing God or Pleasing People?', pp. 42, 47.
37. Hunn, 'Pleasing God or Pleasing People?', p. 48.
38. See Hardin, 'Galatians 1–2', p. 296.

is the thesis of the entire narration, and thus, that this narration functions to demonstrate the divine origin of Paul's gospel, Hunn's view fails to convince because, again, the narration is primarily about Paul himself not the gospel.

Hardin rejects taking Gal. 1–2 as Paul's defence of himself, his gospel, or anything else,[39] suggesting instead that the narration functions as Paul's self-contrast with the agitators in light of 6.12-14 where Paul indicts his opponents as people-pleasers. As Hardin puts it, 'Paul presents himself as a foil for the agitators so the Galatians would realize the folly of chasing after their Judaizing tactics.'[40] In other words, in relation to 1.10, the agitators, rather than Paul, are the ones guilty of being people pleasers.[41]

Hardin, like Hunn, recognizes 1.10 as crucial for understanding the narration. Nonetheless, Hardin's interpretation suffers from at least three weaknesses. First, Hardin does not clearly show how 1.13–2.21 portrays Paul as a God-pleaser, and his arrangement of 1.15–2.21 as a tenuous chiasm does not support his claim.[42] Secondly, Hardin is inconsistent when he condemns the narration-as-a-paradigm view as unsuccessful and yet, referencing 4.12, later claims that Paul's aim in 1.10 and the narration as a whole were to persuade the Galatians, not to follow the agitators but to become like (i.e. imitate) him.[43] Thirdly, Hardin's claim that Paul is not on the defence but on the attack represents an unnecessary and invalid dichotomy. Self-contrast can also be a form of self-defence. In this case, it clearly is. Hardin's appeal to Witherington's comment that 'Paul sees himself as in competition with the agitators over the hearts and minds of the Galatian converts'[44] does not help his case that the narration is not defensive. Witherington himself admits that 'the tone of this material [Gal. 1–2] is somewhat polemical and even

39.   Hardin, 'Galatians 1–2'.
40.   Hardin, 'Galatians 1–2', pp. 298-99.
41.   Hardin, 'Galatians 1–2', p. 299.
42.   Hardin, 'Galatians 1–2', p. 300.
43.   Hardin, 'Galatians 1–2', pp. 292-93 (cf. 299).
44.   Ben Witherington III, *Grace in Galatia* (Grand Rapids: Eerdmans, 1998), p. 130; quoted in Hardin, 'Galatians 1–2', p. 299.

defensive'.[45] In fact, even Gaventa, who privileges the narration-as-a-paradigm view, upholds the defensive character of the material.[46]

Suffice it to say that a valid understanding of Gal. 1–2 must include the notion of self-defence. Further, any assessment of Gal. 1–2 that insists on excluding self-defence faces substantial problems. This article contends that Gal. 1.10–2.21 functions as a self-defensive refutation of a false narrative or notion that impinges on Paul's credibility and ethos.

Galatians 1.10–2.21 as a Rhetorical Unit

Taking Gal. 1.10–2.21 as a rhetorical unit requires clear demonstration, given that only 1.13–2.14 appears to be properly narratival. First, let us recall Hall's point: 'Most ancient rhetoricians would probably prefer to call the first heading (Gal. 1.10–2.21) a narration.'[47] This assertion is supported by ancient rhetorical handbooks. Narration is one of the six parts of a rhetorical speech in the order: *exordium, narratio, partitio, confirmatio, refutatio* and *peroratio*.[48] A narrative or 'Statement of Facts'[49] is more prominent in the forensic genre of rhetorical speeches.[50] As Cicero pointed out, much narration is not needed in deliberative cases.[51] Cicero defines it as 'an exposition of events that have occurred or are supposed to have occurred' (*Inv.* 1.27).[52] Quintilian echoes this definition, 'A Narrative is an exposition, designed to be persuasive, of an action done or deemed to be done' (*Inst.* 4.2.31).[53] In other words, a narrative does not necessarily recount factual events but they

---

45. Witherington, *New Testament Rhetoric,* p. 125. This negates a previous claim that 'the rhetorical function of this material is not defense' (*Grace in Galatia,* p. 184).

46. See Gaventa, 'Galatians 1 and 2', p. 326.

47. Hall, 'Rhetorical Outline', p. 286.

48. Cicero, *Inv.* 1.14.19. In his more mature discussion, Cicero identifies only four divisions: the first (*exordium)* and the last (*peroration)* for arousing emotions, and the second (narrative) and third (proof) for procuring belief in what is said (*Part. or.* 27).

49. *Rhet. Her.* 1.12.

50. Narration is discussed mainly in this genre.

51. Cicero, *Part. or.* 13.

52. Cicero, *Inv.* 1.27 (Hubbell, LCL).

53. Quintilian, *Inst.* 4.2.31 (Russell, LCL).

must be narrated as though they actually happened.[54] Ancient rhetoricians permitted the invention of fictitious events. However, they advised that such inventions must be believable and not contradictory. [55] According to Quintilian, 'We must ... make just as much effort to make the judge believe the true things we say as to make him believe what we invent' (*Inst.* 4.2.34-35).[56]

Cicero identifies three forms of narrative: (1) a narrative which concerns just the case and the whole reason for the dispute; (2) a narrative in which a digression is made beyond the strict limits of the case for the purpose of attack, comparison, amusement or amplification; and (3) a narrative wholly unconnected with the issue but meant 'solely for amusement'.[57] The author of *Rhetorica ad Herennium* identifies three types: (1) a type in which every detail is set for one's advantage; (2) a type which aims at winning belief or incriminating adversaries; (3) a third type which is only composed for practice in the form of *progymnasmata*.[58] This third type, in turn, consists of two kinds—one based on the facts and the other based on the persons. The treatises of classical *progymnasmata* are agreed on the six 'elements' (στοι-χεῖα) that constitute a narrative: the person(s), action done, place, time, manner and cause of the action done by the person(s).[59] Here, the implication is that whether a narrative is factual or fictional, historical, or legendary, it revolves around a person(s) or an actor(s).

There is also a significant degree of consensus on the requirements for a narrative. Three basic virtues of a narrative are brevity (avoiding any detail that would detract from the case), clarity (chronological organization), and plausibility (credibility).[60] To achieve credibility, one must maintain the

54. See Kennedy, *Progymnasmata*, p. 28.

55. Quintilian, *Inst.* 4.2.88-97. For further discussion on this, see Robert G. Hall, 'Historical Inference and Rhetorical Effect: Another look at Galatians 1 and 2', in Duane F. Watson (ed.), *Persuasive Artistry* (JSNTSup, 50; Sheffield: Sheffield Academic Press, 1991), pp. 308-20.

56. Quintilian, *Inst.* 4.2.34-35 (Russell, LCL).

57. Cicero, *Inv.* 1.27 (Hubbell, LCL, p. 55).

58. *Rhet. Her.* 1.12.

59. See Kennedy, *Progymnasmata*, pp. 28, 96-97, 137, 184.

60. According to Quintilian, some add grandeur (*megaloprepeia*) and vividness (*enargeia*). Quintilian does not favour the former, but he would prefer to include the latter with clarity (see Quintilian, *Inst.* 4.2.61-65 [Russell, LCL]; *Rhet. Her.* 1.14).

characters' proper qualities, provide plain reasons for their actions, and ensure that the story fits the nature of the actors and the habits of ordinary people.[61]

However, not all classical rhetoricians necessarily agreed on all theoretical points regarding narration. For example, Aristotle ridiculed the rule of brevity, and the followers of Theodorus rejected the rules of brevity and clarity.[62] Quintilian, in his more extensive discussion, rejected the rule of chronological arrangement,[63] only requiring, 'I want written Narrative to be as carefully composed as possible' (*Inst.* 2.4.15)[64]—that is, with the aim to persuade. Against Cicero's many types, Quintilian subscribed to only two narrative types in forensic cases—one involving the exposition of the Cause itself, the other the exposition of matters relevant to the Cause.[65]

In fact, there are even variations in what a narrative is and does. According to Apollodorus, a narrative 'is a speech instructing the hearer on what is in dispute'.[66] Some nuances can be observed as we move from Cicero to the first century. For example, Quintilian writes, 'In our day … speakers take the narrative as offering, as it were, a free field, and choose this as the best moment to flex the voice, throw back the head, thump the sides, and indulge in every possible play of ideas and words and composition' (*Inst.* 4.2.39).[67] He further states,

> It will be useful also to sow some seeds of the proofs, but in such a way
> that we never forget that this is still the narration and not the proof. We
> may however sometimes confirm an assertion by some Argument, but
> it must be a simple, short one … We can, in fact, give a taste in the
> narration of everything that we shall be treating in the proof: person,
> motive, place, time, means, opportunity (*Inst.* 4.2.54-57).[68]

61. Cicero, *Inv.* 1.29 (Hubbell, LCL).
62. See Quintilian, *Inst.* 4.2.32-33 (Russell, LCL).
63. Quintilian, *Inst.* 4.2.83-84 (Russell, LCL).
64. Quintilian, *Inst.* 2.4.15 (Russell, LCL).
65. Quintilian, *Inst.* 4.2.11 (Russell, LCL).
66. Cited by Quintilian, *Inst.* 4.2.31-32 (Russell, LCL).
67. Quintilian, *Inst.* 4.2 (Russell, LCL).
68. Quintilian, *Inst.* 4.2.54-57 (Russell, LCL).

Quintilian also notes that a narrative is a preliminary statement of proof but it should not include argumentation.[69]

This brief overview shows one aspect of the fluidity of ancient rhetorical theory.[70] However, several critical points emerge from the survey. While narrative may be used in deliberative speeches, it is not typically present or necessary, since narrative deals with the past, while deliberative speeches deal with the future.[71] A narrative must be believable even if it is not factual. It does not simply recount events; it is an exposition of them, elucidating reasons and relevant matters of the dispute, including elements of proof and argument. Perhaps, more importantly, narratives focus mainly on persons, their actions, circumstances and rationales for those actions.

Viewing the first two chapters of Galatians in light of the observations made above leads to at least two implications. First, considering the emphasis on persons and their actions in rhetorical theory, at least from the standpoint of classical *progymnasmata*, the narration properly expands on 1.10. This verse sets the autobiographical tone of the narration, leading all the way to 2.21. In this case, Paul is the central figure, and every other component of the narration (including the origin of the gospel) serves to accentuate his ethos. Secondly, 2.15-21 is not a digression. Rather, it directly flows out of v.14, reflecting Paul's theological reason for resisting Cephas.

It should be noted that the term Ἰουδαῖοι in 2.15 immediately picks up and extends the Jewish (Ἰουδαῖος, Ἰουδαϊκῶς, ἰουδαΐζειν) identity theme in 2.14. Similarly, the first person plural ἡμεῖς in its emphatic (vv. 15-16) and inflectional uses (ἐπιστεύσαμεν ['we have believed'], δικαιωθῶμεν ['we may be justified'] [v. 16]; εὑρέθημεν ... αὐτοί ['we ourselves have been found'] [v. 17]) continues the emphasis on Jewish identity from v. 14. This thematic continuity makes a demarcation between v. 14 and v. 15 improbable. Nor must 2.15-21 necessarily be designated *propositio* rather than *narratio*. As the survey above shows, the *narratio*, which is an exposition of events and actions of a person(s), includes the reason(s) for such events or actions. A

69. Quintilian, *Inst.* 4.2.79, 108-109.

70. As Margaret M. Mitchell rightly observes, such 'fluidity and variety of possibilities of rhetorical composition in Greco-Roman antiquity can be brought to bear on ... analysis' (*Paul and the Rhetoric of Reconciliation: An Exegetical Investigation of the Language and Composition of 1 Corinthians* [Louisville: Westminster John Knox Press, 1991], p. 9).

71. Cicero, *Part. or.* 13.

narration could also include elements of the disputed issue and even argument, all of this without ceasing to be narration. Thus, the disconnection of 1.10 from 1.11-12, on the one hand, and the exclusion of 2.15-21 from the narration, on the other, are unwarranted. Against such demarcations, as seen in the outlines above, 1.10–2.21 coheres as a rhetorical unit and should be taken as such.[72]

A few things need to be pointed out here following Kennedy's third step:[73] While Galatians as a whole is pragmatically deliberative, the narration exhibits a forensic tone. Also, while all species of rhetoric may make use of a narrative for different purposes and in different ways,[74] the epideictic genre rarely needs a narrative,[75] and the deliberative genre requires a narrative only in particular situations. Quintilian made a distinction between a private deliberation and a public one, saying, 'A narrative is never needed in private deliberations ... In public assemblies, a narrative explaining the order of events is often essential' (*Inst.* 3.8.10-12).[76] Galatians 1–2 fits into Quintilian's second category,[77] but it is also true that the defensive tenor of this section gives it a forensic character without implying a juridical *Sitz im Leben*.

Rhetorical Situation

The false narrative against which Paul is reacting is discernible from the text. First, Paul's opponents were persuading the new Gentile followers of Jesus to submit to the Mosaic law of circumcision.[78] Paul describes these op-

---

72. De-emphasizing mechanistic structuring, Mitchell decries what she calls the 'quest for "divisions" of a text as specified in a frozen model, without attention to the varied requirements of genre, content, and rhetorical situation' (*Paul and the Rhetoric of Reconciliation*, p.11).

73. See n. 5 above.

74. Kennedy, *New Testament Interpretation*, p. 145.

75. Mitchell, *Paul and the Rhetoric of Reconciliation*, pp. 9-11.

76. Quintilian, *Inst.* 3.8.10-12 (Russell, LCL).

77. For a cogent discussion favouring the deliberative genre, see Hall, 'Rhetorical Outline', pp. 278-82; Witherington, *New Testament Rhetoric*, pp. 124-25.

78. On this, many interpreters agree. See John M.G. Barclay, *Obeying the Truth: Paul's Ethics in Galatians* (Edinburgh: T. & T. Clark, 1988), pp. 65-66; G.W. Hansen, *Abraham in Galatians: Epistolary and Rhetorical Contexts* (JSNTSup, 29;

ponents as τινές ... οἱ ταράσσοντες ὑμᾶς καὶ θέλοντες μεταστρέψαι τὸ εὐαγγέλιον τοῦ Χριστοῦ ('certain men confusing you and wishing to pervert the gospel of Christ' [1.7]) and οἱ ἀναστατοῦντες ('the agitators' [5.12]) who desire to put up a good showing in the flesh to avoid persecution (6.12). They are probably the same ψευδαδέλφους ('false brothers') mentioned in 2.4, or those sharing the same or similar views.[79]

Secondly, while the protest against mirror reading should be taken seriously, we do gain a reasonably accurate understanding of what the issue is by considering Paul's language, especially the rhetorical questions he employs. Ancient rhetoricians recognized the importance and use of rhetorical questions. Quintilian, for example, identified two types of question—a simple question that asks for a response and a figured [rhetorical] question asked not to acquire information but to emphasize a point.[80] When a speaker uses this second device, no answer is usually required, although sometimes the speaker himself or herself may provide a response.[81] A rhetorical question is also used to add force to a point; using rhetorical questions, 'Demosthenes forces his listener into a sort of corner, so that he seems to be cross-examined and unable to reply' (Demetrius, *Eloc.* 279).[82] In this sense, it might appear that rhetorical questions only make hypothetical points from the perspective of the speaker. However, it has been demonstrated that rhetorical questions are used to pre-empt an opponent's argument and refute it before it is made. They can also serve for defensive rebuttal of an opposing argument that has already been made.[83] This usage appears to be the case in

Sheffield: JSOT Press, 1989), pp. 158-60; Douglas J. Moo, *Galatians* (Grand Rapids: Baker, 2013), pp. 19-20; Dunn, *Galatians,* p. 11.

79.   Dunn (*Galatians*, p. 11) describes them as '*Christian-Jewish missionaries who had come to Galatia to improve or correct Paul's gospel and to "complete" his converts by integrating them fully into the heirs of Abraham through circumcision and by thus bringing them "under the law".*'

80.   Quintilian, *Inst.* 9.2.6-7 (Russell, LCL).

81.   Quintilian, *Inst.* 9.2.14-15 (Russell, LCL).

82.   Demetrius, *Eloc.* 279 (Innes, LCL).

83.   See David Sansone, *Greek Drama and the Invention of Rhetoric* (Oxford: Wiley-Blackwell, 2012), pp. 180-84. For a discussion on how rhetorical questions in ancient writers are connected to the disputed issue (i.e. stasis), see Deborah Thompson Prince, '"Why Do You Seek the Living among the Dead?" Rhetorical Questions in the Lukan Resurrection Narrative', *JBL* 135 (2016), pp. 123-39;

Galatians.[84] Two pivotal rhetorical questions used by Paul illuminate the false perspective that some Galatians have adopted, which are 1.10 and 5.11:

Gal 1.10	Gal 5.11
Ἄρτι γὰρ ἀνθρώπους πείθω ἢ τὸν θεόν; ἢ ζητῶ ἀνθρώποις ἀρέσκειν; εἰ ἔτι ἀνθρώποις ἤρεσκον, Χριστοῦ δοῦλος οὐκ ἂν ἤμην.	Ἐγὼ δέ, ἀδελφοί, εἰ περιτομὴν ἔτι κηρύσσω, τί ἔτι διώκομαι;
For do I now persuade people or God? Or do I seek to please people? If I were *still* pleasing people, I would not be a slave of Christ.	But I brethren, if I am *still* preaching circumcision, why am I *still* persecuted?

In context, these two passages indicate that Paul was refuting a rhetorical logic by which the Galatians were being persuaded to embrace circumcision, namely, *that Paul is a people-pleaser and that his double-standard with respect to circumcision is proof enough.*[85] One may allege a case of mirror reading here. However, the thematic manner in which 5.11 re-enforces 1.10 and the ensuing narration lends credence to the assertion. So, what we have may properly be identified as an exegetical or text-warranted mirror reading as opposed to mere presumptive mirror reading.

Considering the 'pleasing' theme in 1.10a, the words πείθω and ἀρέσκειν should be understood as parallels, both having the idea of seeking to please or win favour. Cicero recommended such parallels, repetitions or restate-

Wilhelm H. Wuellner, 'Paul as Pastor: The Function of Rhetorical Questions in First Corinthians', in A. Vanhoye (ed.), *L'Apôtre Paul: Personnalité, style et conception du ministére* (BETL, 73; Leuven: Leuven University Press, 1986), pp. 49-77.

84.   Arguably, Paul was also knowledgeable on the Old Testament use of rhetorical questions for stating an opinion or presupposition meant to be refuted. For an example of such use, see Walter A. Brueggemann, 'Jeremiah's Use of Rhetorical Questions', *JBL* 92 (1973), pp. 358-59.

85.   Cf. Acts 16.3; Paul's circumcision of Timothy likely occurred before Galatians was written. If not, this account at least indicates that Paul's tendency or practice was well-known. Here, in a missional context, Paul allowed the circumcision law clearly to please the Jews.

ments as an effective rhetorical style.[86] The crux of the matter is whether Paul pleases people or God. In other words, the point is not that Paul no longer persuades men, let alone God, as R.D. Anderson claims.[87] As regards how 1.10 relates to its context, although no complete separation from what precedes can be argued, this verse is logically conjoined to the preceding verses by γάρ. This is so because the adverb ἄρτι in 1.10a defines not literary immediacy but time in Paul's life—the present as opposed to his former career in Judaism (1.13 [cf. v. 23]).

The link between v. 10 and the preceding material is further buttressed by the next adverb ἔτι in v. 10b, which indicates that Paul has in mind a juxtaposition between his former and present life. Thus, we have no reason to expect the tone or content of 1.6-9 to provide a demonstration either that Paul does not please people but God or that his gospel is genuine.[88] In other words, 1.10 is not necessarily 'calling attention to the fact that the proem [1.6-9] does not seek favor with the audience'.[89] The conditional clause in v.10b is an indirect denial calling for substantiation. Paul must demonstrate, in practical terms, that he pleases none other than God and therefore is a slave of none other than Christ, hence the rest of the section culminating in 2.21. Only by demonstrating his own ethos as one approved of God could the question of the validity of his gospel be settled.

Not only do we have the theme of 'pleasing' (ἀρέσκειν [1.10]; εὐδόκησεν [1.15])[90] in the narrative, but we also have explicit references to the theme of circumcision (2.3, 7, 8, 9, 12). The significance of this becomes clear when we consider Paul's comment in Gal. 5.11, which reveals that circumcision is central to the problem that necessitated the writing of this letter. Considering the adverb ἔτι ('still'), 5.11 suggests a real crisis of confidence instigated by the ψευδαδέλφους. They promoted the false notion that Paul's allowance of circumcision to please people is evidence of their claims. Thus, it is not simply that Paul's apostolic authority was being questioned (although this can hardly be excluded), it is that Paul's ambivalence regarding circumcision provided the Galatians enough ground to consider it a requirement to make

86. See Cicero *Part. or.* 21-22, 72.
87. R.D. Anderson Jr., *Ancient Rhetorical Theory and Paul* (Kampen: Kok Pharos, 1996), p. 127.
88. Contra Vos, 'Paul's Argumentation', p. 10.
89. Contra Kennedy, *New Testament Interpretation,* p. 148.
90. Cf. ἵνα θεῷ ζήσω ('in order that I might live to/for God' [2.19]).

their faith complete. Only by manipulating the Galatians to think that Paul himself preached circumcision could the agitators' false narrative persuade the Galatians.[91] Paul's description of the deceptive argument of the agitators as bewitchment (βασκαίνω [3.1]) makes sense in this light.

Paul not only denies any suggestion that he *still* either pleased people or preached circumcision, but he also demonstrates that he is not a people-pleaser by recalling how he vehemently resisted the circumcision of Titus (2.3) and the circumcision party (2.12) to safeguard the gospel. Galatians 6.11-17 supports this understanding in such a way as to sum up the essential elements of the narration.[92] There, Paul turns the case against the agitators, characterizing them as the actual people-pleasers. These agitators are the actual people-pleasers because they seek to make a good showing in the flesh and thus to avoid persecution (6.12-13, 15). In contrast, Paul shows how he not only resisted the circumcision agenda without fear of those who would insist on it (2.3, 5, 11-14), but also boasts in the cross of Christ without fear of persecution (6.14 [cf. 2.20]). One who does such things cannot be accused of being a people-pleaser (per 1.10). The contrast between Paul and his opponents in Gal. 6.11-17 serves to strengthen the defensive character of the narrative in chs. 1–2. It also suggests that the rhetorical situation described above is not a product of conjectural mirror reading.

Demonstrating Paul's Ethos as No People-Pleaser in Galatians 1.11–2.21

In the foregoing, I have laid a broad foundation for the thesis of this article. In what follows, I highlight three aspects of Gal. 1.11–2.21 that compel strict connection to 1.10 and substantiate the argument that 1.10–2.21, taken to-gether as a cohesive rhetorical unit, (1) serves to demonstrate Paul's self-understanding as no longer a people-pleaser and (2) represents his self-defensive refutation of the claims of his opponents.

1. Galatians 1.11-14 as Substantiation for 1.10
The relationship between 1.10 and the *narratio* is key to the thesis of this article. Hester argues that γνωρίζω in v. 11 is a disclosure formula and

91.   See Bruce, *Galatians*, p. 27.
92.   Witherington (*New Testament Rhetoric*, p. 126) rightly designates 6.12-17 as *peroration.*

therefore signals a division point.[93] However, the conjunction γάρ pragmatically indicates 'substantiation' or 'support' in relation to what precedes.[94] In this case, what follows from v. 11 is meant to provide support for Paul's implied claim that he is no longer a people-pleaser in v. 10. Galatians 1.1 already sets the stage for the claim—neither Paul's calling nor his gospel originates in humans. In Paul's view, this makes pandering to people inconceivable for him. The divine calling of Paul and the divine origin of Paul's gospel exclude any obligation to seek human approval. Paul is no longer in that business.

But why is Gal. 1 not primarily about the gospel and its divine origin? Undoubtedly, the gospel's origin δι᾽ ἀποκαλύψεως Ἰησοῦ Χριστοῦ (1.12)[95] is a major motif in the chapter. This notwithstanding, the thrust of Paul's rhetorical argument is autobiographical from start (1.10) to finish (2.21). The inflectional point for this autobiographical emphasis is in 1.10. Thus, despite the fact that a substantiating γάρ opens the verse and connects it to the preceding verses, a demarcation from this point is justified, especially considering the frequency of the first-person plural (pronominal and verbal forms) in vv. 8-9. The autobiographical shift is further accentuated in 1.13-14, which highlights Paul's history, with the implication that what he used to be, he no longer is.

Moreover, 1.24 coheres with this autobiographical emphasis because it says that it was on account of Paul, not of the gospel, that God was glorified. The self-referential character of the passage clearly puts Paul at the center of the narrative. Paul seems to understand the rhetorical axiom expressed by Quintilian to the effect that a speaker does the best service to his Cause if his

93. Hester, 'Presence of Epideictic', p. 298. For a discussion of disclosures in the New Testament, see T.Y. Mullins, 'Disclosures: A Literary Form in the New Testament', *NovT* 7 (1964), pp. 44-50.

94. Stephen H. Levinsohn (*Discourse Features of the New Testament: A Course on the Information Structure of the New Testament* [Dallas: SIL International, 2nd edn, 2003], p. 91) notes, 'the presence of γάρ constrains the material it introduces to be interpreted as strengthening some aspect of the previous assertion, rather than as distinctive information.'

95. This construction is a subjective genitive, by which Paul means not the revelation given by Jesus but the revelation whose content is Jesus himself, as 1.16 shows.

character lends it credibility.[96] Thus, just arguing for the divine origin of the gospel would have no persuasive effect if Paul's credibility were in question.

2. Galatians 1.15–2.17 as Further Evidence That Paul Does Not Please People But God

Paul presents ample evidence that he is not a people-pleaser. The first evidence for this is that he did not confer with anyone to validate his apostolic call. This claim moves from general to particular—'I did not consult with flesh and blood' (1.16) to 'nor did I go up to Jerusalem, to the apostles before me' (1.17). 'Even when, after three years, I went to Jerusalem to acquaint myself with Cephas', Paul seems to say, 'I did not see [any] other of the apostles except James' (1.18-20). Paul seals this denial with an oath, 'That which I am writing to you, before God, I am not lying' (1.20).   As regards this oath, Paul is probably aware of the permission to invent fictitious narratives as we saw in the survey above.[97] This oath would thus amount to a denial of this practice on his part; the issue in question evokes anything but amusement. It also indicates that Paul senses a contradiction in saying that he did not consult with flesh and blood but became acquainted (just three years later) with Cephas and even saw James—the key leaders of the church. The oath, therefore, offsets any notion of contradiction or inconsistency.[98]

When Paul finally goes to Jerusalem, fourteen years after, it is not to consult with flesh and blood for clarification or tutoring, but to 'set forth' or 'present' (ἀνατίθημι) his gospel before the esteemed apostles (2.1-2, 6, 9).

---

96.   See Quintilian, *Inst.* 6.2.18.

97.   See Quintilian, *Inst.* 4.2.88-97; Cicero, *Inv.* 1.27, divides an amusement narrative into two: events (*fabula* [untrue], *historia* [remote recollection], *argumentum* [fictitious but could have occurred]), and persons.

98.   While Paul's oath gives a sense of accuracy, it is debated whether Paul's letters, especially Gal. 1–2, represent an accurate chronology of Paul's life as opposed to the account in Acts. Some scholars think so. See, for example, John Knox, *Chapters in a Life of Paul* (repr., Macon, GA: Mercer University Press, 1987), p. 19; Robert Jowett, *A Chronology of Paul's Life* (Philadelphia: Fortress Press, 1979); Gerd Lüdemann, *Paul, Apostle to the Gentiles: Studies in Chronology* (Philadelphia: Fortress Press, 1984). For a critique of this view, see Hall, 'Historical Inference'. Hall argues that narratives do not necessarily require facts, only persuasion. Thus, Paul is not under any obligation to report all the times he visited Jerusalem, especially if doing so will detract from his case.

Paul is careful to point out that it was κατὰ ἀποκάλυψιν ('by revelation' [2.2]) that he went to Jerusalem. This information would be unnecessary except to highlight the fact that going to Jerusalem was not an obligation he owed anyone such as the apostles, to please them. He owed it to God alone.

The second evidence lies in Paul's stance with respect to circumcision itself. Recall the proposed thesis regarding the issue in Galatians: *a notion was being purveyed by certain agitators that, in allowing circumcision sometimes, Paul not only pleases people but also approves it as a valid law for Christians*. Paul demonstrates the falsity of this idea by narrating how vehemently he resisted the circumcision of Titus to preserve the sanctity of the gospel (2.3-5). Paul intends to show that he no longer pleases people, whoever they may be. Even the reputed apostles cannot claim Paul's allegiance because 'they contributed nothing to me' (ἐμοὶ ... οὐδὲν προσανέθεντο [2.6]). They only saw (ἰδόντες [2.7]) and realized (γνόντες [2.9]) God's grace in Paul and gave him a hand of fellowship.

Paul's third evidence that he sought to please no one but God is in 2.11-17. Notice here that the word εὐαγγέλιον ('gospel') occurs four times (vv. 2, 5, 7, 14), but we hear nothing of its origin. Instead, the narrative remains autobiographical.[99] Galatians 2.11-14 portrays Paul *contra mundum*—not, in the least, a people-pleaser. It represents a syncrisis, that is, a contrast or antithesis: Cephas and 'the rest of the Jews' (v. 13) of Antioch act hypocritically to please certain men from James, but Paul acts with the integrity of a non-people-pleaser. Paul's rebuke of Cephas is further grounded in vv. 15-17. As shown in the table above, many interpreters demarcate vv. 11-14 from vv. 15-21, designating the latter as the *propositio*. However, such separation and designation are questionable. Galatians 2.15-21 includes details of the debated matter, especially in vv. 15-16, yet such details do not nullify it as part of the narration.[100] As shown above, Quintilian allows seeds of the proofs in the narration as well as 'a taste of everything that we shall be treating in the proof' (*Inst.* 4.2.54-57).[101] In fact, according to Quintilian, it is not always

99. Lyons (*Pauline Autobiography*, p. 171) considers the whole of 1.13–2.21 as autobiographical.

100. Witherington (*Grace in Galatia*, p. 171) rightly points out six key terms that are introduced in these verses: δικαιοσύνη, δικαιόω, νόμος, ἔργον, πίστις and ζάω.

101. Quintilian, *Inst.* 4.2.54-57 (Russell, LCL).

essential to make use of a *propositio*.[102] From Quintilian's perspective, the narration in Gal. 1–2 would be Paul telling the story not as a witness but as an advocate.[103] It is no wonder, therefore, that Chrysostom (350–407 CE) did not consider 2.15-21 a *propositio*.[104] Kennedy, apparently following Quintilian (*Inst.* 4.4.1-2), describes it as an *epicheireme* ('argument with the parts fully stated') which provides the conclusion to the first heading (i.e. 1.11-12). He objects to calling it a *propositio* on the basis that it is argumentative.[105] If by 'argumentative', Kennedy means quarrelsome or extended argument, 2.15-21 is hardly such. The passage, in line with

102. Quintilian, *Inst.* 4.4.2. However, it does seem that the climactic statement that concludes this narrative (i.e. 2.21) represents the *propositio* since it sufficiently meets the criteria of brevity, completeness, and conciseness as recommended by Cicero. Cicero discusses proposition under the *partition*, which takes two forms: one which shows points of agreement, and the other which is a methodical statement of topics to be discussed. This second form must have the qualities of brevity, completeness, and conciseness (*Inv.* 1.22.31-32). According to Richard A. Lanham (citing Peacham), 'Sometimes *propositio* is used simply as a figure, rather than the part of an oration, to indicate a brief proleptic summary "which compriseth in few words the sum of that matter, whereof we presently intend to speak"' (*A Handlist of Rhetorical Terms* [Berkeley: University of California Press, 2nd edn, 1991], p. 122). Galatians 2.21 also adequately sets the agenda for the next section in the same way that 1.10 does for what follows up to that point.

103. Quintilian, *Inst.* 4.2.109. This comports well with Hall's view that 'most ancient rhetoricians would probably prefer to call the first heading (Gal. 1.10–2.21) a narration' ('Rhetorical Outline', p. 286).

104. For an extensive discussion of Chrysostom's view and a critique against the designation of 2.15-21 as a proposition, see J. Fairweather, 'The Epistle to the Galatians and Classical Rhetoric: Parts 1 and 2', *TynBul* 45 (1994), pp. 1-38. Fairweather adduces two reasons for why 2.15-21 does not constitute a proposition: 'First, the phrase, ἡμεῖς φύσει Ἰουδαῖοι καὶ οὐκ ἐξ ἐθνῶν ἁμαρτωλοί, makes good sense as a continuation of Paul's address to Cephas, a fellow Jew: it makes no sense at all as a way of addressing Galatian congregations which certainly included Gentiles. Secondly, if we had the opening of a *propositio* in Galatians 2.15, one would expect the beginning of this major new rhetorical paragraph to be signaled in some way: by a particle at least, or alternatively by some form of address to the recipients of his letter, or an indication in the preceding sentence that a paragraph has just been concluded' (p.14).

105. Kennedy, *New Testament Interpretation,* pp. 148-49.

Quintilian's view, represents only 'some seeds of the proofs' or full-scale argument that Paul begins to make from ch. 3. Moreover, defensive reasoning is not strictly prohibited in a narrative. Quintilian makes this point when he further states, 'Argumentation in Narrative ... we shall never use; Argument we shall sometimes' (*Inst.* 4.2.108-109).[106]

3. *Galatians 2.18-20 as the Climax of Paul's Claim of Pleasing God*

Historically, Gal. 2.19-20 has been regarded as a summary of Paul's teaching on justification and the spiritual life.[107] Most interpreters easily read Rom. 6–7 into this passage. Those who take the narration as paradigmatic consider Gal. 2.20 as what it means to imitate Paul based on 4.12.[108] Witherington regards it as an example of how the Galatians should interpret their conversion experience.[109] However, it is not clear that Rom. 6 and 7 should be superimposed upon Gal. 2.19-20. Betz seems to caution against such an interpretative move, although he regards it as an *expositio* of the elements of Paul's theological position with himself as a prototypical example of what applies to all Pauline Christians.[110] For the many reasons laid out above, the paradigmatic view of the narrative is not convincing.[111]

This paper contends that this final part of the narration represents the climax of Paul's demonstration of his personal ethos—a rousing portrayal of himself as a God-pleaser. What Paul rhetorically claims in 1.10 is grounded in 1.11-14, demonstrated in 1.15–2.17 and amplified in 2.18-20. While 2.18 is Paul's final, albeit indirect, rejection of the opponents' 'claim' that he legitimized circumcision and/or only hypocritically shied away from it, vv.19-21 represents the climactic *peroration* of the whole narration. The

106. Quintilian, *Inst.* 4.2.108-109 (Russell, LCL).

107. Philip A. McClendon, 'Galatians 2.20 as a Corrective to Selected Contemporary Views of Christian Spirituality' (PhD diss., Southern Baptist Theological Seminary, 2012), p. 23.

108. See Gaventa, 'Galatians 1 and 2', p. 322.

109. Witherington, *Grace in Galatia*, p. 188.

110. Betz, *Commentary*, pp. 121, 123.

111. Again, see Vos, 'Paul's Argumentation', p. 15; Hardin, 'Galatians 1–2', pp. 292-93; Brian J. Dodd, 'Christ's Slave, People Pleasers and Galatians 1.10', *NTS* 42 (1996), pp. 90-104 (n. 28); Karl O. Sandnes, *Paul—One of the Prophets? A Contribution to the Apostle's Self-Understanding* (WUNT, 2/43; Tübingen: Mohr Siebeck, 1991), pp. 49-50.

latter apparently forms an *inclusio* with 1.10 and thus represents Paul's final self-defensive refutation of the notion that he is a people-pleaser:

Gal 1.10	Gal 2.19-20
I please God	I live for God
I am a slave of Christ	I am crucified with Christ

These two ends of the passage complement and illuminate each other. What is claimed on the one hand is affirmed on the other. Paul's death to the law enables him to live for God (2.19), that is, to please God. The expression, 'crucified with Christ', is to be understood as Paul's idea of what it means to be a slave of Christ. Paul's depiction of himself in 2.20 as one in whom Christ lives out his life (ζῇ δὲ ἐν ἐμοὶ Χριστός [cf. 1.16]) implies identification with Christ. Indeed, for Paul, this is what slavery to Christ means. By identifying with Christ in this way, Paul portrays himself as a God-pleaser, just as Christ was, in his life and ministry. This understanding may be verified by Paul's own claims in Galatians, and 1.15-16 is particularly instructive in this regard.

First, it is not simply that Paul now pleases God, it is also that God himself affirmed his pleasure in him by revealing his Son in him. Notice that the word εὐδόκησεν ('he was pleased') in 1.15 is synonymous with ἀρέσκειν ('to please') in 1.10. Secondly, Paul's declaration that God was pleased to reveal his Son in him (1.16) may properly be taken to mean that Paul himself is 'Christ' revealed. Thus, the idea is that it pleased God to make Paul an express epiphany of Christ. This comports well with the argument that Gal. 1.11-24 is not merely about the content of the gospel, understood as divinely disclosed to Paul (although 1.11-12 implies this), but especially about Paul being the embodiment of the gospel/Christ from God. This would explain why he does not say that God revealed his Son/gospel ἐμοί/μοι (*to* me) but rather ἐν ἐμοί (*in me*). Third, Paul's claim that God set him apart from the womb (1.15) represents a rhetorical allusion to Christ, the suffering servant of Isaiah.[112] The intentionality here is perceptible. Paul is setting forth himself as a type or model of Christ. There is no surprise here, since Paul can dare the Galatians

---

112. Quintilian mentions the use of allusion in *Inst.* 5.11.14-17. For a discussion of allusions, see Richard B. Hays, *Echoes of Scripture in the Letters of Paul* (New Haven: Yale University Press, 1989).

to recall how they welcomed him ὡς Χριστὸν Ἰησοῦν ('as Christ Jesus' [Gal. 4.14]; cf. 6.17).[113]

Such a self-understanding could only have been compelled by a real problem regarding the character and credibility of Paul, especially in relation to the question of circumcision. If in these terms we evaluate the success of the rhetorical unit in line with Kennedy's fifth step,[114] we can clearly see that Paul's response not only comports with the rhetorical situation described above but also successfully deals with the specific issue the letter was meant to address.

Conclusion

The disconnection of Gal. 1.10 from the narration in chs. 1–2 obscures the rhetorical intent of Paul and the function of the narration. This article has argued that Gal. 1.10 belongs to the *narratio* and that 1.10–2.21 coheres as a rhetorical unit. Thus, the narration functions primarily to portray Paul as a pleaser of God rather than people. This claim is grounded in the divine origin of the gospel and demonstrated in Paul's actions and ultimately in his likeness to Christ. Paul seeks to assert his ethos as one who embodies Christ—the one of whom God said, 'in him I am well-pleased' (Mt. 3.17). In all this, Paul aims to refute a false narrative or notion about himself by which the Galatians are being led astray, to dissuade them from embracing the adulterated gospel advocated by the agitators.

113. Cf. Col. 1.24.
114. See n. 5 above.

[*JGRChJ* 19 (2023) 128-60]

The Expansion of Associations and Christianity in the Book of Acts: A Comparative Study

John D. Doss[*]

Asbury Theological Seminary, Wilmore, KY

Introduction

Greco-Roman Associations

John S. Kloppenborg relates the story of how Edwin Hatch, relying on the pioneering work of Georg Henrici and Paul Foucart, posited in the 1880 Oxford Bampton Lectures that Paul modeled his churches on Greco-Roman associations. Hatch's thesis was widely rejected and basically forgotten for almost a century until Robert L. Wilken and Abraham J. Malherbe began to revive it.[1] Over the last thirty years, Kloppenborg and his students—Richard S. Ascough and Philip A. Harland, for example—have become leading scholars of Greco-Roman associations in the English-speaking world.[2] A sizable

---

[*]   My gratitude goes to Craig S. Keener for reading this paper and providing his feedback, most of which I have tried to incorporate.

1.   Cf. John S. Kloppenborg, 'Edwin Hatch, Churches and Collegia', in Bradley H. McLean (ed.), *Origins and Method: Towards a New Understanding of Judaism and Christianity* (JSNTSup, 86; Sheffield: JSOT Press, 1993), pp. 212-24. Cf. also Richard S. Ascough, *What Are They Saying about the Formation of Pauline Churches?* (New York: Paulist Press, 1998), pp. 79-93; H.C.G. Matthew, 'Hatch, Edwin (1835–89), Theologian' (September 2004), see online: https://doi.org/10.1093/ref:odnb/12589.

2.   Their work includes, but is certainly not limited to, a projected five-volume translation and commentary of hundreds of inscriptions and papyri on Greco-Roman associations arranged geographically, of which three have been published. Cf. John S. Kloppenborg and Richard S. Ascough (eds.), *Greco-Roman Associations: Texts, Translations, and Commentary: I. Attica, Central Greece, Macedonia, Thrace*

amount of literature on associations has been generated,[3] and many New Testament scholars who were initially critical now agree that they are crucial for understanding early Christianity.[4]

Providing a definition is not easy, given the wide array of organizational structures and nomenclature found among associations in antiquity.[5] Nevertheless, Sandra Walker-Ramisch helpfully describes voluntary associations as follows:

> A voluntary association might be defined as *an organized association of persons who come together on a voluntary, contractual basis* (rather than kinship, caste, national, or geographic association) *in the pursuit of common interests, both manifest and latent. To the association each*

(BZNW, 181; Berlin: de Gruyter, 2011); Philip A. Harland (ed.), *Greco-Roman Associations: Texts, Translations, and Commentary: II. North Coast of the Black Sea, Asia Minor* (BZNW, 204; Berlin: de Gruyter, 2014); John S. Kloppenborg (ed.), *Greco-Roman Associations: Texts, Translations, and Commentary: III. Ptolemaic and Early Roman Egypt* (BZNW, 246; Berlin: de Gruyter, 2020).

3. See the annotated bibliography in Richard S. Ascough, Philip A. Harland and John S. Kloppenborg, *Associations in the Greco-Roman World: A Sourcebook* (Waco, TX: Baylor University Press, 2012), pp. 277-359.

4. One of the most conspicuous examples is that of Meeks, who initially rejected associations as a model for the Christian ἐκκλησία but later retracted this view. Cf. Wayne A. Meeks, *The First Urban Christians: The Social World of the Apostle Paul* (New Haven: Yale University Press, 1983), pp. 75-84; cf. Wayne A. Meeks, 'Taking Stock and Moving On,' in Todd D. Still and David G. Horrell (eds.), *After the First Urban Christians: The Social-Scientific Study of Pauline Christianity Twenty-Five Years Later* (London: T. & T. Clark, 2009), pp. 134-46.

5. E.g. ἔρανος/ἐρανισταί, αἵρεσις, ἑταῖροι, ὁμότεχνον, κοινά/κοινόν, κοινωνία, κολλέγιον, μελανηφόροι, ὀργεῶνες, φυλή, πλατεῖα, πλῆθος, πολίτευμα, προεδρία, σπεῖρα, σύλλογος, συμβίωσις, συναγωγή, συνέδριον, συνεργασία/ἐργασία, συνέργιον, συνήθεια, συγγένεια, σύνοδος, συντεχνία, συντέλεια, σύστημα, τάξις, τέχνη and θίασος/θιασῶται in Greek; *coetus, collegium, conventus, corporati, corpus, curia, doumos, factio, familia, phratra/phratria/phratores* and *secta* in Latin. Cf. John S. Kloppenborg, *Christ's Associations: Connecting and Belonging in the Ancient City* (New Haven: Yale University Press, 2019), p. 33; Ascough, Harland and Kloppenborg, *Associations in the Greco-Roman World*, pp. 374-75; Ralph J. Korner, *The Origin and Meaning of Ekklēsia in the Early Jesus Movement* (AGJU, 98; Leiden: Brill, 2017), p. 52 n. 129.

> member contributes, by contractual agreement, a part of his/her time
> and resources.[6]

Associations were thus voluntary and private, not state-mandated or demanding exclusive allegiance. They were local and formally organized to meet certain needs of adherents, such as meaningful and profitable social interaction, shared interests, religious devotion, public service and recognition, identity and a proper burial.[7] While several taxonomies have been proposed for the numerous kinds of Greco-Roman associations, Kloppenborg's fivefold categorization around common ethnicity, religious affiliation, vocation, address and family has replaced more traditional efforts at categorization.[8] These are

6.   Sandra Walker-Ramisch, 'Graeco-Roman Voluntary Associations and the Damascus Document: A Sociological Analysis', in John S. Kloppenborg and Stephen G. Wilson (eds.), *Voluntary Associations in the Graeco-Roman World* (London: Routledge, 1996), pp. 128-45 (131) (emphasis in original). Cf. also Richard S. Ascough, 'Voluntary Associations and the Formation of Pauline Christian Communities: Overcoming the Objections', in Andreas Gutsfeld and Dietrich-Alex Koch (eds.), *Vereine, Synagogen und Gemeinden im kaiserzeitlichen Kleinasien* (Studien und Texte zu Antike und Christentum, 25; Tübingen: Mohr Siebeck, 2006), p. 151 n. 9; Ascough, *What Are They Saying*, pp. 74-78.

7.   Cf. Stephen G. Wilson, 'Voluntary Associations: An Overview', in John S. Kloppenborg and Stephen G. Wilson (eds.) *Voluntary Associations in the Graeco-Roman World* (London: Routledge, 1996), pp. 7-14; Eckhard J. Schnabel, *Early Christian Mission: Jesus and the Twelve* (2 vols.; Downers Grove, IL: IVP Academic, 2004), I, pp. 648-50.

8.   I.e. (1) Diasporic or immigrant associations; (2) Cultic associations; (3) Occupational guilds; (4) Neighborhood associations; and (5) *Collegia domestica*. Cf. Kloppenborg, *Christ's Associations*, pp. 24-40. Cf. also Kloppenborg (ed.), *Greco-Roman Associations*, pp. 574-84. This is very similar to Harland's five categories of (1) Household, (2) Ethnic, (3) Neighborhood, (4) Occupational and (5) Cult or temple connections. Cf. Philip A. Harland, *Associations, Synagogues, and Congregations: Claiming a Place in Ancient Mediterranean Society* (Minneapolis: Fortress Press, 2003), pp. 29-53. This replaced the traditional, threefold taxonomy of (1) Occupational, (2) Cultic and (3) Burial associations. In Marcus Tod's 1931 lectures at the University of London, given at a time when he claimed there was no comprehensive work on ancient associations in English, he made the oft-repeated mistake of likening guilds to modern trade unions and categorized associations according to the names of their (1) Gods, (2) Founders and (3) Location. Cf. Marcus N. Tod, *Ancient Inscriptions: Sidelights on Greek History: Three Lectures on the Light Thrown by Greek In-*

flexible and often overlapping categories. From their legendary origins under King Numa (715–673 BCE),[9] Greco-Roman associations exploded across the Mediterranean from the fifth century BCE to the fourth century CE.[10] Kloppenborg notes that Poland lists 1,200 associations and Waltzing 2,500 *collegia*, while Robert S.J. Garland's study of Piraeus identified over fifty cultic associations in the Athenian port alone between the fifth and the first centuries BCE.[11] Peter Richardson notes that on Delos, the smallest island of the Cyclades, twenty-four different associations have been identified.[12] The size of each association varied considerably, from fifteen to two or three hundred, yet most of them had less than a hundred members.[13]

Associations and the Book of Acts
Among the growing literature on associations and early Christianity, several studies have focused specifically on the book of Acts. Markus Öhler provides a fascinating comparative study of ancient associations and the *Jerusalemer Urgemeinde*.[14] Ascough uses the lens of ancient associations to interpret the accounts of Ananias and Saphira (5.1-11) as well as the Jerusalem Council (15.1-35).[15] Justin K. Hardin argues that the judicial episode in Thessalonica

scriptions on the Life and Thought of the Ancient World (Chicago: Ares, 1974), pp. 71-93.

9. See Plutarch, *Num.* 17.1-3.

10. See Ascough, Harland and Kloppenborg, *Associations in the Greco-Roman World*, pp. 252-53.

11. Robert Garland, *The Piraeus from the Fifth to the First Century BC* (London: Duckworth, 2nd edn, 2001), pp. 101-38; cf. John S. Kloppenborg, 'Collegia and Thiasoi: Issues in Function, Taxonomy, and Membership', in John S. Kloppenborg and Stephen G. Wilson (eds.), *Voluntary Associations in the Graeco-Roman World* (London: Routledge, 1996), pp. 16-30 (23); Kloppenborg, *Christ's Associations*, p. 29.

12. Peter Richardson, 'Building "an Association (Synodos) ... and a Place of their Own"', in Richard N. Longenecker (ed.), *Community Formation in the Early Church and the Church Today* (Peabody, MA: Hendrickson, 2002), pp. 36-56 (46).

13. Kloppenborg, 'Collegia and *Thiasoi*', pp. 25-26; Kloppenborg, *Christ's Associations*, pp. 106-30.

14. Markus Öhler, 'Die Jerusalemer Urgemeinde im Spiegel des antiken Vereinswesens', *NTS* 51 (2005), pp. 393-415.

15. Richard S. Ascough, 'Benefaction Gone Wrong: The "Sin" of Ananias and Sapphira in Context', in Stephen G. Wilson and Michel Desjardins (eds.), *Text and*

(17.6-9) is best understood as relating to imperial policy concerning illegal associations.[16] Finally, Dirk Schinkel posits that the illegal ἐκκλησία in the Ephesian theater (19.23-40) was dissolved by the γραμματεύς of the local silversmith *Verein*, not the civic official.[17] Hence, association research has forged exciting new avenues for Acts studies as well as of the New Testament in general.

The book of Acts, as Keener explains, is an ancient historiography of the expansion of Christianity from its origins in Jerusalem to Rome, the capital of the ancient world.[18] The narrative represents the transition of the new faith from a Jewish 'sect' (αἵρεσις, cf. Acts 24.5, 14; 28.22) to what Martin D. Goodman calls a 'universal, proselytizing mission'.[19] The purpose of this paper is to compare Luke's account of the growth of Christianity in Acts with that of other ancient associations. Part I demonstrates that early Christianity primarily understood itself and was understood by outsiders as an association. Part II surveys the epigraphic and archaeological data on how associations grew. This leads to the third and final part, namely, the expansion of Christianity in Acts as compared with that of other associations. The crucial role of social networks, influential converts, patronage, the marginalized and divine guidance in the growth of ancient associations is also reflected in the expansion of early Christianity as reported in the book of Acts.

Artifact in the Religions of Mediterranean Antiquity: Essays in Honour of Peter Richardson (ESCJ, 9; Waterloo, ON: Wilfrid Laurier University Press, 2000), pp. 91-110; Richard S. Ascough, 'The Apostolic Decree of Acts and Greco-Roman Associations: Eating in the Shadow of the Roman Empire', in Markus Öhler (ed.) *Aposteldekret und antikes Vereinswesen: Gemeinschaft und ihre Ordnung* (WUNT, 280; Tübingen: Mohr Siebeck, 2011), pp. 297-316.

16. Justin K. Hardin, 'Decrees and Drachmas at Thessalonica: Illegal Assembly in Jason's House (Acts 17.1-10a)', *NTS* 52 (2006), pp. 29-49.

17. Dirk Schinkel, 'Kanzler oder Schriftführer? Apg 19,23-40 und das Amt des γραμματεύς in griechisch-römischen Vereinigungen', in David C. Bienert, Joachim Jeska and Thomas Witulski (eds.), *Paulus und die antike Welt: Beiträge zur zeit- und religionsgeschichtlichen Erforschung des paulinischen Christentums* (FRLANT, 222; Göttingen: Vandenhoeck & Ruprecht, 2008), pp. 136-49.

18. Craig S. Keener, *Acts: An Exegetical Commentary* (4 vols.; Grand Rapids: Baker Academic, 2012–2015), I, pp. 90-115.

19. Martin D. Goodman, *Mission and Conversion: Proselytizing in the Religious History of the Roman Empire* (Oxford: Clarendon, 1994), p. 7.

I. *Christianity as an Association*

I present four reasons why Greco-Roman associations were the primary organizational model for early Christian churches. First and secondly, both outsiders and insiders understood Christianity as an association. Thirdly, associations were the primary influence on the development of the Jewish synagogue from which Christianity emerged. Finally, the shared terminology between Christians and associations suggests that the former defined themselves in terms of the latter.

Outsiders Understood Christianity as an Association

What is striking about the earliest Roman sources concerning Christianity is
the similar terminology used to describe the new sect. The first mention of
Christians in extant Latin literature is found in Pliny the Younger's correspondence with Trajan (112 CE). The procurator of Bithynia and Pontus con-
sulted Caesar's council as to how to deal with those who currently or formerly
identified as Christians. Pliny repeatedly refers to Christianity as a *superstitio*
which, like a disease, has 'infected through contact … a great many individuals of every age and class, both men and women'.[20] He groups Christianity
together with other new *collegia*, which Trajan had earlier prohibited Pliny
from tolerating.[21]

Also writing at the outset of the second century, Tacitus and Suetonius use
the term *superstitio* to refer to Christianity. Both accounts concern the same
incident of the Great Fire of Rome (64 CE), which Nero blamed on the Christians, lethally persecuting them. Suetonius refers to Christians as 'a class of
men given over to a new and mischievous superstition'.[22] Tacitus is even

---

20. Pliny the Younger, *Ep. Tra.* 10.96 (Radice, LCL).

21. 'But they [i.e. the Christians] had in fact given up this practice since my
edict, issued on your instructions, which banned all political societies' (*Ep. Tra.*
10.96 [Radice, LCL]). The edict refers to Trajan's refusal to grant Pliny's request for
a 'company of firemen' (*collegium fabrorum*) in 10.33, responding in 10.34 (Radice,
LCL), 'You may very well have had the idea that it should be possible to form a company of firemen [*collegium fabrorum*] at Nicomedia on the model of those existing
elsewhere, but we must remember that it is societies [*factionibus*] like these which
have been responsible for the political disturbances in your province, particularly in
its towns. If people assemble for a common purpose, whatever name we give them
and for whatever reason, they soon turn into a political club [*hetaeria*].'

22. Suetonius, *Nero* 16.2 (Rolfe, LCL).

more critical, referring to the faith as a 'pernicious superstition' and a 'horrible or shameful ... disease'.[23]

Wilken elaborates on the significance of all three of the earliest Latin sources referring to Christianity using the same term. He writes,

> On the lips of an educated Roman or Greek the term *superstitio* had many connotations. Most frequently it designated religious groups or practices foreign to the Romans, e.g., Jews, devotees of Isis, et al. Such religions were thought to be fanatical—Jews refusing to fight on the sabbath—and exotic, irrational, and incompatible with Roman ideals or simply at variance with established religious rites and ceremonies. Superstition was at odds with genuine religion.[24]

The reference to Jews not fighting on the Sabbath is to Plutarch's description of the Delphic priest grouping Judaism together with other ancient religions that have a negative effect on their adherents (cf. Plutarch, *Superst.* 8). Likewise, Cicero clearly distinguished between *superstitio* and *religio*, noting that the latter deserves approval while the former deserves censure (cf. *Nat. d.* 2.72). Hence, from the outset, the Romans classified Christianity together with other foreign, eastern religions. Thus, they were viewed as new associations or *collegia* that were not to be tolerated per imperial decree.[25]

---

23.   Tacitus, *Ann.* 15.44 (Jackson, LCL). Ascough also cites the example of Severus, *Hist. Aug.* 49 (cf. 'Voluntary Associations', p. 151).

24.   Robert L. Wilken, 'Collegia, Philosophical Schools, and Theology', in Stephen Benko and John J. O'Rourke (eds.), *The Catacombs and the Colosseum: The Roman Empire as the Setting of Primitive Christianity* (Valley Forge, PA: Judson, 1971), pp. 268-91 (271). Cf. Kloppenborg, *Christ's Associations*, pp. 15-16, 328-29; Kim D. Bowes, *Private Worship, Public Values, and Religious Change in Late Antiquity* (Cambridge: Cambridge University Press, 2008), pp. 44-48; E.A. Judge, *The First Christians in the Roman World: Augustan and New Testament Essays* (ed. James R. Harrison; WUNT, 229; Tübingen: Mohr Siebeck, 2008), p. 599; Harland, *Associations, Synagogues, and Congregations*, pp. 211-12.

25.   For a helpful overview of the history and complicated relationship between Rome and associations, see Wendy Cotter, 'The Collegia and Roman Law: State Restrictions on Voluntary Associations, 64 BCE–200 CE', in John S. Kloppenborg and Stephen G. Wilson (eds.), *Voluntary Associations in the Graeco-Roman World*, (London: Routledge, 1996), pp. 74-89; cf. Harland, *Greco-Roman Associations II*, pp. 161-73; Markus Öhler, 'Römisches Vereinsrecht und christliche Gemeinden', in Michael Labahn and Jürgen Zangenberg (eds.), *Zwischen den Reichen: Neues*

Early Christians Understood Themselves as an Association

The Roman stance towards early Christianity is crucial for understanding the way the church fathers described their faith. Tertullian's *Apology* is one of the most conspicuous examples that Christians understood themselves as an association. He asks, 'Should not this school [*secta*] have been classed among tolerated associations [*factiones*]?'[26] In light of the imperial ban on associations due to their perceived danger to public order, Tertullian devotes this chapter to emphasizing the peaceful and non-threatening nature of the Christian religion.

The description of Christianity as an association continues in *Apol.* 39, even as it opens with, 'I will now show you the proceedings with which the Christian association (*factio*) occupies itself.'[27] Tertullian begins with the Christian assembly (*congregatio*), order (*disciplina*) and leadership (*seniores*), key components of any association.[28] He then moves on to the 'treasury' (*arca*), explaining how it differs from that of other associations. That is, instead of mandatory entrance fees, Christians take up a voluntary offering. Instead of spending the money 'on feasts, and drinking-bouts, and eating-houses' as the associations do, 'God's school' (*dei sectae*) spends their collection on the poor.[29]

Testament und römische Herrschaft. Vorträge auf der Ersten Konferenz der Euro-pean Association for Biblical Studies (TANZ, 36; Tübingen: Francke Verlag, 2002), pp. 51-71; Ascough, 'Apostolic Decree', pp. 299-306; Keener, *Acts*, I, pp. 450-51. For a survey of primary sources concerning imperial policy towards associations, see Ascough, Harland and Kloppenborg, *Associations in the Greco-Roman World*, pp. 252-75.

26. Tertullian, *Apol.* 38.1 (Glover and Rendall, LCL).

27. Tertullian, *Apol.* 39.1 (Glover and Rendall, LCL).

28. Markus Öhler, 'Iobakchen und Christusverehrer: Das Christentum im Rahmen des antiken Vereinswesens', in Rupert Klieber and Martin Stowasser (eds.), *Inkulturation: historische Beispiele und theologische Reflexionen zur Flexibilität und Widerständigkeit des Christlichen* (Theologie: Forschung und Wissenschaft, 10; Vienna: LIT, 2006), pp. 63-86; Luke Timothy Johnson, *Among the Gentiles: Greco-Roman Religion and Christianity* (AYBRL; New Haven: Yale University Press, 2009), pp. 138-40.

29. Tertullian, *Apol.* 39.6 (ANF 3/46; Glover and Rendall, LCL). For finances in associations as they relate to early Christian churches, see the section below on 'Benefaction and Financial Support'; cf. also Eva Ebel, *Die Attraktivität früher*

The third and lengthiest section of *Apol.* 39 is devoted to the Christian 'dinner' (*coena*) called *agape* in 'the three-bench dining room (*triclinium*)'.[30] Udo Schnelle observes, 'Just as social life in Roman-Hellenistic antiquity took place in associations and reached its high point and central focus in communal meals, communal life among Christians was structured around the communal meal.'[31] Tertullian concludes where he started, by asking once again what reason there is to equate Christianity with 'like assemblies of the illicit sort',[32] when indeed it differs completely from them. It is worth noting that even though Justin Martyr does not refer to churches as associations, his description of Christian worship in *1 Apol.* 67 is remarkably similar to Tertullian's.

Origen's *Contra Celsum* is another primary example that early Christianity understood itself and was understood by others as an association. Indeed, the lengthy apology opens with a response to Celsus's accusation that 'the Christians secretly make associations [συνθῆκαι] with one another contrary to

christlicher Gemeinden: Die Gemeinde von Korinth im Spiegel griechisch-römischer Vereine (WUNT, 178; Tübingen: Mohr Siebeck, 2004), pp. 63-64.

30. Tertullian, *Apol.* 39.15-16 (Ascough, Harland and Kloppenborg, *Associations in the Greco-Roman World*, p. 250). For more on the *triclinium* in early Christian worship, see L. Michael White, *The Social Origins of Christian Architecture* (2 vols.; HTS, 42; Valley Forge, PA: Trinity Press, 1996), I, pp. 107-10, 119-22.

31. Udo Schnelle, *The First One Hundred Years of Christianity: An Introduction to Its History, Literature, and Development* (trans. James W. Thompson; Grand Rapids: Baker Academic, 2020), pp. 245-46; cf. Kloppenborg, *Christ's Associations*, pp. 209-44. First Corinthians has received more attention from scholars of Greco-Roman associations than any other New Testament book, especially the meal instructions (11.17-32) (see Richard Last, *The Pauline Church and the Corinthian Ekklēsia: Greco-Roman Associations in Comparative Context* (SNTSMS, 164; New York: Cambridge University Press, 2016); Dace Balode, *Gottesdienst in Korinth* (Greifswalder Theologische Forschungen, 21; Frankfurt am Main: Lang, 2011), pp. 21-98; Matthias Klinghardt, *Gemeinschaftsmahl und Mahlgemeinschaft: Soziologie und Liturgie frühchristlicher Mahlfeiern* (TANZ, 13; Tübingen: Francke Verlag, 1996); Ebel, *Attraktivität*, pp. 151-213; Stephen J. Chester, *Conversion at Corinth: Perspectives on Conversion in Paul's Theology and the Corinthian Church* (London: T. & T. Clark, 2005), pp. 245-52.

32. ANF 3/47.

the laws.'[33] Like Tertullian, Origen must also respond to the accusation that Christians are a secret association posing a threat to the *Pax Romana*. His response is that even though forming new associations may be illegal in Rome's eyes, it is necessary according to 'the true law' of God: 'Therefore, it is not wrong to form associations [συνθῆκαι] against the laws for the sake of truth.'[34] Hence, Origen openly admits that Christianity is an association, even of the kind prohibited by imperial policy. The magisterial apology contains multiple passages in which Christianity is referred to using association terminology, whether by Origen himself or in his citations of Celsus.[35]

Finally, Eusebius concludes the opening praise of his tenth book concerning God's triumph over his enemies by the 'heavenly light' that 'shone down upon the churches of Christ throughout the whole world', as well as 'even [to] those outside our society [θίασος]'.[36] Hence, the writings of the early church fathers are compelling evidence that Christianity was primarily understood by both insiders and outsiders as an association.[37]

Synagogues as Associations
The third reason why associations were the primary model of early Christianity is that they were also the predominant social institution responsible for the formation of the Jewish synagogue. Much research has been conducted on synagogues as associations.[38] Richardson surveys the literary, archaeological and epigraphic evidence around the Mediterranean indicating that, in their terminology, structure, functions and architecture, 'synagogues looked and

33. Origen, *Cels.* 1.1 (Henry Chadwick [trans.], *Origen: Contra Celsum* [Cambridge: Cambridge University Press, rev. edn, 1980], p. 7). Chadwick uses italics to indicate the passages in which Origen is believed to be quoting Celsus.

34. Origen, *Cels.* 1.1 (Chadwick).

35. Cf. Origen, *Cels.* 1.1, 7, 9, 11, 62, 64, 69; 3.12, 13, 23, 29, 30, 81; 4.79, 89, 97; 6.24, 34, 53; 8.15-17, 20, 47.

36. Eusebius, *Hist. eccl.* 10.1.7 (οὐδέ τις ἦν καὶ τοῖς ἔξωθεν τοῦ καθ' ἡμᾶς θιάσου φθόνος συναπολαύειν; Oulton, LCL).

37. Cf. Kloppenborg, *Christ's Associations*, pp. 4-19; Ascough, *What Are They Saying*, pp. 95-99.

38. Cf. Harland, *Associations, Synagogues, and Congregations*, pp. 177-228; Klinghardt, *Gemeinschaftsmahl*, pp. 175-267.

behaved like voluntary associations.'[39] In his exhaustive study *The Origins of the Synagogue*, Anders Runesson concludes that synagogue and 'synagogue terms were used for two basic types of institution: public city/town/village assemblies and (semi-public) voluntary associations.'[40] The latter were various 'denominations' of Judaism, which emerged in the Hellenistic period and used the former as a kind of forum to put forth their views and gain adherents.[41] It is in this context that Christianity emerged among other Jewish denominations. Runesson notes, 'with Jesus and his earliest followers, we witness the birth of a new voluntary association, gathering around one teacher and his message.'[42]

Besides the denominations of the Pharisees, Sadducees, Essenes and the early Jesus movement, associations also had a profound influence on Jewish sects. Moshe Weinfeld's study of Greco-Roman voluntary associations and the Qumran sect shows the remarkable degree of overlap between the two.[43] Runesson agrees, using Matthias Klinghardt's study to conclude that 1QS is

39.   Richardson, 'Building an Association', p. 54; cf. Peter Richardson, *Building Jewish in the Roman East* (Supplement to the Journal for the Study of Judaism; Waco, TX: Baylor University Press, 2004); Peter Richardson, 'Early Synagogues as Collegia in the Diaspora and Palestine', in John S. Kloppenborg and Stephen G. Wilson (eds.), *Voluntary Associations in the Graeco-Roman World* (London: Routledge, 1996), pp. 90-109; Peter Richardson and Valerie Heuchan, 'Jewish Voluntary Associations in Egypt and the Roles of Women', in John S. Kloppenborg and Stephen G. Wilson (eds.), *Voluntary Associations in the Graeco-Roman World* (London: Routledge, 1996), pp. 226-51.

40.   Anders Runesson, *The Origins of the Synagogue: A Socio-Historical Study* (ConBNT, 37; Stockholm: Almqvist and Wiksell, 2001), p. 395. Korner agrees with Runesson and uses his twofold definition of the synagogue as the basis for his study of ἐκκλησία in Jewish sources (cf. *Origin and Meaning*, p. 85).

41.   Cf. Runesson, *Origins of the Synagogue*, pp. 398-400; cf. the helpful *Forschungsgeschichte* on synagogue research in Anders Runesson, Donald D. Binder and Birger Olsson, *The Ancient Synagogue from its Origins to 200 C.E.: A Source Book* (AGJU, 72; Leiden: Brill, 2008), pp. 1-19.

42.   Runesson, *Origins of the Synagogue*, p. 483.

43.   Cf. Moshe Weinfeld, *The Organizational Pattern and the Penal Code of the Qumran Sect: A Comparison with Guilds and Religious Associations of the Hellenistic-Roman Period* (NTOA, 2; Göttingen: Vandenhoeck & Ruprecht, 1986).

'a statute of a Hellenistic voluntary association'.[44] He ends his study declaring, concerning Judaism and Christianity, that 'the conclusion must be that the Graeco-Roman voluntary association, as an institutional type, rather than the public "synagogue", was the birthplace of two world-religions.'[45] The book of Acts also bears witness to this historical development.[46]

Shared Terminology between Christianity and Associations
Familial and Leadership Terminology. In his earlier work, one of Meeks's principal critiques against viewing Christian churches as associations was 'the almost complete absence of common terminology for the groups themselves or for their leaders'.[47] However, this has since been amply rebutted since the shared terminology between Christianity and associations is now rather compelling.[48] The crucial term ἐκκλησία will be discussed last on account of the contested issue of its use in Greco-Roman associations. The book of Acts bears record that both Christians and Jews commonly referred to one another as 'brother' (ἀδελφός).[49] Likewise, the epigraphic evidence

44. Runesson, *Origins of the Synagogue*, p. 371 (cf. pp. 331-37); see also Matthias Klinghardt, 'The Manual of Discipline in the Light of Statutes of Hellenistic Associations', in Michael O. Wise et al. (eds.), *Methods of Investigation of the Dead Sea Scrolls and the Khirbet Qumran Site: Present Realities and Future Prospects* (Annals of the New York Academy of Sciences, 722; New York: New York Academy of Sciences, 1998), pp. 251-67.
45. Runesson, *Origins of the Synagogue*, p. 488.
46. Acts 6.8-10; 9.2, 20-21; 13.5, 13-47; 14.1; 17.1-3, 10-11, 17; 18.4-6, 19-20, 26; 19.8; 22.19; 26.11; cf. Runesson, *Origins of the Synagogue*, p. 483 and Markus Öhler, 'Antikes Vereinswesen', in Kurt Erlemann et al. (eds.), *Neues Testament und Antike Kultur: Band 2. Familie, Gesellschaft, Wirtschaft* (Neukirchen-Vluyn: Neukirchener Verlag, 2004), pp. 83-85.
47. Meeks, *First Urban Christians*, p. 79.
48. See Richard S. Ascough, 'Redescribing the Thessalonians' Mission in Light of Graeco-Roman Associations', *NTS* 60 (2014), pp. 61-82 (66); cf. Ascough, *What Are They Saying*, pp. 86-89; Philip A. Harland, *Dynamics of Identity in the World of the Early Christians: Associations, Judeans, and Cultural Minorities* (New York: T. & T. Clark, 2009), pp. 64-67, 158-59; Kloppenborg, 'Edwin Hatch', pp. 222-24.
49. Acts 1.14, 16; 2.29, 37; 3.17, 22; 6.3; 7.2, 23, 25, 26, 37; 9.17, 30; 10.23; 11.1, 12, 29; 12.17; 13.15, 26, 38; 14.2; 15.1, 3, 7, 13, 22, 23, 32, 33, 36, 40; 16.2, 40; 17.6, 10, 14; 18.18, 27; 20.32; 21.7, 17, 20; 22.1, 5, 13; 23.1, 5, 6; 28.14, 15, 17, 21; cf. Öhler, 'Jerusalemer Urgemeinde', pp. 399-401.

demonstrates the prominence of familial terminology among members of associations.[50] Also, one of the most prolific self-designations for associations is τὸ κοινόν, which is attested in numerous inscriptions.[51] Öhler explains that Luke's description of the *Urgemeinde* having 'all things common' (εἶχον ἄπαντα κοινά) in Acts 2.44 and 4.32 intentionally calls to mind the Aristotelian *Freundschaftsideal* toward which the Pythagoreans, Epicureans and other Greek philosophical associations strove.[52] Keener also observes that Luke's original audience would have not only thought of associations when they read the initial description of the church's fellowship (κοινωνία), sharing of meals and possessions (2.42-47), but also understood the church as a fulfillment of Hellenistic friendship and community ideals.[53]

Leadership terminology within Christian churches, borrowed from Judaism, was also common among Greco-Roman associations. It is important to understand that there is no standard leadership structure or common nomenclature between the vast array of different associations in antiquity.[54] The central church leadership office in the New Testament is the 'elder' (πρεσβύτερος) or 'overseer' (ἐπίσκοπος).[55] Ascough discusses several examples of associations using ἐπίσκοπος to refer to their leaders, though he notes that the title carries no implicit job description.[56] However, ἐπίσκοπος only occurs once in Acts (20.28; cf. 1.20). Instead, the predominant term for

---

50.   E.g. IBosp 104; 1283-1284; ICiliciaBM 201. Cf. Harland, *Greco-Roman Associations II*, pp. 32-39, 415-16; cf. Richard S. Ascough, *Paul's Macedonian Associations: The Social Context of Philippians and 1 Thessalonians* (Eugene, OR: Wipf and Stock, 2020), pp. 76-77; Ascough, 'Voluntary Associations', pp. 160-61; Harland, *Associations, Synagogues, and Congregations*, pp. 31-33.

51.   See (*inter alia*) IG 2.2.1261-1263, 1275, 1277-1278, 1291-1292, 1297-1298, 1314, 1316-1317, 1323, 1325-1327, 1334, 1343, 1368, 2354, 2960. Cf. Kloppenborg, *Greco-Roman Associations III*, pp. 589-90, 650.

52.   Öhler, 'Jerusalemer Urgemeinde', pp. 401-3.

53.   Keener, *Acts*, I, pp. 1000-1023.

54.   Kloppenborg, *Greco-Roman Associations III*, pp. 600-612.

55.   Phil. 1.1; 1 Tim. 3.1-2; 5.1-2, 17, 19; Tit. 1.5, 7; Jas 5.14; 1 Pet. 5.1, 2, 5; 2 Jn 1.1; 3 Jn 1.1.

56.   E.g. IDelos 1522; IG 12.1.49-50, 731; 12.3.329; IGL 1989; 1990; 2298; OGIS 2.611; 2.614. Cf. Ascough, 'Voluntary Associations', pp. 164-65; Ascough, *Paul's Macedonian Associations*, pp. 80-81.

church leaders is πρεσβύτερος, which is used thirteen times.[57] Many associations in Ptolemaic and early Roman Egypt also used πρεσβύτερος as a title for their leaders.[58] The office of deacon is not reported in Acts (though see 6:1-4; 19:22), yet the rest of the New Testament bears ample witness to the διάκονος as a standard leadership role in the early church.[59] Ascough cites numerous inscriptions demonstrating that διάκονος was also a common title used for assistants and functionaries in cultic associations.[60]

Associations as Ἐκκλησίαι? One of the primary self-designations of early Christianity was the 'church' (ἐκκλησία), which occurs twenty times in Acts.[61] Meeks's major reason for once rejecting associations as the primary model of early Christianity is the fact that the former never used ἐκκλησία as a self-designation.[62] Kloppenborg and other scholars refuted this claim, positing five inscriptions as examples of associations using ἐκκλησία to refer to themselves and their gatherings.[63] However, the evidence is not as conclusive as they maintain. In his recent monograph on ἐκκλησία in early Christianity, Ralph J. Korner provides a thorough analysis of the epigraphic

57. Acts 11.30; 14.23; 15.2, 4, 6, 22, 23; 16.4; 20.17; 21.18; 23.14; 24.1; 25.15. The other occurrences of πρεσβύτερος (4.5, 8, 23; 6.12; 23.14; 24.1; 25.15) refer to the elders of the Jews.

58. See IAlexImp. 92; IFayum 2.122; OGIS 2.729; P.Hamb. 1.34; P.Mich. 5.313; PSI 8.901; P.Stras. 5.341; SB 1.996. Cf. Kloppenborg, *Greco-Roman Associations III*, pp. 28-29, 105-7, 229-32, 267-76, 304-7, 315-16, 331-34, 411-12, 609.

59. Rom. 16.1; 1 Cor. 3.5; 2 Cor. 3.6; 6.4; 11.15, 23; Gal. 2.17; Eph. 3.7; 6.21; Phil. 1.1; Col. 1.7, 23, 25; 4.7; 1 Thess. 3.2; 1 Tim. 3.8-13; 4.6.

60. E.g. CIG 1793b; 1800; 3037; IG 4.774; IG 9.1.486; IMagnMai 109, 217; Μουσεῖον 93, 100; RIG 122; cf. Ascough, 'Voluntary Associations,' pp. 165-66; Ascough, *Paul's Macedonian Associations*, pp. 82-83; cf. Kloppenborg's discussion of ἐπίσκοπος and διάκονος in Kloppenborg, 'Edwin Hatch', pp. 231-34.

61. Acts 2.47; 5.11; 8.1, 3; 9.31; 11.22, 26; 12.1, 5; 13.1; 14.23, 27; 15.3, 4, 22, 41; 16.5; 18.22; 20.17, 28.

62. Meeks, *First Urban Christians*, p. 79.

63. I.e. IGLAM 1381-1382; OGIS 2.488; Samos/OGIS 119; CIG 2271. Cf. Ascough, 'Voluntary Associations', p. 159; Richard S. Ascough, 'Greco-Roman Philosophic, Religious, and Voluntary Associations', in Richard N. Longenecker (ed.), *Community Formation in the Early Church and the Church Today* (Peabody, MA: Hendrickson, 2002), pp. 3-19 (14); Harland, *Associations, Synagogues, and Congregations*, pp. 106, 182; Kloppenborg, 'Edwin Hatch', p. 231.

data, concluding, 'there does not appear to be inscriptional attestation of a community of people using *ekklēsia* as a collective designation prior to the first century CE.'[64] He demonstrates that the first three inscriptions (i.e. IGLAM 1381-1382; OGIS 2.488) use the term in its traditional sense of a formal, civic assembly. IDelos 1519 is the only clear example of an association using ἐκκλησία (cf. also *Samos* 119; *Sinuri* 73.8). However, it is used in reference to their meetings and not as a general self-designation.[65]

The closest parallel Korner identifies to the early Christian use of ἐκκλησία is not Greco-Roman associations but Diaspora synagogues. He surveys the usage of the term in the LXX, the Deuterocanonical books of Judith, Sirach and 1 Maccabees, as well as Josephus, Philo and Paul. These books primarily use ἐκκλησία to refer to the civic gatherings of the nation of Israel from the Exodus to the post-exilic period which, unlike the Greek formal assembly, included women and slaves.[66] Intriguingly, he notes that Philo's use of ἐκκλησία—in *Virt.* 108; *Spec.* 1.325; *Deus Imm.* 111—indicates that Alexandrian synagogues used the term both in reference to their non-civic, private, religious gatherings and 'to self-identify collectively as an *ekklēsia hiera*'.[67] Korner spells out the implications for the Christian use of the term:

> If a 1st century CE voluntary association with a *corpus mixtum* of Jews and gentiles, or even one with an exclusively gentile composition, adopted an *ekklēsia* ident ity, its members could have been viewed as being in continuity with a Jewish, and not simply with a Greco-Roman, heritage.[68]

Hence, though Meeks was correct in asserting that ἐκκλησία was not used by Greco-Roman associations, the Christian use of the term reflects its Jewish heritage. In conclusion, there is substantial literary, archeological, and epigraphic evidence to support the claim that early Christianity, in both its Jew-

---

64. Korner, *Origin and Meaning*, p. 68.
65. Korner, *Origin and Meaning*, pp. 53-68.
66. Korner, *Origin and Meaning*, p. 98.
67. Korner, *Origin and Meaning*, p. 148. Origen's wordplay on ἐκκλησία in *Cels.* 3.29-30 is interesting, comparing 'the assemblies of superstitious, licentious, and unrighteous men' in Athens and elsewhere to the 'far superior ... Churches of God in all places' (Chadwick, *Origen*, p. 147).
68. Korner, *Origin and Meaning*, p. 149.

ish origin and its Greco-Roman milieu, understood itself and was understood by others as an association,

II. *The Expansion of Associations*

This part transitions from Christianity as an association to a study of how associations grew. First, I will use Ascough's article on the architectural and epigraphic evidence that demonstrates the impressive growth of many associations.[69] Secondly, two case studies of association growth will be offered in order to identify potential causes.

Epigraphic and Archeological Evidence

There is abundant evidence indicating the expansion of numerous associations across the Roman empire before, during and after Christianity emerged. For instance, the addition of new names on a fourth-century BCE Athenian inscription demonstrates the growth of seven or eight θίασοι over time.[70] Another intriguing example is Dionysodoros of Alexandria (second century BCE), who was the head (ἀρχερανιστάς) of both the club (ἐρανιστάν) of the Haliasts and Haliads for twenty-three years as well as of the κοινόν of Paniasts for eighteen years.[71] Both associations honor their benefactor with a golden crown for having 'increased' the club.[72] Another inscription dating to 147–49 CE in the Italian port city of Misenum suggests that the *collegium* of the Augustales had a waiting list of around a hundred people desirous of membership.[73]

---

69.   Richard S. Ascough, '"A Place to Stand, A Place to Grow": Architectural and Epigraphic Evidence for Expansion in Greco-Roman Associations', in Zeba A. Crook and Philip A. Harland (eds.), *Identity and Interaction in the Ancient Mediterranean: Jews, Christians and Others* (NTM, 18; Sheffield: Sheffield Phoenix, 2007), pp. 76-98.

70.   IG 2.2.2345 (Phaleron [Attica]; c. 365–330 BCE); cf. Ascough, *Early Christ Groups*, p. 83; Kloppenborg and Ascough, *Greco-Roman Associations I*, pp. 17-21.

71.   IG 12.1.155 (Rhodes [Dodecanese]; second century BCE).

72.   Ascough, Harland and Kloppenborg, *Associations in the Greco-Roman World*, pp. 156-59; Ascough, *Early Christ Groups*, pp. 83-84.

73.   Ascough, '"Place to Stand"', p. 94; Ascough, Harland and Kloppenborg, *Associations in the Greco-Roman World*, pp. 226-28.

The membership lists of associations (or *alba*) not only attest to their growth but yield insight into the factors behind it. Ascough notes the rise in membership of a professional association in Ostia evidenced by comparing their *alba*, inscribed between 152 and 213 CE.[74] The increase from 125 to 258 names, many of which are fathers and sons, indicates the crucial role of familial relationships in the expansion of associations. He writes, 'the *paterfamilias* was a key component in the recruitment of new members. Father-son or *dominus-libertus* (*liberti*) connections are the primary means that the group grew.'[75] He also discusses two examples of Mithraist *alba* in Virunum (Nordicum) from the second and third centuries CE that likewise attest to the role 'kin and social networks' played in the secret association's rapid growth.[76]

Next, Ascough considers the impressive expansion of the Dionysian associations, relying on the work of Peter Pilhofer. The German scholar refers to this cult as 'ein andres Volk ohne Tempel', a reference to Judaism.[77] That is, he notes the parallel between Judaism, Christianity and the cult in that the last evolved from a temple-based religion to an international movement of small-groups meeting in homes to worship their σωτήρ, Dionysus. In Thessalonica, three second-century CE inscriptions (IG 9.2.1; 185; 309) attest the existence of numerous Dionysian θίασοι in the city.[78] In Pergamon, excavations of a meeting place of the βυκόλοι ('cowherds') reveal that the building was continually renovated and expanded from 27 BCE to the fourth century CE; this

74. I.e. the *Collegium lenunculariorum tabulariorum auxiliariorum* (*CIL* 14.250-251); cf. Ascough, Harland and Kloppenborg, *Associations in the Greco-Roman World*, pp. 201-2.

75. Ascough, *Early Christian Groups*, p. 92.

76. Ascough, '"Place to Stand"', p. 95; for the rise and fall of Mithraism, see David Walsh, *The Cult of Mithras in Late Antiquity: Development, Decline and Demise ca. A.D. 270–430* (Late Antique Archaeology Supplementary Series, 2; Leiden: Brill, 2018).

77. See Peter Pilhofer, 'Ein andres Volk ohne Tempel: Die θίασοι der Dionysos-Verehrer', in Peter Pilhofer, *Die frühen Christen und ihre Welt: Greifswalder Aufsätze 1996–2001. Mit Beiträgen von Jens Börstinghaus und Eva Ebel* (WUNT, 145; Tübingen: Mohr Siebeck, 2002), pp. 123-38.

78. Pilhofer, *Die frühen Christen*, pp. 128-30; Ascough, *Early Christ Groups*, pp. 85-87.

demonstrates the association's steady growth.[79] The last stop in Asia Minor is the capital city of Ephesus. Ascough discusses two examples, an association of fishmongers dedicated to Isis, as well as what appears to be a private Dionysian cult. The epigraphic and archaeological evidence suggests that both groups experienced numerical growth and financial prosperity during the second century CE.[80]

The final stop on Ascough's tour of the expansion of associations is Dura-Europos, relying on L. Michael White's excellent two-volume study.[81] The Roman garrison on the Syrian frontier was destroyed in 256 CE. The site is invaluable as it contains 'the earliest and most completely known pre-Constantinian church building'.[82] The excavation reports explain that the oldest extant Christian worship facility was originally a private house built around 232–33 CE and renovated as a *Domus Ecclesiae* around 241.[83] It is not clear whether the Christians originally worshipped in the house before renovating it. However, White documents several examples from archaeological excavations of ancient churches in Rome, Carthage, Antioch and Hippo of the transition in the Ante-Nicene era from a house church first, then to a renovated church facility still serving as a domicile, and finally to a church building.[84]

Dura-Europas provides archeological evidence of the way in which ancient associations expanded, including Christianity. There is a synagogue and a Mithraeum on the same street as the Christian building. Much more prominent are the three temples of Adonis, Zeus Theos and of the 'Gaddê' (a Palmyrene temple dedicated to their 'gods' [Gaddê]). All these houses of worship were built and rebuilt, renovated and expanded, throughout the city's history beginning in the third century BCE.[85] White observes,

> A survey of the local religious landscape at Dura-Europos over time indicates that this process of gradual appropriation and adaptation was

79. Pilhofer, *Die frühen Christen*, pp. 130-37; Ascough, *Early Christ Groups*, pp. 85-86.

80. I.e. IEph 20, 1503; cf. Ascough, *Early Christ Groups*, pp. 87-90; Harland, *Greco-Roman Associations II*, pp. 249-60.

81. White, *Social Origins*, I and II.

82. White, *Social Origins*, I, p. 7.

83. White, *Social Origins*, II, pp. 123-35.

84. White, *Social Origins*, I, pp. 102-39.

85. White, *Social Origins*, I, pp. 40-45.

> commonly followed ... In case after case, year after year, these small religious associations adapted private domestic structures for public religious or collegial use.[86]

The financial means for such expensive building projects for these local associations, including Christian churches, came primarily through donations from benefactors. He interprets the graffiti found in the Christian assembly hall and baptistry at Dura-Europas as coming 'from patrons and/or artisans who participated in the renovation and decoration of the building for Christian usage'.[87] He notes the evidence from several other excavations of second-to-fourth-century church buildings in Rome, Istria, Arabia, etc. that demonstrate the same pattern of gradual and continual renovation.[88] He concludes, 'access to property through patronage and donation was perhaps the *sina qua non* for the architectural development from house church to *domus ecclesiae.*'[89] Hence, the financial support of patrons and wealthy members of cultic associations, including Christianity, was crucial to the growth of their facilities and thus the size of their group.

Case Study 1: The Agrippinilla Inscription
The epigraphic data not only affirm the impressive expansion of many associations during the rise of Christianity, but also provide illuminating insights into the causes behind it. Four inscriptions in particular serve as case studies of association growth. The first is the Agrippinilla inscription (IGUR 1.160) in the Roman Campagna (Torre Nova), dated 160–70 CE.[90] The marble base contains a list of 402 names of only those Dionysian μύσται who helped finance the statue, hence the total size of the association must have been larger. The statue honors the high priestess and wife of Marcus Gavius Squilla Gallicanus, founder of the household association around 150 CE, a senator and proconsul of Asia Minor, whose ancestry hails from Lesbos (Mytilene).

In the 'first critical edition of the Agrippinilla inscription', Bradley H. McLean discusses the familial structure of the association: 'the principal

---

86. White, *Social Origins*, I, pp. 43-44.
87. White, *Social Origins*, II, p. 134 n. 12.
88. White, *Social Origins*, I, pp. 111-23; White, *Social Origins*, II, pp. 209-28.
89. White, *Social Origins*, I, p. 146.
90. Ascough, Harland, and Kloppenborg, *Associations in the Greco-Roman World*, pp. 215-16.

functionaries are all members of the senatorial family.'[91] This was common
as 'private *collegia* and *thiasoi* were customarily dependent upon aristocratic
individuals or families who established and financed them.'[92] He observes
that 'eighty percent (323 of 402 names) of the cognomina listed in the inscription are of Greek origin.'[93] This suggests that the association was predomi-
nantly made up of foreigners, those who 'had only recently immigrated from
Lesbos as the slaves and freedmen of the Gallicanus household'.[94] Yet the
names and size of the group indicate that many members came from outside
the household of the *paterfamilias*. Ascough observes that this exemplifies
one of the reasons why certain associations grew, namely, 'the desire of those
outside the family ... to be affiliated with a person of great influence and
power'.[95]

The honorific titles listed next to the names display the unique value of
this artifact, as McLean observes: 'the Agrippinilla inscription encompasses
more titles than any other extant Dionysiac inscription.'[96] He identifies
twenty-two of them, most of which are related to the Bacchic procession.[97]
What is striking about the list is the role of women and slaves in the
collegium, both groups making up about one quarter of the whole.[98] This is
substantial since they were generally worse off financially than others, which
means there were probably many other female and slave initiates not en-
graved. However, even among those listed, McLean discusses the prominent

91. Bradley H. McLean, 'The Agrippinilla Inscription: Religious Associations
and Early Church Formation', in Bradley H. McLean (ed.), *Origins and Method:
Towards a New Understanding of Judaism and Christianity* (JSNTSup, 86; Sheffield:
JSOT Press, 1993), pp. 239-70 (247-48) (the Greek text and critical footnotes are
found on pp. 240-45).
92. McLean, 'Agrippinilla Inscription', p. 249.
93. McLean, 'Agrippinilla Inscription', p. 249.
94. McLean, 'Agrippinilla Inscription', p. 254 (cf. the extensive discussion on
pp. 247-57).
95. Ascough, *Early Christ Groups*, p. 92.
96. McLean, 'Agrippinilla Inscription', p. 258.
97. E.g. basket-bearers (κισταφόροι); god-bearers (θεόφοροι); fire-bearers
(πυρφόροι); holy cowherds (βούκολοι ἱεροί); phallus-bearers (φαλλοφόροι); torch-
bearers (δαδοῦχοι); winnowing-basket bearers (λικναφόροι), etc. (cf. McLean,
'Agrippinilla Inscription', p. 262).
98. McLean, 'Agrippinilla Inscription', pp. 251-52, 262.

roles they played. Women bear numerous titles, including two of the four highest offices (e.g. priestess and δαδοῦχος), not to mention the statue's name-sake, Pompeiia Agrippinilla herself.[99]

Likewise, slaves occupy fifteen of the twenty-two titles, including some of the leadership roles.[100] Hence, the inscription is evidence of an oft-observed principle concerning the attraction of some associations and a cause of their growth, namely, the high sense of kinship and equality initiates enjoyed.[101] McLean observes, 'membership in the association served to relativize social distinctions in an otherwise socially stratified society.'[102] The Agrippinilla inscription is only one of numerous examples of associations, both Greco-Roman and Jewish (i.e. Synagogues), that listed women and slaves as members and honored them as both benefactors and leaders in the group.[103]

Case Study 2: The Cult of Serapis
The cult of Serapis on the island of Delos is often exhibited as a case study for the growth of associations. The 220 BCE inscription recounts the story of the cult's founding told by Apollonius II, grandson of the founder, on a

---

99. McLean, 'Agrippinilla Inscription', pp. 262-63.

100. E.g. ἱεροφάνται (leaders of male and female bacchants [ἀρχιβάσσαροι/αι]); ἀρχινεανίσκοι (youth leaders) (cf. McLean, 'Agrippinilla Inscription', p. 256).

101. John S. Kloppenborg, 'Egalitarianism in the Myth and Rhetoric of Pauline Churches', in Elizabeth A. Castelli and Hal Taussig (eds.), *Reimagining Christian Origins: A Colloquium Honoring Burton L. Mack* (Valley Forge, PA: Trinity Press, 1996), pp. 247-63 (252-60); Thomas Schmeller, *Hierarchie und Egalität: Eine sozialgeschichtliche Untersuchung paulinischer Gemeinden und griechisch-römischer Vereine* (SBS, 162; Stuttgart: Katholisches Bibelwerk, 1995).

102. McLean, 'Agrippinilla Inscription', p. 269.

103. For women, cf. IApamBith 35; IJO 2.36, 43, 168; ISmyrna 653–654; MAMA 6.263; SEG 28.953; TAM 3.4, 62; 5.972 (see Harland, *Greco-Roman Associations II*, pp. 50-54, 95-100, 106-14, 150-56, 223-29, 308-11, 385-90); Kloppenborg, *Greco-Roman Associations III*, p. 681. For slaves, cf. BGU 4.1137; IBosp 69, 1021, 1123; IByzantion 31; IEph 20; *IG* 2.2.1365-1366; ILeukopetra 16; SB 22.15460; SEG 46.800; TAM 5.1539 (see Kloppenborg and Ascough, *Greco-Roman Associations I*, pp. 262-78, 335-39, 400-402); Harland, *Greco-Roman Associations II*, pp. 24-32, 178-93, 249-60; Kloppenborg, *Greco-Roman Associations III*, pp. 65-70, 668.

temple column (IG 11.4; 1299).[104] As Hans-Josef Klauck explains, Apollonius I migrated from Memphis around 280 BCE, 'having brought his own god with him', and began venerating the statue of Serapis in rented rooms.[105] Leadership was passed to his son Demetrius, then to his son Apollonius, and the foreign cult grew steadily.

One night, Serapis instructed Apollonius II in a dream that 'he should no longer be in rented rooms as before' and wanted a temple to dwell in.[106] The priest was also given a sign of a mysterious 'note' by which he would know the predestined location 'where you will build for me a sacred enclosure and a famous temple'.[107] The dream was fulfilled and the temple constructed accordingly. But then opposition came as 'certain individuals conspired against' Apollonius, threatening him with monetary and even corporal punishment.[108] Once again in a dream, Serapis told the weeping priest not to be afraid and said that he would defend him. The column concludes by praising Serapis for his 'miracle on that day' of delivering Apollonius 'by divine power'.[109] By the time Delos came under Roman control (c. 166 BCE), the cult of Serapis had become so prominent on the island that it occupied three temples on the Terrace of the Foreign Gods.[110]

Another similar example is found in Thessalonica in the temple of the Egyptian gods (IG 10.2.1).[111] Although the inscription is dated to the first and second centuries CE, Ascough explains that the original version was com-

---

104. Ascough, Harland, and Kloppenborg, *Associations in the Greco-Roman World*, p. 224.

105. Hans-Josef Klauck, *The Religious Context of Early Christianity: A Guide to Graeco-Roman Religions* (trans. Brian McNeil; Minneapolis: Fortress Press, 2003), pp. 63-64. The English translation of IG 11.4, 1299 quoted here is from B. Hudson McLean, 'The Place of Cult in Voluntary Associations and Christian Churches on Delos', in John S. Kloppenborg and Stephen G. Wilson (eds.), *Voluntary Associations in the Graeco-Roman World* (London: Routledge, 1996), pp. 186-225 (206-8).

106. McLean, 'Place of Cult', p. 206.

107. McLean, 'Place of Cult', p. 207.

108. McLean, 'Place of Cult', p. 206.

109. McLean, 'Place of Cult', p. 208.

110. White explains the irony that resulted from this growth as the patrons of the official cult (Sarapeion C) on Delos eventually attempted to shut down the various private associations of Serapis using Sarapeion A (cf. *Social Origins I*, pp. 32-40).

111. Kloppenborg and Ascough, *Greco-Roman Associations I*, pp. 357-62.

posed in the second and third centuries BCE.[112] As in Delos, Serapis appears to a man named Xenainetos in a dream and also gives him a sign involving a secret note or letter, commanding him to give it to his political rival Eurynomos. Upon waking, Xenainetos finds the miraculous letter and gives it to Eurynomos, who is then converted from his skepticism and founds the cult in the household (οἶκος) of a woman named Sosinikē. Ascough explains that the inscription narrates the humble origins of the cult, which, by that time, had become one of the largest temples of Isis-Serapis in the Greco-Roman world.[113]

The phenomenon of associations being founded by divine oracle was not limited to the cult of Serapis. One of the more intriguing examples is the Dionysian household association in Philadelphia (TAM 5.1539, c. 100 BCE).[114] The inscription explains that Zeus the Σωτήρ appeared to Dionysios to give him instructions for 'common salvation' (κοινῆι σωτηρίαι). He commands Dionysios to establish a place of worship in his οἶκος 'giving access ... to men ... and women, free people and household slaves'.[115] Moreover, Zeus reveals a lengthy set of ethical injunctions adherents are to practice, which mainly center around sexual purity.[116] These are just a few of the many examples of the role of divine oracles in the establishment and leadership of ancient associations.[117] Harland concludes, 'the clear message of such stories, including our own from Philadelphia, seems to be that the gods

---

112. Kloppenborg and Ascough, *Greco-Roman Associations I*, p. 360.

113. Kloppenborg and Ascough, *Greco-Roman Associations I*, p. 361.

114. Harland, *Greco-Roman Associations II*, pp. 178-93; cf. Ascough, Harland, and Kloppenborg, *Associations in the Greco-Roman World*, pp. 82-84; Klauck, *Religious Context*, pp. 64-68; White, *Social Origins I*, p. 45.

115. Harland, *Greco-Roman Associations II*, p. 181.

116. Harland warns against 'a moralizing or Christianizing reading of the rules' (*Greco-Roman Associations II*, p. 189), explaining that they relate primarily to ritual purity and defilement (cf. pp. 189-92). For other examples of associations with various regulations pertaining both to their gatherings as well as the ethical behavior of adherents, cf. IG 2.2.1368-1369; SEG 31.122; Kloppenborg and Ascough, *Greco-Roman Associations I*, pp. 229-57; cf. Weinfeld, *Organizational Pattern*, pp. 46-57.

117. E.g. IG 2.2.1283, 1326, 1365-1366; IG 12.3.329; ImagnMai 215; P.Lips. 2.131; SEG 42.157; Kloppenborg and Ascough, *Greco-Roman Associations I*, pp. 125-32, 179-84, 198-203, 262-78; Harland, *Greco-Roman Associations II*, pp. 344-50; Kloppenborg, *Greco-Roman Associations III*, pp. 257-58, 632, 660.

themselves were personally invested in the activities of the group and that the instructions given should therefore be followed closely and taken serious-ly.'[118] Therefore, many cultic associations preserved narratives promulgating divine guidance over the emergence and expansion of their congregation.

III. *Expansion of the Christ Associations in Acts*

The study of the growth of ancient associations in Part II has led to the identification of several common factors that can be used to study the expansion of early Christianity as recorded in the book of Acts. There are five in particular:

> 1. The role of one's social network in recruiting new members, especially family and household relationships.
> 2. The participation of powerful figures, who exercise great influence and contribute substantially to the association.
> 3. The monetary gifts patrons and especially wealthy members contribute to finance the association (e.g. facilities).
> 4. The opportunities for marginalized groups such as women and slaves in some associations to have access to relationships and leadership opportunities otherwise not available to them.
> 5. The role of divine guidance, or at least the perception thereof, in the origin and growth of the association.

Part three explores the role each of these factors plays in the growth of Christianity as recorded in the book of Acts.

1. Οἶκος *and Social Networks*
Many studies have been conducted on the central importance of the οἶκος in Acts, as it relates both to the physical structure and to the Greco-Roman household. [119] The principal meeting places of the first Christians in Jerusalem were in the temple as well as 'from house to house' (cf. Acts 2.46; 5.42). As the movement expanded, the private home served as the primary

---

118. Harland, *Greco-Roman Associations II*, p. 188.

119. Bradley Blue, 'Acts and the House Church', in David W.J. Gill and Conrad H. Gempf (eds.), *The Book of Acts in Its Graeco-Roman Setting* (BAFCS, 2; Grand Rapids: Eerdmans, 1994), pp. 119-222; Keener, *Acts*, I, pp. 1030-31; Ben Witherington III, *The Acts of the Apostles: A Socio-Rhetorical Commentary* (Grand Rapids: Eerdmans, 1998), p. 211; Bowes, *Private Worship*, pp. 191-96.

meeting place for Christianity's early beginnings, just as was the case with associations.[120] Even in Ephesus, where Paul rented 'the hall of Tyrannus' (19.9), he continued meeting with the people 'from house to house' (20.20).[121] Of course, οἶκος is also used to refer to the household, i.e. one's spouse, children and other dependents living in the house, as well as slaves.[122] Κατὰ τοὺς οἴκους thus not only signifies different domiciles but also refers to the various social networks brought into the Christian fold.

Many scholars have noted the importance of the four household conversions of Cornelius (Acts 10.2, 24, 33; 11.14), Lydia (16.14-15), the Philippian jailer (16.31-34) and Crispus (18.8) in Acts, which represent the progress of Christian expansion.[123] Ascough uses the lens of associations to reinterpret the Thessalonian mission (1 Thess. 1.2-10) as a natural spread of the gospel. This took place locally through the Thessalonians' social networks as well as abroad in their personal and business travels, as they 'went everywhere gossiping the gospel', to use Michael Green's phrase.[124] Eckhard J. Schnabel also identifies the οἰκία (or *familia*) and one's social network as well as the ease of travel to be crucial factors of Christian expansion in the second and third centuries CE.[125]

120. Acts 8.3; 10.22-23; 11.3, 12; 12.12; 16.15, 32, 40; 17.5; 18.7; 20.7-8; 21.8; cf. Schnelle, *First One Hundred Years*, pp. 243-45. White's survey of literary sources concerning early Christian assembly is extraordinary (cf. *Social Origins II*, pp. 33-120).

121. Keener, *Acts*, III, pp. 2827-35.

122. *DNTB*, p. 366; Kloppenborg, *Christ's Associations*, pp. 24-25.

123. David Lertis Matson, *Household Conversion Narratives in Acts: Pattern and Interpretation* (JSNTSup, 123; Sheffield: Sheffield Academic, 1996); Keener, *Acts*, III, p. 2399.

124. Michael Green, *Evangelism in the Early Church* (Grand Rapids: Eerdmans, 1970), p. 173; Ascough, 'Redescribing'. Although Luke focuses on the Peter-Paul parallel as part of his apologetic for the latter, he frequently mentions the role of ordinary laypeople in the expansion of Christianity, whose impact cannot be overstated. Cf. Acts 6.8–7.60; 8.4, 5-40; 9.10-18; 11.19-21; 18.2-3, 24-28. Cf. Keener, *Acts*, II, pp. 1485-87, 1832-44.

125. Schnabel, *Early Christian Mission*, II, pp. 1555-61.

2. *Patrons and Prominent Converts*

Related to households is the importance of powerful figures to lend credibility and recruit members for the new association. The mention of influential people in the young churches in Jerusalem (priests and Pharisees in Acts 6.7; 15.5) and Antioch (Manaen, 13.1) presumes their contribution to the new faith's reputation.[126] The Ethiopian eunuch, as a royal court official (8.27), was another convert of prominent status whom tradition holds to have had great impact in his homeland.[127] Although he was not the first Gentile convert, Cornelius represents the beginning of the Gentile mission in Acts. The retired centurion's influence not only led to the conversion of his οἶκος but also converted 'his relatives and close friends' (10.24).[128] Examples abound throughout the account of Paul, from the conversion of Sergius Paulus, the proconsul of Cyprus, at the outset of his mission (13.7, 12),[129] to Publius, 'the chief man of the island' of Malta (28.7-10) at its conclusion.[130] Other noteworthy examples are Dionysius, a member of the Athenian Areopagus (17.34)[131] as well as at least one ἀρχισυνάγωγος or perhaps two in Corinth (cf. Acts 18.8, 17; 1 Cor. 1.1, 14).[132] Luke's frequent mention of prominent people in Paul's Gentile mission is suggestive of the substantial impact they had on the establishment, credibility and spread of the new faith.

3. *Benefaction and Financial Support*

The conversion of such prominent figures benefitted not only the propagation of early Christianity but also its budget. Christian expansion was financed by wealthy converts who became benefactors in the new movement as was seen in other associations. Indeed, the existence of Luke–Acts itself is most likely the product of Luke's patron, Theophilus (cf. Lk. 1.1-4; Acts 1.1).[133]

---

126. Keener, *Acts*, II, pp. 1291-93, 1988-91.

127. Keener, *Acts*, II, pp. 1550-79, 1595.

128. τοὺς συγγενεῖς αὐτοῦ καὶ τοὺς ἀναγκαίους φίλους (cf. Keener, *Acts*, II, pp. 1742-55).

129. Keener, *Acts*, II, pp. 2014-16.

130. τῷ πρώτῳ τῆς νήσου ὀνόματι Ποπλίῳ (see Keener, *Acts*, IV, pp. 3681-93).

131. Keener, *Acts*, III, pp. 2678.

132. Keener, *Acts*, III, pp. 2748-50, 2778-79.

133. Keener, *Acts*, I, pp. 653-68; Darrell L. Bock, *Acts* (BECNT; Grand Rapids: Baker Academic, 2007), p. 52; Darrell L. Bock, *Luke 1:1–9:50* (BECNT; Grand Rapids: Baker Books, 1994), p. 63.

Keener's study of the Asiarchs, who were Paul's 'friends' (19.31), suggests that they were most likely the apostle's benefactors in Ephesus, supporting the new teacher and perhaps financing the rented hall he taught in (19.9).[134]

Nevertheless, Christian benefaction differed markedly from its Greco-Roman counterpart. As Ascough points out, the hapax legomenon εὐεργέτης ('benefactor') occurs in Lk. 22.25, where the Evangelist adapts Jesus' teaching on servant leadership (Mk 10.41-45) to delineate the Christian antithesis to Hellenistic patronage. Instead of giving to receive honor, the third Gospel emphasizes more than any other the 'service-oriented frame of mind', as Frederick W. Danker puts it, that Christians are to adopt in their generosity.[135] Ascough concludes, 'Luke is attempting to transform the culturally defined pattern of patron-client relationships and benefaction in his community.'[136] This motif continues in Acts, where Luke's portrayal of the early church functions as the realization of Jesus' ethic. Keener writes, 'the sharing of goods in Acts thus may fulfill on a literal level what Jesus demanded in an ideal and hyperbolic manner.'[137]

After the second description of ideal generosity and friendship in the Jerusalem church (cf. Acts 4.32-35), Luke provides two models of Christian benefaction. The first is the positive example of Barnabas, who, like others, was content to lay the proceeds from the sale of his property 'at the apostles' feet' (v. 37).[138] The second (5.1-11) is infamously negative. Ascough writes,

> Set within the larger context of both Luke–Acts and the world of voluntary associations, the story of Ananias and Saphira is a cautionary tale about wanting honours for benefaction, and a warning for those who act according to human conventions rather than divine conventions.[139]

134. τινὲς δὲ καὶ τῶν Ἀσιαρχῶν, ὄντες αὐτῷ φίλοι (see Keener, *Acts*, III, pp. 2908-18). The staggering value of the burned magic books in 19.19 suggests the considerable wealth of several converts in Ephesus (cf. Witherington, *Acts*, p. 582).

135. Frederick W. Danker, *Benefactor: Epigraphic Study of a Graeco-Roman and New Testament Semantic Field* (St. Louis: Clayton, 1982), p. 324; cf. Lk. 3.11; 6.24-25; 12.13-21, 33-34, 43-48; 14.7-24, 33; 16.1-13, 19-31; 18.18-30; 19.8-9.

136. Ascough, 'Benefaction Gone Wrong', p. 105.

137. Keener, *Acts*, I, p. 1022.

138. Keener, *Acts*, II, p. 1178.

139. Ascough, 'Benefaction Gone Wrong', p. 105.

It is worth noting that the church buried Ananias and Saphira (5.6, 10), a crucial service provided by associations.[140]

Another major way in which Christian benefaction differed from its Greco-Roman counterpart was in its concern for the poor. Instead of spending the funds primarily on acquiring and renovating church property, Acts emphasizes the primary focus on the needy.[141] As Keener notes, the early Christian collection for the poor was most likely another result of their Jewish heritage.[142] Kloppenborg's study of Paul's *epidosis* (organized contribution) among the Gentile Christian associations for the poor saints in Jerusalem (cf. Acts 20.4; 21.26; 24.17) is fascinating.[143] Not only was it rare for associations to collect funds for the needy locally, but there is 'no evidence of any *epidosis* organized for the benefit of residents of a city or members of an association other than that of the donors themselves'.[144] Even more unparalleled is the appeal for Greek Christians to organize a collection for their remote, Jewish brethren, members of a different ethnic group. Paul's vision behind this revolutionary act, as articulated in 2 Cor. 8–9, is that it would be a tangible expression of the 'equality' (2 Cor. 8.13-14) and thus the transnational identity and unity of the church of Jesus Christ.[145]

4. *Women and Slaves*

The importance of women in Luke–Acts has been the subject of much study.[146] Among the Gospels, Luke's emphasis on the role of women, in-

---

140. Keener, *Acts*, II, pp.1194-95; Kloppenborg, *Christ's Associations*, pp. 265-77; Ebel, *Attraktivität*, pp. 44-46; Pilhofer, *Die frühen Christen*, pp. 207-8.

141. Acts 2.44-45; 3.2; 4.34-35; 6.1-6; 11.28-30.

142. Keener, *Acts*, II, p. 1178. He notes the striking example of CD 14.13-16, the Essene collection for 'the fatherless ... the poor and the needy, the aged sick and the man who is stricken (with disease), the captive taken by a foreign people, the virgin with no near kin, and the ma[id for] whom no one cares' (Géza Vermès [ed.], *The Complete Dead Sea Scrolls in English* [London: Penguin, rev. edn, 2011], p. 145).

143. Acts 20.4; cf. Rom. 15.31; 1 Cor. 16.1-4; 2 Cor. 8–9.

144. Kloppenborg, *Christ's Associations*, pp. 260-61.

145. Kloppenborg, *Christ's Associations*, pp. 245-64.

146. Ivoni Richter Reimer, *Women in the Acts of the Apostles: A Feminist Liberation Perspective* (trans. Linda M. Maloney; Minneapolis: Fortress Press, 1995); Keener, *Acts*, I, pp. 597-638; Witherington, *Acts*, pp. 334-39.

cluding female benefactors (cf. 8.2-3), is preeminent.[147] The motif continues in Acts as Peter raises a woman from the dead in the Jewish port city of Joppa; she was a 'disciple named Tabitha ... full of good works and acts of charity' (9.36). Keener concludes from 9.39 that she was a 'benefactress of widows', who financially assisted them.[148] Thus, she exemplifies Christian benefaction as one who uses one's own wealth to support the poor without expectation of public honor.[149]

In Thessalonica and Berea, Luke mentions many of 'the leading women' and 'women of high standing' among the new converts to the faith (17.4, 12).[150] The influence these female disciples would have exerted for Christianity is exemplified by the power 'the devout women of high standing' in Pisidian Antioch exercised against it, forcing Paul and Barnabas out of the region (13.50).[151] The mention of Damaris among the Athenian converts (17.34) suggests she was a female philosopher or at least 'a member of the elite'.[152] That two of these texts mention women first before men emphasizes the former's prestige.[153]

Yet the most prominent example of an influential benefactress in Acts is undoubtedly Lydia. The 'seller of purple goods' (16.14) must have been a woman of means since she had her own οἶκος as well as a house large enough to serve as the first Philippian worship space (cf. vv. 14-15, 40).[154] Her willingness to serve as a benefactress is suggested by the hospitality she insisted on offering Paul and his team and Paul's epistle to the Philippians has been posited as further evidence of her patronage (cf. 2.25-30; 4.2, 14-17).[155] There are other women noted in Acts for their spiritual influence even though

---

147. Lk. 1.26-56; 2.19, 36-38, 51; 4.25-26, 38-39; 7.11-13, 36-50; 8.19-21, 40-56; 10.38-42; 13.11-16; 15.8-10; 16.18; 18.2-8; 21.1-4; 23.27-31, 49, 55-56; 24.1-11.

148. Keener, *Acts*, II, p. 1718.

149. Reimer, *Women in the Acts*, pp. 31-69.

150. cf. Keener, *Acts*, III, pp. 2542-44, 2562-63.

151. Keener, *Acts*, II, pp. 2103-105.

152. Keener, *Acts*, III, p. 2680.

153. Reimer, *Women in the Acts*, pp. 243-48.

154. Keener, *Acts*, III, pp. 2393-2420.

155. Richard S. Ascough, *Lydia: Paul's Cosmopolitan Hostess* (Paul's Social Network: Brothers and Sisters in Faith; Collegeville, MN: Liturgical Press, 2009), pp. 52-57; Reimer, *Women in the Acts*, pp. 71-149.

nothing is said of their material wealth. Two of the most significant examples are Priscilla, the church planter and teaching minister (cf. 18.2, 18, 26; Rom. 16.3; 2 Tim. 4.19), and Philip's daughters, i.e. the four prophetesses (21.9).[156]

While women feature prominently in Luke–Acts, slaves are rare. Since Christianity was later criticized as a foolish *superstitio* for the lowly and un-educated,[157] Luke's emphasis on converts of high social status (and lack of attention towards slave converts) may stem from his apologetic motivation to correct this broad misperception and present the faith as viable for the edu-cated elite (e.g. Theophilus).[158] The reference at the outset of Peter's Pente-cost sermon to the outpouring of the Holy Spirit 'on my male servants and fe-male servants' (2.18) is best understood figuratively as a general reference to the servants of the Lord (cf. 4.29; 16.17). However, it certainly conveys the New Testament principle that women and those of lower status are full-fledged members of Christ's body.[159]

There are two slave girls (παιδίσκη) mentioned in Acts. The first is Rhoda at Mary's house church (12.12-15). Keener notes that Luke's positive por-trayal of this Christian slave implies that she was a trusted member of the ear-ly church.[160] The other is the woman with the Python spirit in Philippi (16.16), who stands in stark contrast to affluent Lydia.[161] Luke does not re-cord what happened to the young woman after she was delivered, but it is plausible that she became another member of the new Philippian Christ asso-ciation.[162]

Finally, Cornelius sends two of his οἰκέται (household slaves) to fetch Peter, who presumably were converted along with his οἶκος (10.7, 19-23).

156. Reimer, *Women in the Acts*, pp. 195-226; Ben Witherington III, *Women in the Earliest Churches* (Cambridge: Cambridge University Press, 1988), pp. 153-54; Witherington, *Acts*, pp. 566-67.

157. Origen, *Cels.* 3.44-58; Pliny the Younger, *Ep. Tra.* 10.96; Tacitus, *Ann.* 15.44; Suetonius, *Nero* 16.2.

158. Kloppenborg, *Christ's Associations*, pp. 187-89; Green, *Evangelism*, pp. 172-78; Rodney Stark, *The Rise of Christianity: How the Obscure, Marginal Jesus Movement Became the Dominant Religious Force in the Western World in a Few Centuries* (San Francisco: Harper and Row, 1997), pp. 29-47.

159. Keener, *Acts*, I, pp. 882-86.

160. Keener, *Acts*, II, pp. 1904-48; Reimer, *Women in the Acts*, pp. 240-43.

161. See Keener, *Acts*, III, pp. 2422-56.

162. Keener, *Acts*, III, pp. 2466-67; Reimer, *Women in the Acts*, pp. 151-94.

Hence, Christianity, like many other associations, counted women and slaves among its adherents. Yet as Eva Ebel explains, the structure and policy of Christian churches towards women and the marginalized was more attractive than other associations.[163] The ἐκκλησία likewise afforded elite women opportunities to use their wealth and influence to contribute towards the expansion of the uniquely trans-local, Christian movement.[164]

5. Divine Guidance

One of the primary themes in Acts is that Christian expansion is the result of God's guidance not only of the apostles but of members in general, through prophecy, visions, dreams and other means.[165] There are striking parallels between the Lord's guidance of Paul in Acts and the founding of cultic associations, particularly that of Serapis. In Corinth, the Lord appears to Paul in a night vision, saying, 'do not be afraid,' for he would protect him and prosper the new church (18.9-10). The dream is fulfilled by God's deliverance from Jewish legal opposition under Gallio (vv. 12-16). Similarly, Serapis appeared to Apollonius in a night vision, telling him not to be afraid because the deity would fight on his behalf in court and prosper the cult (IG 11.4). Moreover, the narrative of Paul's journey as a prisoner to Rome includes two night-visions in which God promises to protect the apostle and aid him in trial (cf. 23.11; 27.23-24).

The Thessalonian inscription also parallels the Lord's guidance of Paul. As Serapis commanded Xenainetos in a dream to found the household association in Thessalonica (IG 10.2.1), so the Spirit forbids Paul from remaining in Asia and gives him the Macedonian vision (16.6-10). Paul and his team interpret this dream to be the Lord's instructions for the second missionary

---

163. Ebel, *Attraktivität*, pp. 218-19; McLean disagrees (cf. 'Agrippinilla Inscription', pp. 257, 265, 270).

164. 'Als Ergebnis dieser Skizze läßt sich festhalten: Im Wettbewerb mit paganen Vereinen in ihrem Umfeld können christliche Gemeinden vor allem auf ihren Verzicht auf formale Zulassungsbedingungen und auf die größere Intensität ihres Zusammenlebens, die den Christinnen und Christen auch materielle Vorteile einbringt, verweisen' (Ebel, *Attraktivität*, p. 218); Pilhofer, *Die frühen Christen*, pp. 209-11; Keener, *Acts*, III, pp. 2408-22.

165. Acts 1.4-8; 2.1-4, 17; 7.31, 55-56; 9.3-18; 10.3-22; 11.4-17, 27-28; 12.7-11; 13.2; 16.6-10; 18.9-10; 21.9-14; 22.6-21; 23.11; 26.12-18; 27.23-24; cf. Keener, *Acts*, I, pp. 886-916; Witherington, *Acts*, p. 142.

journey, leading to the establishment of Christ associations in Philippi, Thessalonica, Berea and Corinth (cf. 16.11–18.18). Indeed, Paul's conversion and calling as well as the beginning of his Gentile mission are all portrayed in Acts as oracles.[166] More research also needs to be done on the role of miracles and miracle reports in the propagation and expansion of both early Christianity and other cultic associations.[167] Suffice it to say that Luke's account of Paul's ministry, like that of Peter, is characterized by visions and dreams, prophecies and miracles. These are designed to convey the Lord's guidance over the emergence and expansion of the new Christian faith.[168]

Conclusion

The purpose of this paper has been to provide a comparative study of early Christian expansion as recorded in the book of Acts with that of other ancient, Greco-Roman associations. Part I presented four reasons why associations were the primary socio-organizational model for early Christianity. Outsiders (e.g. Pliny, Tacitus, Suetonius) understood Christianity as one of the many new cultic associations spreading around the empire, and the church fathers (e.g. Tertullian, Origen, Eusebius) also described Christianity as an association. Thirdly, numerous scholars have demonstrated that Greco-Roman associations were the primary influence on the development of Jewish synagogues, out of which Christianity emerged. Finally, the New Testament, including the book of Acts, uses common association terminology in reference to the early church.

166. Acts 9.15; 13.2-3; 22.21; 26.15-19.

167. Acts 2.43; 3.1-10; 4.30, 33; 5.12-16; 6.8; 8.13, 18-19; 9.12, 17-18, 32-41; 13.9-11; 14.8-10; 16.16-19; 19.11-12; 20.7-11; 22.13; 28.3-9; cf. Origen, *Cels.* 1.1-2, 6, 25-26, 28, 30, 38, 45-46, 57, 60, 67-68, 71; 2.8-9; 6.40; 7.8; 8.37. See Craig S. Keener, *Miracles: The Credibility of the New Testament Accounts* (2 vols.; Grand Rapids: Baker Academic, 2011), I, pp. 35-82; Robin Lane Fox, *Pagans and Christians* (San Francisco: HarperSanFrancisco, 1995), pp. 118-19, 327-30, 570-71; Howard Clark Kee, *Miracle in the Early Christian World: A Study in Sociohistorical Method* (New Haven: Yale University Press, 1983), pp. 128-31, 202-6, 211-18, 267-71; A.D. Nock, *Conversion: The Old and the New in Religion from Alexander the Great to Augustine of Hippo* (Oxford: Clarendon, 1933), pp. 83-98.

168. Acts 4.31; 5.17-20; 10.1-33; 11.4-11; 12.6-11. For the Lukan Peter-Paul parallelism, see Keener, *Acts*, I, pp. 561-74.

Part II surveyed the epigraphic and archaeological evidence for the growth of Greco-Roman associations as well as case studies that provide insight into its causes. Five factors were identified as being of particular importance: (1) family and social networks, (2) influential converts, (3) financial support, (4) opportunities for the marginalized and (5) divine guidance. Part III interpreted the account of early Christian expansion in the book of Acts through the lens of these five factors. Scholars continue to debate why Christianity emerged among so many other cultic associations to become the religion of Rome.[169] This study confirms some assumptions about the uniqueness of early Christianity and the causes of its rapid growth while challenging others. It is hoped that a greater knowledge of Christianity's past leads to enhanced understanding of its role today.

169. Ebel, *Attraktivität*, pp. 214-21; Pilhofer, *Die frühen Christen*, pp. 194-211. However, Kloppenborg expediently criticizes the 'Pilhofer-Ebel model' (cf. *Christ's Associations*, pp. 236-37).

INDEX OF ANCIENT SOURCES

OLD TESTAMENT

APOCRYPHA

NEW TESTAMENT

9.23	51	13.13-47	139
9.30	139	13.15	139
9.31	141	13.26	139
9.32-41	159	13.38	139
9.36	156	13.44–18.17	47
9.39	156	13.50	156
10.1-33	159	14.1	139
10.2	152	14.2	139
10.3-22	158	14.8-10	159
10.7	157	14.19-21	62
10.19-23	157	14.23	141
10.22-23	152	14.27	141
10.23	139	15.1-35	131
10.24	152-53	15.1	139
10.33	152	15.2	141
11.1	139	15.3	139, 141
11.3	152	15.4	141
11.4-17	158	15.5	153
11.4-11	159	15.6	141
11.12	139, 152	15.7	139
11.14	152	15.13	139
11.19-21	152	15.22	139, 141
11.22	141	15.23	139, 141
11.26	51, 55, 141	15.32	139
11.27-28	158	15.33	139
11.28-30	155	15.36	139
11.29	139	15.40	139
11.30	141	15.41	62, 141
12.1	141	16.2	139
12.5	141	16.3	118
12.6-11	159	16.4	141
12.7-11	158	16.5	141
12.12-15	157	16.6-10	158
12.12	152	16.11–18.18	159
12.17	139	16.14-15	152, 156
13.1	141, 153	16.14	156
13.2-3	159	16.15	152
13.2	158	16.16-19	159
13.5	139	16.16	157
13.7	153	16.17	157
13.9-11	159	16.31-34	152
13.12	153	16.32	152

2.88	30	*War*	
		1.419	30
JOSEPHUS		1.420	30
Ant.		2–6	100
4.55	31	2.14.3-4	41
9.243	31	2.14.5-9	41
15.324	30	2.19.2	41
18	101	2.19.9	41
18.3	51	2.57-59	97
18.63-64	98	4.614	31
18.344	31	5.449-551	69
20.11.1	41	6.4.3	41
20.182-196	43	6.299-300	97
20.195	41	6.312-313	96
		7.176	31
Life		7.294	31
13-16	43		

OTHER EARLY JEWISH AND CHRISTIAN AUTHORS

Hermas, *Vis.*		4.13.18	58
1.1.1	57	4.26.2-14	58
		8.6	58
CLEMENT OF ROME		10.1.7	137
1 Clem.			
5	52, 57, 59, 66	JEROME	
25	70	*Vir. ill.*	
		1	69
EUSEBIUS			
Hist. eccl.		JUSTIN MARTYR	
2.22.2-8	64	*1 Apol.*	
2.25	66	13	99
2.25.4	58	67	136
2.25.7	66		
3.1	69	ORIGEN	
3.1.2	58	*Cels.*	
3.31.4	66	1.1-2	159
3.33.1-4	58	1.1	137

38	54		18.63-64	96, 103
Vesp.			*Hist.*	
4–5	97		1.47.2	51
4	42		5	100
5.6	97		5.5	100
			5.9	97
TACITUS			5.13	96
Ann.				
5.10	41		THUCYDIDES	
5.13	41		*Hist.*	
15.44	47-51, 94-95, 100, 103, 134, 157		2.77.4	17, 31
15.61	42			
16.6	43			

PAPYRI, OSTRACA, AND INSCRIPTIONS

BGU			1283-1284	140
4.1137	148		IByzantion	
CIG			31	148
1793b	141			
1800	141		ICiliciaBM	
2271	141		201	140
3037	141		IDelos	
IApamBith			1519	142
35	148		1522	140
IAlexImp			IEph	
92	141		20	145, 148
			1503	145
IBosp				
69	148		IFayum	
104	140		2.122	140
1021	148			
1123	148